Cognitive-Behavioral Play Therapy

D1565032

Cognitive–Behavioral Play Therapy

SUSAN M. KNELL, PH.D.

JASON ARONSON INC.
Northvale, New Jersey
London

Production Editor: Judith D. Cohen

PLAY-DOH ® is a registered trademark of Tonka Corporation. Copyright © 1993 Playskool, Inc. Used with permission.

1995 Softcover Edition
Copyright © 1993 by Jason Aronson Inc.

10 9 8 7 6 5 4 3 2

Library of Congress Cataloging-in-Publication Data

Knell, Susan M.
    Cognitive-behavioral play therapy / by Susan M. Knell.
       p.   cm.
    Includes bibliographical references and index.
    ISBN 1-56821-719-6
    1. Play therapy. 2. Cognitive therapy for children. i. Title.
    [DNLM: 1. Cognitive Therapy—in infancy & childhood. 2. Play Therapy—in infancy & childhood. 3. Play Therapy—methods.   WS 350.2 K68c]
RJ505.P6K6   1993
618. 92'89165—dc20
DNLM/DLC
for Library of Congress   92-49558

Manufactured in the United States of America. Jason Aronson Inc. offers books and cassettes. For information and catalog write to Jason Aronson Inc., 230 Livingston Street, Northvale, New Jersey 07647.

To Martin and Sylvia Globus Knell

and Robert Shafran

for their love and support

Contents

Author's Note

The names and other identifying details in individual case histories have been changed to protect the privacy of the children and families presented.

A wide variety of "cognitive" and "cognitive-behavioral" therapies have been developed. To avoid confusion, the term "Cognitive Therapy" is used when referring to the work of Aaron T. Beck, M.D. The term "cognitive-behavioral" therapy is used generically to refer to a wide range of approaches based on cognitive and behavioral principles and intervention strategies. Because the present work is based on the integration of cognitive, behavioral, and play therapy, the term "Cognitive-Behavioral Play Therapy" has been chosen.

Acknowledgments

When Charles Schaefer, Ph.D., first asked me to contribute to his series on child psychotherapies, I was delighted at the prospect of introducing the notion of Cognitive-Behavioral Play Therapy to other child clinicians. I appreciate his support and assistance in this project, and his encouragement of my work.

I am especially grateful to James Overholser, Ph.D., who reviewed many chapter drafts with attention to detail and stylistic acumen. Jim has been a wealth of knowledge, and a tremendous resource.

Richard Paulson, Executive Director of the Child Guidance Center, and his staff have been immeasurably encouraging and supportive of my work. My association with this dedicated group of professionals has been most rewarding.

In the early stages of this work, I talked with a number of individuals about the idea of integrating cognitive-behavioral interventions with play therapy. E. Klonoff, Ph.D., provided some useful thoughts that led me to think more systematically about the integration of cognitive and behavioral interventions with very young children. Douglas Moore, Ph.D., contributed to my understanding of the encopretic child described in Chapter 7. Doug and I also spent much time talking about the idea of Cognitive-Behavioral Play Therapy. Discussions with Linda Hartman-Makovec, LISW, regarding psychotherapy with sexually abused children contributed to my thinking as well as to the work done by members of the Sex Abuse Treatment Team at the Child Guidance Center of Greater Cleveland. The chapter on sexually abused children by Christine Ruma, M.S., M.S.S.A., includes a number of cases treated by Linda. Chris shares my enthusiasm for the integration of cognitive-behavioral interventions and play therapy, and has been a pioneer in her application of this approach with children who have been sexually molested.

A number of students provided technical support, and at times their enthusiasm could not help but be contagious. I would particularly like to thank Laura Hubbert DiCarlo, who provided library assistance and transcribed audiotapes of clinical sessions with painstaking detail.

Finally, I have learned from the children and families with whom I have worked over the years. This book would never have been possible without them. Cognitive-Behavioral Play Therapy grew out of an effort to find a "better match" to the needs of the individual children and families I have seen. I hope that my search for new treatment options has been helpful to them and ultimately will be helpful to others.

PART I

PLAY THERAPY

The chapters in Part I serve to introduce the field of Cognitive-Behavioral Play Therapy by discussing the history of play therapy. Additionally, issues related to the use of play therapy with preschool-age children are considered. It is noteworthy that play has been used in the psychotherapeutic treatment of young children for over 50 years. Chapter 1 traces the historical development of play in child psychotherapy, as well as the emergence of play therapy. The varying schools of thought, including psychoanalytic, structured, relationship, nondirective, limit setting, group, and behavioral therapies, are considered. A number of trends in play therapy are presented. These include the focus on short-term interventions, treatment used for preventive purposes, feedback mechanisms (e.g., videotape), and increasing emphasis on finding a match between therapy type and child. A renewed interest in the field of play therapy has generated numerous books and articles, and the formation of a national association of play therapy.

Chapter 2 discusses a number of special issues in therapeutic work with preschool-age children. Many of these issues involve developmental concerns about normal development and individual differences in cognitive and language development. Because of the wide range of behavior problems considered normal in young children, it is imperative to differentiate between common, transient problems and more serious childhood disturbances. Cognitive functioning, as well as affective and emotional development, must be considered in therapeutic work with children. In some recent studies, Piaget's work on the child's understanding of conservation as it relates to measurable properties has been applied to the child's understanding of affective functioning. This work has important implications for the child's understanding of emotional and social phenomena. Clinical implications of the child's cognitive, linguistic, and affective development are related to treatment planning. Other clinical issues such as referral factors and sources of assessment data are discussed and their implications for cognitive-behavioral therapy are considered.

1

Approaches to
Play Therapy

PLAY AND ITS IMPORTANCE IN CHILDHOOD

Is it possible to consider play therapy without first understanding what is meant by play? Perhaps not, but defining play is a difficult task. There is no single, accepted definition of play, although it seems easier to define play by what it is not than by what it is. Play is considered the opposite of work. It is fun and pleasurable. It has no extrinsic goals. It is, according to Webster, "action or exercise for amusement; recreation; sport." And according to Erikson (1964), "in its own playful way, it tries to elude definition" (p. 4).

In the context of play, children practice new roles, express emotions, try to make sense of experiences, and deal with both reality and fantasy. A child's play is influenced by parental factors, experiences with peers, available materials, school, and the media (Rubin et al. 1983). The multifaceted nature of play and its meaning make it an invaluable, if complicated tool for use in therapy.

USE OF PLAY IN THERAPY WITH CHILDREN

If the meaning of play is unclear, its use as a therapeutic intervention may be even more complex. Despite differences in the theoretical conceptua-

7

lization of play, it is widely accepted that play is an attempt by the child to explore, gain mastery, and develop understanding. In practice, therapists assume that a child's play is a reflection of feelings, conflicts, thoughts, and perceptions of reality. These are expressed through play because the child is not yet able to express them verbally. In many therapies, play is a means of communication. In others, such as behavior therapy, play may be used as a means through which particular strategies, such as contingency management, are applied.

The use of play as an assessment and treatment modality is fairly standard in individual psychotherapy with young children. Even with this common ground, the traditional practice of child psychotherapy has changed dramatically over the past 75 years of its existence. In this chapter we will briefly consider the history of play therapy before moving on to a discussion of recent trends and current applications.

HISTORICAL PERSPECTIVE

Psychoanalytic Therapy

Although he never personally saw a child in psychotherapy, Sigmund Freud (1909) was probably the first to recognize the therapeutic possibilities play held for children. Much of his thinking about play was gathered from his work with adults, reconstructing psychological developments from infancy and childhood. Freud also referred to the significance of play in his discussion of Little Hans (Freud 1909). Little Hans's play activities, as reported by his father, were used by Freud to assess the child's intrapsychic conflicts.

In his early writings, Freud saw play as a reflection of unconscious concerns and conflicts. Later he expanded his view of play to include its role in the process of mastery and abreaction, where children repeat in play the things that have made an impression on them in their daily lives. Play allows the child to escape reality and explore new possibilities in a safe context.

Freud's thinking about play was often embedded in considerations of other issues more central to his theory. For example, Freud's notion of the repetition compulsion, the need to reenact painful experiences in words or acts, addressed the mastery aspects of play. The repetition compulsion is manifested through children's play, for as Freud contended, "children repeat in their play everything that has made a great impression on them in actual life, that they thereby abreact the strength of the impression and so to speak make themselves masters of the situation" (Freud 1922, p. 15).

Other psychoanalytic theorists, such as Erik Erikson, expanded upon Freud's work. For both Freud and Erikson, play served the role that dreams do for the adult, that is, as the "road to the unconscious." However, Erikson, the principal theorist dealing with the mastery aspects of play, saw play as an ego function that represented the child's efforts to deal with traumatic experiences. Erikson (1950) contended that child's play is "the infantile form of the human ability to deal with experience by creating model situations and to master reality by experiment and planning" (p. 222).

Play was first used directly in therapy with children by Hug-Hellmuth (1921), who felt it was an essential part of child analysis. Hug-Hellmuth saw children over 6 years of age in their own homes. She used drawings and play materials, often toys that belonged to the child, but did not develop a specific play technique per se. Although Hug-Hellmuth is credited with stressing the importance of play activities in child treatment, her written work provides little elaboration. The contributions of others, particularly Melanie Klein, Anna Freud, and Margaret Lowenfeld, are better known, largely through their writings.

Both Anna Freud (1928, 1946) and Melanie Klein (1932) did extensive work incorporating play into their analytic sessions, although their approaches were somewhat divergent. Anna Freud used play to get children interested in therapy. She felt that play was essential to the development of a therapeutic alliance. After this alliance was established, the analyst could move the child from play to verbalizations. Thus, play was a means to an end, namely the solid therapeutic relationship.

In contrast, Melanie Klein (1932) felt that play was a direct substitute for verbalizations, or the equivalent of adults' "free association." She used play as a means of communication, the manner by which the child made his or her thoughts known. One major difference was that Anna Freud treated older children with more well-developed verbal skills, whereas Klein worked with children with more limited verbal abilities, many of whom were as young as 2½ to 3 years old.

Another disagreement between A. Freud and Klein was about whether the preoedipal child could be analyzed. Anna Freud's position was that a child who could not form an oedipal object relationship with the therapist could not be analyzed; therefore play therapy was not truly analysis. Klein argued that analytic work could be done with very young preoedipal children.

Despite these differences, both Klein and A. Freud made significant contributions to the field of child therapy. However, Anna Freud's work appears to have had the greater influence on analytically oriented child therapists in this country. It is her work that is most often quoted in discussions of play in child analysis, and which has set the stage for more recent trends in psychoanalytically oriented play therapies.

In summary, the early child psychoanalysts, most notably A. Freud and Klein, incorporated play into their treatment sessions in order to adapt traditional psychoanalysis for use with children. Ultimately, the goal of psychoanalytic therapy was to help the child gain insight in order to facilitate optimal development. Despite differences in the meaning and use of play among various psychoanalytic theorists, this was accomplished by making the child's conflicts conscious.

Structured Therapy

During the 1930s and 1940s, a school of structured therapy developed whose interventions were based largely on psychoanalytic theory. Later the focus expanded to include more goal-directed interventions. Therapists in structured therapy played a more active role than in the analytic therapies, although still believing in the cathartic properties of play. The therapist supplied the child with materials that were felt to be helpful in working through conflicts. Structured therapists felt that in play the child must repeatedly reenact a conflict in order to overcome it, a notion that was derived from the psychoanalytic concept of the repetition compulsion.

As it was first developed, this type of play therapy was neither totally structured nor goal directed. Rather, the therapist guided the child toward what was considered to be the focal point of the child's problems and supplied structure in order to break through the child's defenses (Nickerson 1973). It was, however, more structured and goal directed than other play therapies in existence at that time.

Levy (1938, 1939) developed the first structured play therapy with his "release therapy," in which he worked with children traumatized by discrete events who presented with specific symptoms of fairly short duration. Levy dealt primarily with night terrors and fears, and worked with children whose own methods of dealing with their anxiety had been unsuccessful. His patients were usually under 10 years of age and suffering from the sequelae of a past specific trauma, not from an ongoing situation. Levy was primarily interested in the method from a research perspective, although others, such as Hambridge (1955), further elaborated the technique for clinical purposes.

Hambridge's (1955) interventions were quite directive, with the therapist creating specific situations and then having the child reenact these scenarios. For example, Hambridge would tell the child that two dolls were the mother and father asleep in their bedroom. A child doll (self-doll) is invisible in the parents' bedroom. The child is then asked, "What happens?" or "What does the child see?" (Hambridge 1955). Any of a number of conflict situations, derived from information about the child, could be presented in dramatic play. Such directive interventions were used in the middle phases of an already ongoing therapy, when the therapeutic relationship was well established. Hambridge did not introduce such structure until the child had the ego resources to manage what he considered to be a very intrusive act. He also allowed the child free play time after the reenactment so that there was time to "recover" before leaving the therapy room.

Variations on structured play therapy include Gardner's (1971, 1972) Mutual Storytelling technique. In this therapeutic technique, the child tells a story, the therapist interprets its meaning, and then the therapist repeats a different story using the same characters but with a healthier resolution of conflicts. Gardner's work differs in that it uses storytelling as a metaphor for the child's conflicts, rather than having the child act out these conflicts through play. It does, however, provide the structured presentation of such situations to the child, with the goal of providing the child insight into the difficulties. Also, because of the nature of the task, the technique is appropriate only for older, more verbal children.

Other examples of structured play interventions use role playing and/or more dramatic techniques. Woltman (1969, 1972) used puppets in play therapy, stressing that the child related to, identified with, and ultimately worked through feelings via puppets. Besides using puppets in individual therapy, Woltman also devised puppet shows that incorporated audience reactions for use in group therapy.

The structured play therapies can be summarized by their common themes. They were based on psychoanalytic theory; assumed, at least in part, a cathartic property of play; and were structured such that the therapist took an active role in helping the child achieve the therapeutic goals. These interventions were directive, in that the therapist chose play materials and created scenarios that would enable a child to reenact previous experiences. They differed in the materials used, the manner in which they were presented, and varying degrees of verbal skills required by the child.

Relationship Therapy

The 1930s gave rise to a number of play therapies that fell under the broad category of relationship therapies. These interventions, based on early work by Otto Rank (1936), stressed the importance of the birth trauma in development. Rank contended that the stress of birth led the individual to cling to the past and to fear individuation. Rank deemphasized the importance of transference and the understanding of past events for the client. Instead, the focus of these therapies was on the patient's current life and the relationship between therapist and client in the present time.

Several play therapists (e.g., Taft 1933, Allen 1942, Moustakas 1959) adhered to this school of thought. They believed that the child's ability to form positive social relationships was influenced by the trauma of birth. These theorists all contended that some children had difficulty in developing healthy relationships with their primary caretakers. The therapeutic relationship provided them with the opportunity to develop a significant relationship in a safe environment. Despite some differences, these theorists all stressed the importance of the positive therapeutic relationship in helping the child deal with the prior trauma.

The relationship therapies were also tied quite strongly to psychoanalytic theory. However, the therapeutic relationship was seen as the most important aspect of therapy, and, as stated above, the emphasis in treatment was not on past conflicts, but on the present. Because the effectiveness of these therapies was assumed to be based on the quality of the therapeutic relationship, not in the introduction of specific materials or goals, they differed significantly from the previous structured therapies.

Nondirective Therapy

This emphasis on the therapeutic relationship was also characteristic of the nondirective therapies. The core of these therapies was the notion that individuals are basically motivated to reach their highest potential. The nondirective or client-centered school of thought was originally developed for work with adults by Carl Rogers (1951). In the client-centered approach, personality change is considered to begin within the individual, and thus the impetus for change comes from the client, not the therapist. The therapist merely creates therapeutic conditions that are favorable to change.

A play therapy approach based on the theories of Rogers was developed by Axline (1947). Nondirective play therapy accepts the child's capacity for self-determination. In nondirective therapy, the child uses play as a natural medium of self-expression and to act out feelings. The eight therapeutic principles of nondirective play therapy espoused by Axline highlight that it is the atmosphere created by a nonjudgmental, permissive therapist, not therapeutic techniques per se, that promote change in the child. The principles for nondirective therapists are that they:

1. Must develop a warm, friendly relationship with the client, in which rapport is established as soon as possible.
2. Accept the child as he or she is.
3. Establish a feeling of permissiveness in order for the child to freely express feelings.
4. Recognize feelings the child expresses and reflect those feelings back to the client so that the child may gain insight.
5. Maintain respect for the client's ability to solve problems if allowed to do so. It is the child's responsibility to make choices and changes.
6. Do not direct the child in any way. The child leads; the therapist follows.

7. Recognize that therapy is a gradual process, and no attempt is made to hurry the process.
8. Establish only those limitations necessary to "anchor the therapy to the world of reality" so that the child is aware of his or her responsibility in the relationship. [Axline 1947]

The nondirective play therapy movement blossomed in the 1940s and 1950s. Its popularity became even greater in the mid-1960s with the publication of Axline's (1964) book *Dibs in Search of Self*. This account of play therapy with an exceptionally bright, disturbed young boy provides a very real sense of the actual process of nondirective play therapy as practiced by Axline.

The importance of the relationship between child and therapist was a hallmark of nondirective play therapy. Although previously mentioned therapies stressed the importance of the therapeutic relationship, Axline's approach added the assumption that individuals strive for self-actualization. As part of this philosophy, the nondirective therapist merely reflected the child's feelings, so that the child could gain insight that promoted problem solving and behavior change. The impetus for change clearly came from the child. The therapist was not the source of interpretations (psychoanalytic) or direction (structured), but essentially served as a mirror for children to view their own reflections as they grew emotionally.

Limit-Setting Therapy

The importance of limit setting as a mechanism of change in therapy was highlighted by Bixler (1949). It is common to have children in therapy who cannot accept limits on their behavior, and such children were discussed by various therapists (e.g., Allen 1942, Axline 1947). Although earlier writings considered the role of limits or the fact that they are often broken, Bixler was the first to emphasize what the therapist should do when a child does not accept limits. Bixler contended that limits were essential, although they should be minimal, and should be determined by the therapist's own comfort level. For Bixler, limits included rules about not destroying property or hurting the therapist, adhering to time constraints, and removing toys from the therapy room.

Ginott (1959, 1961) also stressed the importance of limits in child psychotherapy. He felt that children needed clear guidelines in therapy, as well as in everyday life, about which behaviors are acceptable and which are not. Ginott contended that by enforcing limits in therapy, the child viewed adults as protectors. For the acting-out client, therapy was felt to help the child experience negative feelings without negative consequences, thus helping the child gain control. The introduction of the notion of limits in therapy suggested a critical change in the history of play therapy. To that point, limits had never been considered a primary intervention in therapy sessions. In combination with the structured therapies, limit-setting therapies might be considered the earliest examples of therapists taking an active role while using very structured, goal-directed interventions.

Group Therapy

Play therapy in groups developed in part because patterns of behavior emerged in groups of children that were not present in the play of each individual child. Slavson (1948) wrote about the catalytic effect that each child had on others in the play group. One aspect of groups was the support that children gave to each other; sometimes such support involved hostility toward the therapist, which was not as easily expressed in individual therapy. Group therapy is not a theoretical orientation, such as psychoanalytic or behavioral, but rather a technique or format for applying a particular intervention. Therapists from a variety of orientations conducted group therapy sessions, incorporating their own theories into such interventions (e.g., Axline 1947).

Group therapy with children has grown rapidly in recent years. It is probably safe to say that whatever approaches have been used in work with individual children have been incorporated into a group therapy format. The nature of group interaction suggested that some therapeutic tasks that cannot be accomplished in individual therapy may be accomplished in a group environment. Additionally, most group therapists assume that the interactive experience of a group has therapeutic value.

Behavioral Therapy

Behavioral therapies for children developed in part as an effort to help children and parents translate the knowledge gained in treatment into the development of more adaptive behavior patterns outside of the therapist's office (Russo 1964). Based on principles of learning theory, the behavior therapies practiced in the 1960s relied largely on operant conditioning. Behavioral approaches were either taught to parents and/ or teachers so that they might apply these techniques to the child outside the therapy setting, or they were used directly by the therapist with children in the office. Some therapists even worked in a play setting that included the presence of parent, child, and therapist (Russo 1964). Regardless of how the behavioral interventions were applied, the therapist would attempt to discover the factors that reinforced and maintained the child's problematic behaviors so that these behaviors could then be altered. Regardless of the setting, play was used in behavioral play therapy, mainly as a way to engage the child in treatment, and thus was more of a means to an end rather than inherently valuable in and of itself.

Behavior therapists have widened their sphere, which now includes social learning theory (e.g., Bandura 1977). Emphasis on learning through observation contributed to the development of cognitive-behavioral interventions in which cognitions play an important role in the development of problems. This recent emphasis on cognitions led to the cognitive-behavioral interventions with children, a focus that has only recently been applied with very young children in play therapy.

RECENT TRENDS AND CURRENT APPLICATIONS

During the past 20 years, attention has been focused on new approaches, techniques, and conceptualizations of play therapy. Changes have occurred in the settings where play therapy takes place, the types of clients served, the specific therapeutic techniques employed, and the foci of interventions. Although a complete discussion of recent trends in play therapy is beyond the scope of this chapter, the reader is directed toward a number of excellent reviews describing these many new approaches (e.g., Schaefer and O'Connor 1983). Several of these trends will be briefly discussed below.

One trend has been toward the use of short-term interventions. Once considered superficial and useful only on a temporary basis until long-term treatment could begin, briefer psychotherapies are now viewed more positively, and often as the treatment of choice. Even adaptations of psychoanalytic therapy, usually referred to as the psychodynamic therapies, have included some shorter term approaches. These interventions have typically involved fewer sessions per week and an increased emphasis on presenting problems. The shorter term therapies often are more focused on specific problem resolution rather than on more global interventions (see Koss and Butcher 1986).

A trend toward short-term interventions is logical for the preschool population, since many preschoolers have transient and mild problems. In such situations, short-term interventions may be used to deal rapidly and efficiently with problems that do not require extensive intervention.

Another trend has been toward the use of play therapy for preventive purposes. Much of this work has occurred in the school setting, where practitioners such as school psychologists and counselors are conducting individual and group play interventions for children. Many of these efforts have a particular focus (e.g., children of divorced parents), while others are geared for the more general school-age population.

Other preventive work has taken place in hospital settings where children often face a variety of intrusive, painful medical procedures. There is little question that preparation to reduce the trauma of hospitalization and medical procedures is important. Various programs have been successful in reducing anxiety associated with the hospital experience (Siegel 1976). Much of the initial impetus for such programs came from the child-life movement, which focused on the psychological as well as physical well-being of hospitalized children (Plank 1971). Currently, many child-life programs in hospital settings are designed to help children use play to cope with the traumatic effects of medical treatment.

The use of feedback mechanisms is a growing trend, reflecting in part the advances in electronic technology that have made it possible. The introduction of audiotape and videotape recorders in therapy may allow children to learn by listening and/or observing, and discussing segments of their therapy session. Nickerson (1973) noted how much young children reveal when talking on a telephone or into a tape recorder. The latter seems especially helpful when the child is allowed to play back the tape and listen to what was said. This type of feedback may be particularly useful in group therapy where the therapist guides the children through a discussion of what they observe in their own interaction with each other.

Finally, there is a growing trend toward finding the best fit between patient and therapist characteristics, and conditions under which therapy is conducted. Schaefer and Millman (1977) argued for a "prescriptive approach" to therapy, in which the therapist, choosing from an array of theories and techniques, determines the most appropriate therapy for each child. This makes intuitive sense, but also has clinical and empirical support (Schaefer and O'Connor 1983).

Clearly, child therapists have been using play therapy interventions since their inception over 70 years ago. Yet, the continued development of the field of play therapy seemed to have remained static during the 1960s, 1970s, and early 1980s. In the last five years, play therapy has once again assumed prominence in child psychotherapy. The recent trends discussed above reflect this awakening by highlighting the growing interest in new techniques and approaches in working with young children therapeutically through play. Additional evidence of this interest can be found in the foundation in 1982 of the National Association for Play Therapy. Further support is seen in the recent publication of several important books in this area, such as *The Handbook of Play Therapy* (Schaefer and O'Connor 1983); *The Play Therapy Primer* (O'Connor 1991); and *Play Diagnosis and Assessment* (Schaefer et al. 1991).

EVALUATING PLAY THERAPY

With this growing interest in play therapy, the ultimate question about its effectiveness remains unanswered, in part because the task of evaluating play therapy is complicated. All therapy outcome research is complex, although the very nature of play therapy makes it a particularly difficult subject to study. Early studies were largely concerned with nondirective play therapies (e.g., Cox 1953, Dorfman 1958). Very little systematic research has taken place with other types of play therapy and with regard to process and outcome issues. Child psychotherapy research does not always include play therapies, and when it does, play interventions are often not distinguished from other approaches or are given minimal attention (see Phillips 1985). Further, most child psychotherapy research is focused on the school-age population with little attention to treatment of preschoolers. This lack of attention is striking, given the increasing interest in play therapy from a clinical perspective.

2

Therapy with Young Children

Play therapy is used with a wide range of age groups, although as the child's linguistic skills improve, more emphasis may be placed on verbal, rather than play, interventions. Play therapy is primarily used with children between the ages of 3 to 10 years, although this range is by no means inflexible. Many 8- to 10-year-old children are reluctant to engage in play with a therapist. At the other end of the age continuum, adolescents and even adults, especially those with developmental delays, have benefited from play therapy. Clearly, there are no steadfast rules. However, it is safe to say that most preschoolers in therapy will need an approach based on play.

Psychotherapy with children and adolescents presents many unique challenges not present with adults. It is no more appropriate to think of preschoolers merely as "little children," than to think of school-age children as "little adults." Preschool-age children present with a unique set of abilities and limitations, such that principles related to working with school-age children and adolescents cannot merely be extrapolated to apply to younger children.

In this chapter, special issues in therapeutic work with preschoolers will be considered. Some of these issues involve developmental concerns, such as the notion of what constitutes normality or individual differences in children's cognitive abilities to engage in psychotherapy.

Others relate to clinical factors, such as referral and assessment sources. The impact these issues have on designing and implementing treatment plans for young children in play therapy will be discussed.

DEVELOPMENTAL ISSUES

Normality versus Normal Development Gone Awry

Wenar (1982) contends that when problems occur in children, the effect can best be described as "normal development gone awry" (p. 198). In such situations, normal development, as we expect it to unfold, takes another direction. The many challenges facing the young child are met by different children in a variety of ways: some children quickly show mastery with little evidence that the challenge was other than momentary; other children exhibit transient difficulties while struggling to deal with the challenge; for still other children, more serious and continuing problems emerge. The task of the therapist is to understand how the child's development has gone awry, and to determine what can be done about it.

Epidemiologic studies and large-scale surveys of the behavior problems of young children suggest that behavior problems are quite common in preschoolers (e.g., Jenkins et al. 1980, Lapouse and Monk 1958, 1959, 1964, MacFarlane et al. 1954). Frequent areas of concern for parents of preschoolers are the youngster's eating, sleeping, toileting, and noncompliant behaviors. Additional problems frequently exhibited by young children involve fears, aggression, nightmares, speech difficulties, and impulsivity.

Many children exhibit problem behaviors at some point in time, although few will exhibit such behaviors to the extent that they are considered indicative of serious psychopathology (Campbell 1990). Although potentially quite upsetting for the parent, these behaviors are usually relatively transient and are not exhibited at high intensities and/or frequencies, or for long periods of time. Other behaviors (e.g., pervasive lack of responsiveness to others; gross deficits in language) are rarely exhibited, and when they do occur, they are more likely to reflect a more serious problem. Intensity, frequency, and duration of a problem, as well as how often others of the same chronological and mental age exhibit the same behavior, are important factors in determining its seriousness.

When do common, transient problems become more serious ones presenting cause for concern? When is a child exhibiting problems that will require mental health intervention? These questions are particularly thorny because of the ever-changing nature of the child during the preschool years. They can only be answered on the basis of a knowledge of child development, which provides a foundation from which to make decisions regarding the appropriateness, on a "normality–normal development gone awry" continuum, of a given child's behaviors.

In part because the early childhood years are a time of enormous growth and change, the therapist is faced with many such decisions. Determining if normal development has gone awry is the first consideration. However, behaviors that are typically suggestive of psychopathology may in fact be adaptive responses to traumatic events. Therapy may or may not be indicated in such situations. Similarly, even for the child developing within normal limits, therapy may still be appropriate if the child and/or the family's struggle can be helped by professional intervention.

Cognitive Issues

Probably the most critical issue related to young children in therapy is that of their cognitive functioning. Obviously, the therapist must always be mindful of the cognitive level of any individual in treatment, although as the individual develops, these issues become less critical because most average adult clients exhibit the minimum cognitive skills necessary to benefit from psychotherapy. However, for very young children, strengths and limitations in the cognitive sphere are crucial issues in developing appropriate treatment modalities.

Despite the importance of the role that cognitive developmental level plays in treatment planning, child therapists have not been as actively interested in cognitive development as have their colleagues in developmental psychology. Shirk (1988) attributes this partly to the rapid expansion of play therapy, which in some ways has obscured the need to understand a child's cognitive development. Because of the use of play in place of verbalization in therapy, the cognitive differences between children and adults are often not addressed. Thus, by not emphasizing spoken language in therapy, the therapist may fail to focus on the child's cognitive limitations.

Theoretic underpinnings of therapy also influence therapists' thinking about the importance of cognitions. If abreaction, or emotional release, is considered to be the sole means of therapeutic change, then the cognitive differences of children compared with adults are not as problematic. Play may then substitute for words as a mechanism of emotional release. However, if increased understanding or insight is a goal of therapy, then *all* treatments, even those relying on play, must involve cognitive activities (Shirk 1988). These cognitive components may be less sophisticated for children, but Shirk contends nonetheless that they must exist.

Thus, understanding of cognitive development is a crucial aspect of therapy, not only for treatment planning and therapy process, but also in terms of therapy outcome. Understanding the effectiveness of therapy, particularly as it relates to measuring these changes in children, relies on a sense of what the child is capable of grasping cognitively. It is not that most therapists deny the cognitive changes that are taking place in children. Rather, by focusing on other aspects of the child's functioning, the therapist does not have to deal directly with the challenges presented by the young child's cognitive limitations.

Piagetian Perspective

The theories of Jean Piaget have shaped much of our thinking about the cognitive development of children (e.g., Piaget 1926, 1928, 1930. Overview of Piagetian theory may be found in Flavell 1963, Wadsworth 1989). In Piaget's theory, cognitive development can be divided into four broad periods or stages, with cognitive changes occurring in a cumulative manner. What the child learns in each stage is used as a building block for learning in the next stage of development. Piaget viewed the preschooler as in the stage of preoperational thought (ages 2–7 years). This period is characterized by rapid conceptual and language development, although the child's thought is not yet adultlike. By definition, Piaget compared this period with the previous stage, sensorimotor intelligence, wherein the child between birth and 2 years explores the environment predominantly through sensory and motoric means. The preoperational stage is also contrasted with the next stage, concrete operations (7–11 years), in which the child is able to perform certain tasks, albeit from a concrete, rather than abstract, perspective.

Children in the preoperational stage are frequently compared with older children and adults, and described by how relatively "illogical" and egocentric their thinking is. Children in the preoperational stage of development do exhibit advances from the earlier (0–2 years) sensori-motor stage. Symbolic thought and representation are emerging, and language is taking on a critical role in the child's ability to distinguish between objects and their labels. There are major advances in the child's ability to symbolically represent objects in their absence and to reason symbolically rather than motorically. Rather than thinking of preopera-tional-stage children in terms of what they cannot do, some theorists (e.g., Gelman and Baillargeon 1983) have suggested that this view underestimates the child's abilities. These theorists argue that despite preschoolers' limitations, children should be understood based on what they can, rather than cannot, do.

Even so, there are striking limitations in the preoperational child's thinking, many of which are thought to interfere with the child's ability to benefit from more verbally focused psychotherapy. Preoperational-stage children cannot reason logically or deductively. Their judgments are strongly influenced by their perceptions and appear to be based on illogical thinking. For example, events may appear related to the pre-operational-stage child because they occur together in time, not because of any true cause–effect relationship.

An example from the everyday life of a preschool child can be used to highlight the child's thinking. A family with young children had relatives visiting from out of town for several days. To deal with cramped quarters, they moved some beds around and let the 7-year-old child sleep on the sofa in the living room. Her bed was given to her aunt for several days, and the child seemed delighted by the unusual chance to sleep in the living room. However, her 5-year-old brother seemed puzzled by the changes. After the relatives left, he commented to his parents, "What happened to Maggie?" The parents were puzzled but realized by talking with him that he was confused. The temporal se-quence of his sister's move out of her room and the relatives' visit implied to him that something had "happened" to her.

The egocentrism of the preschool-age child also presents problems, because taking another's perspective is difficult for the preoperational child, who is caught up in an "egocentrism with respect to symbols" (Elkind 1981). The child lacks a clear differentiation between symbols and their referents (e.g., words). To the preoperational child, words carry inherent meaning; the word itself is believed to carry information about the properties it is meant to represent. As the child moves into concrete operations, the differentiation between symbols and referents is accomplished by the emergence of concrete operations. One consequence of concrete operations is the ability to hold in mind more than one property or element at the same time. Prior to this, children can only attend to one attribute or dimension at a time and cannot deal with two pieces of information that may appear contradictory on the surface. Piaget's theorizing about this inability to accept contradictory information was focused only on physical quantities/mathematical issues. This inability to conserve, as Piaget referred to it, is a crucial aspect of his theory.

Extrapolation of Piaget's Theory to the Affective Domain

Although Piaget's focus was on the preoperational child's inability to conserve as it related to physical and mathematical properties, there are important implications for thinking about more emotional qualities. Harter (1977, 1983) extrapolated Piagetian principles and applied them to affective spheres. The cognitive limitations that lead the child to faulty logic and errors in understanding events have been adapted to describe the child's understanding of such social phenomena as social relationships, perspective taking, and conventions.

In the same way that children have difficulty understanding that the quantity of liquid does not change when it is poured from a tall, thin container to a short, fat one, so will they have difficulty focusing on two affective dimensions. Can a preschooler recognize two different emotions, especially contradictory ones? For example, can children feel both love and anger toward a parent at the same time? Can they feel both dumb and smart? Harter contends that because young children can focus on only one of two opposite affective dimensions at a given time, their understanding of affective material is largely characterized by all-or-nothing thinking (e.g., "I am always dumb"; "My dad is always mad at me").

Thus, without conservation of affect, the child may be greatly influenced by single environmental events. These may dramatically alter the child's reference points so that, for example, when the popular young boy does not get picked by his peers for a ball game one day, he may believe he is always unliked. Or when the bright young girl does poorly on a test, she may believe that she is always stupid. Such examples can be dramatic (and frustrating) until the child develops the ability to conserve affect. Eventually, with affective conservation, "particular events do not transform the entire emotional system, even though they may distort the balance of feelings temporarily" (Harter 1977, p. 423).

Emotional recognition and differentiation in self and others develops through a sequence of levels, as it moves from concrete and egocentric to complex, abstract, and other-oriented. These levels, similar to those proposed by Selman (1980, 1981) in the development of friendship, are used by Harter (1983) to characterize the young child's growing ability to understand feelings. Clearly, the younger preschool-age child has difficulty differentiating his or her own feelings from those of the parent and sees others as defined by concrete, not psychological, attributes. As the child gets older, there is increasingly more differentiation between self and parent and an understanding of the attributes of others.

This differentiation is encouraged by the child's growth through experience. The primary task for the child at the preoperational stage of development is an ability to use language to organize experiences. This ability develops gradually over this stage, as the child has difficulty comparing and contrasting experiences and cannot yet manipulate knowledge *about* experiences.

In understanding the preschooler's abilities, it is important to distinguish between behaviors that are spontaneously exhibited in the environment, and those that the child is capable of, but must be prompted to exhibit. Clearly, preschoolers are more advanced in their skills than Piaget suggested; however, they are generally concrete and cannot easily generalize from one experience to another. The lack of language to explain what they know may further limit children who understand certain relationships or feelings, but may not have the words to explain what they know. The ability to self-reflect and understand contradictory emotional information may not ordinarily be seen. Nonetheless, the preschooler may be capable of exhibiting some of these skills under certain circumstances. It is possible for play therapy to provide one set of experiences that facilitates this understanding of contradictory emotions.

Clinical Implications

Within the therapeutic context, this manipulation and experimentation can be encouraged and fostered by the therapist. Children enter therapy with a history of experiences from which they have constructed some set of explanations. Although their understanding of such experiences is marked by their own unique past and cognitive level, these experiences are affected by various environmental influences. Therapy can provide a positive opportunity for the child to explore and develop more adaptive coping abilities.

The child's cognitive developmental sophistication must be considered in designing intervention strategies (e.g., Bierman and Furman 1984). A good match between the developmental level of the child and the level of complexity of the intervention chosen is critical. For preschoolers to benefit from therapy, therapists must capitalize on children's strengths and abilities, rather than focus on weaknesses. Obviously, therapies incorporating play and de-emphasizing complex cognitive capabilities are likely to be the most useful for children of this age. Therapy must be more experiential than verbal. Tasks and toy materials should be familiar to the child, and the child should be allowed to interact without the need for complicated language skills. Given these factors, the egocentric functioning normally seen at this age may be decreased and reasoning abilities may improve.

One opportunity for therapeutic intervention is in encouraging and facilitating the child's language to describe experiences and emotions. Although one sees dramatic growth in general vocabulary during this period, knowledge about words describing emotions is still limited. Most preschoolers' vocabulary about feelings is limited to a simple triad: happy, mad, and sad, and perhaps minor variations on these three. Many youngsters do not even have these rudimentary words to express their feelings.

At this age, young children need more than a vocabulary to express their feelings. They may also benefit from efforts to help them match their behaviors with their feelings, and learn to express certain maladaptive behaviors in more adaptive, language-based ways. A common example for the preschooler is the expression of anger through aggression. One child is angry about the birth of a new sibling, so he tries to kick the baby carriage and thus hurt his new sister. Another child is mad about being left with a baby-sitter when her parents go out for the evening, so she tries to break a toy. Teaching these youngsters to understand that they are angry, what it means to be angry, and how to say it in words instead of behavior may be a beginning to helping them deal with their feelings. This is not to negate the importance of looking at the environmental/family situation, which may be contributing to the child's behavior. It does, however, acknowledge that children at this age benefit from a sense of control, and that using language rather than aggressive behaviors may provide some of this sense of mastery and control.

In therapy, learning may take place for the child in a very experiential way. Children can practice different facial expressions as modeled by the therapist, drawings, or puppets, and learn to associate these expressions with appropriate words. The boy mentioned above can play with puppets and toys and thereby demonstrate his feelings toward his new sister. While the child is acting out his anger by kicking the play carriage, a punching bag, or a puppet representation of his sister, the therapist can help the child label his feelings. Merely acting aggressively in therapy does not teach the child that there are alternatives. Labeling the aggression and learning other verbal and nonverbal ways to cope can offer the child some other, more adaptive way of dealing with his frustration and anger.

OTHER CLINICAL ISSUES

Referral Factors

How individuals decide to enter therapy, and the process through which they are referred, may play an important part in the course of therapy. A multitude of factors may influence the adult individual's decision to enter treatment; and because preschoolers do not self-refer for therapy, these factors are even more complicated, with significant adults playing a key role in the referral process. Most frequently, parental concern regarding a child is what prompts referral. If the child's behavior is problematic in settings outside the home, the parents are more likely to seek mental health treatment. This is especially true if it is a nursery school teacher, day-care provider, pediatrician, or other professional who perceives the child's behavior as problematic. Children who are seen as possibly intellectually or linguistically delayed are also more likely to be referred (Campbell 1990).

Numerous other factors will influence parents' decision whether to seek mental health services. Two important factors are the parents' developmental expectations for their child and the parents' tolerance levels for the problem behavior. Other factors, such as the parents' own history, understanding of the development of their other children, psychiatric family history, perceptions of mental health care, perception of available resources, and their own mental status play important roles.

These referral issues raise important questions for the child therapist. Children behave differently around different adults in different settings. Further, there is relatively low agreement between parents on child rating scales (Achenbach et al. 1987). Thus, understanding the referral means knowing *how* the child behaves, with *whom*, and in *what* setting. Understanding the background of the referral and its meaning for the family can also provide invaluable information regarding the identified child patient.

Sources of Assessment Information

Assessment is a critical component of the treatment process. Typically, in assessing young children for therapy, therapists talk with parents, referral sources, and significant adults (e.g., teachers) in the child's life. Included as part of the assessment may also be observations of the child and standardized behavior checklists or developmental/intellectual tests. Although most therapists will be interested in the child's sense of his or her own problem, information from other sources is considered to be more reliable. The parental report often provides more accurate and complete information than the child can offer.

Even when the focus of treatment is parent guidance, the child will usually be included, although in a limited way, in the evaluation process.

This may involve the child being observed in play or in interaction with the parent(s), with the information thus obtained being used to provide support for parental perceptions or to offer the therapist new understanding of the situation. Such assessment, however, does not take into account various aspects of the child's perceptions, which may be critical to the therapist.

Indeed, much may be lost if the assessment does not include the child's perception of the presenting problems. Further, the child's self-statements, attributions, and self-evaluation are themselves important factors, which are difficult to glean from parental report. This is not to imply that they are easy to gather from the young child! However, efforts to gather this information in a developmentally sensitive way will often provide information that is critical to treatment success.

Gathering such information when evaluating young children relies on a well-trained therapist who understands child development and is comfortable interacting with young children. In Chapter 6, we will consider the ways in which assessment of preschoolers can be developmentally sensitive and potentially maximize the information available to the evaluator.

THE IMPACT OF THESE ISSUES ON COGNITIVE-BEHAVIORAL THERAPY

The issues discussed above present some unique challenges for psychotherapy with preschool-age children. Nonetheless, a multitude of young children have been seen in therapy over the past 75 years. As new types of interventions have been developed, clinicians of various theoretical orientations have contributed to an understanding of various developmental and clinical issues involved in psychotherapy with preschoolers.

Cognitive therapy with adults is relatively new, with the first work in this area dating back to the early 1960s (Beck 1963, Ellis 1962). Most adults in psychotherapy are self-referred, able to provide history regarding their presenting problems, and cognitively able to respond to the structured, directive approach of cognitive therapy. Thus, the use of cognitive-behavioral therapy with children raises issues that are not typically encountered when the approach is used with adults.

Is cognitive-behavioral therapy appropriate for use with preschool-age children? Are there developmental issues that make it impossible for a youngster of this age to benefit from such interventions? Individual differences in development and the transient nature of many common problems during the preschool period make treatment planning difficult. The fact that children are not self-referred means that the therapist must engage them in treatment and facilitate the child's working with the therapist, although the "collaborative empiricism," as described by Beck and his colleagues (Beck et al. 1979), is clearly of a very different nature than the approach used with adults. Finally, the cognitive abilities of children at this age make a cognitive-behavioral approach open to question because of the component of these interventions that relies heavily on more sophisticated cognitive abilities (e.g., hypothesis testing).

The merger of cognitive and behavioral interventions and play therapy for preschoolers, the thrust of this book, is a new, albeit promising, one. Some authors (e.g., Campbell 1990, Cohen et al. 1981) contend that cognitive-behavioral therapies are beyond the grasp of most preschoolers. Others (e.g., Knell and Moore 1989, 1990) argue that when presented through play therapy in a developmentally sensitive way, cognitive-behavioral interventions can be used appropriately with young children. In a review article on play therapy research, Phillips (1985) hypothesized that the incorporation of cognitive-behavioral techniques into play interventions offered a promising direction for the field. He contended that the specificity of treatment goals and methods of study may account for the positive outcomes noted with studies incorporating such techniques. Berg (1989) has presented some clinical work in which he combines cognitive therapy and play interventions, although his target population is school-age children.

Clearly, the integration of cognitive, behavioral, and play therapies must involve a flexibility in implementation that takes into account the unique nature of the child in the preschool years. The proposed integrated approach, Cognitive-Behavioral Play Therapy, is considered in Chapter 3. The chapters in Part III, Clinical Applications, provide specific case examples of how Cognitive-Behavioral Play Therapy is conducted with preschoolers.

PART II

COGNITIVE-
BEHAVIORAL PLAY
THERAPY (CBPT)

Part II presents the theoretical framework for Cognitive-Behavioral Play Therapy (CBPT) as it is currently conceptualized. CBPT as an integration of cognitive, behavioral, and play therapy approaches is discussed in Chapter 3. In this chapter the attributes of CBPT are presented, and the similarities and differences between CBPT and other types of play therapy are discussed. The importance of a positive therapeutic relationship and the use of play as a means of communication are discussed, as are differences among play therapies, which are based on varying philosophies related to the goals, direction, and educational components of treatment, as well as such considerations as the use of praise, and various play materials. The underlying components of behavioral and cognitive interventions are presented in Chapters 4 and 5, respectively. Chapter 4 provides an overview of behavioral interventions based on classical conditioning, operant conditioning, and social learning theory. Systematic desensitization, a type of classical conditioning, is considered. A case example highlighting systematic desensitization with a young child is presented. Operant approaches, including contingency management, shaping, stimulus fading, extinction, differential reinforcement of other behavior, time-out, and response prevention are discussed. The significance of modeling, whose origins lie in social learning theory, is emphasized as a method of delivery in CBPT.

Chapter 5 describes cognitive-behavioral interventions and their application with preschool-age children. A number of interventions, such as
self-monitoring and activity scheduling, are more behaviorally based.
The more cognitive methods, including recording thoughts, cognitive
change strategies, coping self-statements, and bibliotherapy, are considered. Finally, the focus on teaching children to develop more adaptive
coping skills, particularly through the use of positive self-statements, is
highlighted as a critical component of CBPT.

Chapter 6 considers the role of assessment in CBPT. First, basic
principles in the assessment of young children are described. Specific
assessment measures are considered, including those that rely on parent
report and those that involve individual administration of tests with
children. A new sentence-completion task employing puppets is described, which presents a traditional measure in a more developmentally
sensitive manner. The use of feeling scales, drawings, and other concrete
materials is considered from the perspective of assessing younger, less
verbally sophisticated children. Play assessment, developmentally sensitive interviewing, and the implications for clinical assessment in
cognitive-behavioral therapy are discussed. A number of these issues are
highlighted in the case description of the clinical assessment of a 4½-
year-old who had temper tantrums and was afraid of attending nursery
school.

3

Integration of Cognitive-Behavioral Interventions and Play Therapy

Psychotherapists working with young children often rely on play to achieve therapeutic goals. Traditionally, play therapy has been largely unstructured, as in the psychoanalytic (A. Freud 1928, 1946, Klein 1932) or nondirective (Axline 1947) approaches. As noted, the more recent play therapy literature has introduced discussion of more directive, structured interventions. The extension of behavioral, and more recently, cognitive, interventions into play therapy offers an important focus for structured psychotherapy with preschool-age children.

TRADITIONAL ROOTS

Traditionally, psychotherapies with preschool-age children have relied either on work with the parent (usually the mother) around the child's problems or direct work with the child. Although the case of Little Hans is considered to mark the advent of the modern child psychotherapy movement, Little Hans was actually treated by the child's father, who observed the child and consulted with Freud (1909). The indirect approach to treatment was common in the early Child Guidance movement. One Child Guidance Clinic study found that in 40 percent of the cases, the mother alone was the only member of the family in treatment (Levitt et al. 1959).

There are several reasons for this focus on parent-implemented treatments. Shirk (1988) contends that treatment of the child by way of the parent may be explained by the acceptance of parental neurosis as a causal factor in child psychopathology. Alternatively, he suggests that therapeutic techniques developed for adults may not have been applicable to children, thus necessitating that therapeutic work be done with the parent, not the child. Other reasons may involve differences in the child's motivation, and therefore investment, in being in treatment, since it is usually the parents' discomfort that brings the child into therapy.

Traditional psychodynamically oriented child psychotherapy with the child as client is based on the same theoretical underpinnings as adult treatment. That is, self-understanding and insight are the road to emotional and behavioral change. Insight is believed to be gained via self-observation, recovery of repressed memories, and the reconstruction of the past as it relates to the present (Neubauer 1979). Other psychodynamic therapists emphasized the importance for the patient of a corrective emotional experience (e.g., Alexander and French 1946). Still others saw play in general as the child's attempt to actively master situations that had been experienced more passively earlier in the child's life (e.g., Erikson 1950). Self-understanding in traditional psychodynamic play therapies was achieved via interpretation (Erikson 1964, A. Freud 1928), the therapeutic nature of play itself (Erikson 1950) or in the case of nondirective play therapy, as the consequence of the uncritical, accepting therapeutic relationship (Axline 1947).

BEHAVIORAL ROOTS

Behavioral interventions with preschoolers have taken the same two directions, namely, treating the child via the parent and direct work with the child. A large and growing body of behavioral literature with preschoolers supports the use of treatments implemented by the parent (or other significant adult) to effect changes in child behaviors (e.g., Forehand and McMahon 1981, Bernal et al. 1980). Such approaches have proven effective with problems such as child noncompliance. Other presenting problems of preschoolers may be less responsive to such interventions, particularly if parent-implemented treatment is met with resistance by the child. This may be particularly true if the child's problem is particularly aversive to the parent (e.g., Knell and Moore 1988), if the parent–child relationship has inhibited development of the child's self-mastery (Klonoff et al. 1984, Klonoff and Moore 1986), or if issues of control are prominent. O'Leary and Dubey (1979) argue that in addition to changing the environment, behaviorists are increasingly emphasizing the need to help children change their own behavior.

Child behavior therapy provides a potentially powerful arena for children to change their own behavior. Direct behavioral intervention with young children has expanded greatly since the early work of Mary Cover Jones (1924). As the range of behavioral techniques with adults has increased, many similar interventions have been proven effective with young children. With preschoolers these treatments often involve the simple application of a behavioral procedure within the play therapy setting (e.g., systematic desensitization, positive reinforcement). Such interventions typically do not integrate behavior therapy and play therapy. Rather, they use behavioral techniques within the *context* of play but not as part of a larger behavioral play therapy paradigm.

These behavioral interventions may prompt behavior change but may not adequately encourage the child's involvement. The need for children to change their own behavior and be active participants in treatment has not been adequately addressed either in parent- or therapist-implemented behavioral interventions.

COGNITIVE ROOTS

Cognitive therapy is a structured, focused approach that helps make changes in one's thinking and perceptions and ultimately in one's behavior. The earliest cognitive therapy literature was focused on adults, beginning with depressed (Beck 1963) and neurotic (Ellis 1958) individuals and now dealing with a wide array of diagnoses, ranging from anxiety to personality disorders (Freeman et al. 1990). In recent years, the literature on cognitive treatment has expanded its focus to include the treatment of children and adolescents as well as adults. All too frequently, however, it has been assumed that interventions suitable for adults require only minor modifications to be appropriate for use with children. This may have some validity with older children and adolescents, but it has not been the case with younger children and preschoolers. Among the current applications of cognitive therapies specifically geared to children are those developed for depressed (e.g., Emery et al. 1983) and impulsive (Kendall and Braswell 1985) children. Consideration of developmental issues is of course critical in such adaptations of interventions originally designed for adults.

For children, the interaction of psychological problems and developmental abilities adds to the complexity of psychotherapy. This complexity may be highlighted in cognitive therapies, since the interventions assume certain levels of cognitive abilities, such as abstract thinking. The abilities needed for cognitive therapy (e.g., hypothesis testing, looking at alternatives, and problem solving) may be seen in many adolescents. The cognitive therapist who works with adolescents makes modifications based as much on the teenager's social and interpersonal issues as on cognitive limitations.

Adapting cognitive therapy for younger children is even more complicated, since at first glance, one might assume that young children lack the cognitive skills to engage in such interventions. Yet, there is ample evidence that the ability of preschoolers and young school-age children to understand complex problems is enhanced by such techniques as providing more concrete examples and using less open-ended questions. Rather than assuming young children lack the cognitive abilities to engage in cognitive therapy, we must consider ways to make cognitive interventions more developmentally appropriate, and therefore accessible. Issues related to the preschool-age child's ability to benefit from cognitive interventions were discussed in the previous chapter. More information on developmentally sensitive assessment and interviewing of children can be found in Chapter 6.

THE NEED FOR COGNITIVE-BEHAVIORAL PLAY THERAPY

The significance of a child's involvement in treatment may be understood from several perspectives. Developmentally, children need to demonstrate a sense of mastery and control over their environment. Such mastery can be seen as children exhibit increasing levels of self-management of their own behavior. In a cogent description of cognition and self-management with children, Ollendick and Cerney (1981) delineated a number of reasons why teaching children to regulate their own behavior has received increasing interest. They note evidence that controlling one's own behavior may be more efficient (Lovitt and Curtis 1969), more durable (Drabman et al. 1973), and may permit significant adults to engage in more positive activities with the child. Finally, when a parent administers a program, that adult may become the source of discriminative cues for the child to emit the appropriate behavior or suppress an inappropriate one. Thus, children may only behave in certain ways when these cues are present (Kazdin 1975).

Despite the growing body of literature regarding behavioral and cognitive interventions with young children, these recent ventures seem to ignore the need to view the child as an active participant in change. Further, there has been a lack of integration of behavioral and cognitive approaches with preschoolers. In fact, such an integration might provide the missing link to promoting the child's active involvement in a focused, goal-directed treatment.

THE NATURE OF COGNITIVE-BEHAVIORAL PLAY THERAPY

Cognitive-Behavioral Play Therapy (CBPT), as the name clearly suggests, incorporates cognitive and behavioral interventions within a play therapy paradigm. Play activities as well as verbal and nonverbal forms of communication are used in resolving problems. (In subsequent chapters we will explore how specific behavioral and cognitive interventions can be used in play therapy.) Cognitive-Behavioral Play Therapy is more than the use of cognitive or behavioral techniques, however; it provides a theoretical framework based on cognitive-behavioral principles and integrates these in a developmentally sensitive way.

Cognitive-Behavioral Play Therapy places a strong emphasis on the child's involvement in treatment in a way that many other behavioral therapies for young children do not. The behavioral and cognitive components of the treatment may serve diverse purposes. Behavioral interventions may prepare the child to benefit from treatment; they may also influence the child directly. For example, a behavioral intervention such as modeling may provide the child access to information that might not otherwise be available if the therapist needed to rely solely on verbal means. Thus, modeling may facilitate the child's access to treatment. Alternatively, some behavioral interventions (e.g., shaping, positive reinforcement) may promote behavior changes by virtue of their psychological properties.

Cognitive therapy may provide a framework for the child's involvement in treatment by addressing issues of control, mastery, and responsibility for one's own behavior change. By incorporating the cognitive components, the child may become an active participant in change. For example, children who are helped to identify and modify irrational beliefs may experience a sense of personal understanding and empowerment. Integrating cognitive and behavioral interventions, with the resultant effects of the combined properties of all approaches, seems warranted. Certainly, more empirical study of the specific properties of CBPT is needed.

The potential efficacy of Cognitive–Behavioral Play Therapy may be related to six specific properties. These properties, highlighted in clinical examples presented in Part III, are:

1. *CBPT involves the child in treatment via play.* With the child an active participant in therapy, issues of resistance and noncompliance can be addressed. Additionally, the therapist can deal with the child's issues directly, rather than via a parent or significant adult. For example, the encopretic child discussed in Chapter 7 offers an example of how a child's resistance to change is dealt with within the context of therapy.

2. *CBPT focuses on the child's thoughts, feelings, fantasies, and environment.* In this way it is possible to focus on a combination of situation-specific factors (e.g., soiling, phobia) as well as the child's feelings about the problem (e.g., anger, sadness). It is focused neither on feelings nor on thoughts exclusively, nor only on situations or environmental circumstances. For example, treatment of the elective mute child (Chapter 8) focused on the child's feelings and perceptions of her situation, as well as her symptom of silence.

3. *CBPT provides a strategy or strategies for developing more adaptive thoughts and behaviors.* Through CBPT, the child is taught new

strategies for coping with situations as well as feelings. As a result of successful CBPT, the child becomes able to replace maladaptive ways of coping with more adaptive approaches. An example is the cognitive strategy of replacing maladaptive thoughts with positive self-statements. Learning more positive adaptive coping skills is highlighted in all cases employing CBPT and is frequently taught through modeling positive self-statements by means of toys and puppets. In clinical use, the puppets present situations that are similar to the child's and then model adaptive coping strategies as well as appropriate verbal expression of feelings.

4. *CBPT is structured, directive, and goal-oriented, rather than open-ended.* The therapist works with the child and family to set goals and helps the child work toward these goals. Direction toward the goals is an important part of CBPT and can be seen in the case examples presented throughout this book.

5. *CBPT incorporates empirically demonstrated techniques.* Drawing heavily upon the behavioral and cognitive traditions, CBPT employs, whenever possible, empirically demonstrated interventions. One of the most commonly used, well-documented, and perhaps most powerful techniques is modeling (Bandura 1977). Modeling (i.e., through puppets and dolls by the therapist) is the basis of much of CBPT because of the need to demonstrate concretely, nonverbally, and specifically for preschoolers.

6. *CBPT allows for an empirical examination of treatment.* The importance of using techniques that can be evaluated cannot be overstated. Paul's (1967) statement, "What treatment, by whom, is the most effective for this individual with that specific problem, under which set of circumstances?" is the ultimate question in psychotherapy outcome research. Cognitive-Behavioral Play Therapy offers the opportunity to study the specific effects of well-defined interventions for well-delineated problems.

SIMILARITIES

Although quite different from traditional play therapies, CBPT incorporates many of the assumptions underlying traditional interventions, while positing other assumptions that run counter to the premises on which traditional interventions are based. Let us first turn to a discussion of the similarities between CBPT and traditional therapies, before considering the differences among these approaches. An overview of these similarities is presented in Table 3–1.

The Therapeutic Relationship

The development of a positive therapeutic relationship is critical in psychotherapy and is considered to be most predictive of good treatment outcome (Brady et al. 1980, Rogers et al. 1967). Play therapy is no exception, in that the therapist attempts to establish a positive therapeutic contact with a child via play. Psychoanalytic play therapy, particularly as practiced by Anna Freud (1928) and her followers, emphasized play as the means of establishing the therapeutic relationship. Axline (1947), influenced primarily by the Rogerian school, believed that the therapist should develop a warm, friendly relationship with the child, establishing good rapport as soon as possible. Similarly, the therapeutic relationship is of utmost importance in CBPT. The therapist must make contact with the child, engage the child, and engender his or her trust if treatment is to be effective.

Play as Communication

In play therapy, play is not only the treatment modality but also the means through which child and therapist communicate. Observing the

TABLE 3–1
Cognitive-Behavioral Play Therapy vs. Traditional Play Therapy: Similarities

- Therapeutic relationship: Establish contact with child, engage child in treatment, engender child's trust.
- Communication via play: Play is treatment modality as well as means by which child and therapist communicate.
- Therapy as a safe place: Play therapy provides the child with a sense of security and safety.
- Obtain clues to understanding child: How child views self and others, conflicts and fantasies, problem-solving approaches.

child's play offers the therapist an understanding of the child's thoughts, feelings, and view of the world. The implications of children's play are endless: Play is the window through which we see how children view themselves and others, how they interact with the therapist, how they approach problems, how they understand the world around them. Children bring their conflicts and fantasies into treatment, and the less able they are to verbalize these, the more one sees through play. All schools of thought within play therapy see play as providing a body of information about the child.

Therapy as a Safe Place

Play therapy should provide the child with a sense of security and safety. It is important for the child to know that therapy is a safe place to deal with problems. Criticisms and uncertainties are part of the real world; they should be in the therapy setting only in that the child brings them there and can deal with them in a more comfortable, less threatening way.

DIFFERENCES

As noted in Chapter 1, there are many types of play therapies. Currently, the most widely used forms of play therapy are those based on nondirective approaches (Axline, 1947) and the psychoanalytically oriented approaches (A. Freud 1928, 1946, Klein 1932). It is beyond the scope of this chapter to contrast CBPT with every type of play therapy. Because nondirective and psychoanalytic approaches have attracted the most attention in the literature and in clinical settings, let us now turn to a discussion of the differences between these approaches and CBPT. Table 3–2 highlights these differences.

Direction and Goals

In traditional Axlinian play therapy, direction from the therapist is not accepted. Axline felt that direction came only from the child; she felt that direction imposed on the child by the therapist did not accept the child as he or she is. In CBPT, therapeutic goals are established and direction

TABLE 3–2

Cognitive–Behavioral Play Therapy vs. Traditional Play Therapy: Differences

Psychoanalytic	Nondirective (Axline)	Cognitive–Behavioral Play Therapy
	Directions and Goals	
Direction does not come from the therapist.	Direction is not accepted because it imposes on child; does not accept child as he/she is.	Therapeutic goals are established, direction toward goals is basis of intervention.
	Play Materials and Activities	
Therapist is "participant observer," not playmate. Therapist does not suggest any materials or activity.	Play materials, activities, direction of play *always* selected by child.	Both child and therapist select materials and activities.
	Play as Educational	
Play is not used to educate. Education is not the goal of therapy.	Education is not appropriate because it is a form of direction.	Play is used to teach skills and alternative behaviors.
	Interpretations/Connections	
Interpretation as ultimate tool.	Not made by therapist unless child introduces them first. Therapist communicates unconditional acceptance, *not* interpretation of symbolic play.	Introduced by therapist. Therapist brings conflict into verbal expression for child.
	Praise	
Not considered appropriate.	Praise should not be used by therapist. Praise communicates to child that therapist does not accept child, but rather wants child to be a certain way.	Praise is crucial component. Praise communicates to child which behaviors are appropriate and reinforces child.

toward those goals is an integral part of treatment. Whereas goals and direction are counter to the basic philosophy of Axlinian play therapy, they form the basis of CBPT. The cognitive-behavioral therapist's selection of a direction may be based on the child's lead or on knowledge of the child's situation gleaned from an outside source. In CBPT it is acceptable for the therapist to introduce themes based on parent or teacher report of the child's behavior in situations outside the therapy setting. For example, the cognitive-behavioral play therapist may provide direction by purposefully and systematically employing a puppet that behaves in certain ways or verbalizes issues that the child reportedly is exhibiting.

Play Materials and Activities

In Axlinian play therapy, the child always selects the play material, activities, and direction of play. Similarly, in psychoanalytic play therapy, the therapist is a "participant observer," not a playmate (Esman 1983). The therapist is expected to maintain a position as a neutral observer in order to understand the child's behavior. Thus, the psychoanalytic therapist does not suggest the use of any particular play material, in that he or she must maintain a position as neutral and permissive but not directive. In CBPT, both the child and therapist play a role in the choice of play materials and activities. From the child's spontaneous use of particular toys and activities, the cognitive-behavioral therapist gleans information that is then used to structure play sessions geared specifically for the child.

Play as Educational

In psychoanalytically oriented play therapy, play is not used to educate a child. Esman (1983) notes that play in nontherapeutic contexts can be used for instructional purposes. However, play in psychoanalytic therapy is intended to resolve conflicts that may interfere with a child's ability to maximize use of educational materials. Although educational benefits may be derived secondarily from therapeutic processes, education is not the goal of therapy. Similarly, for nondirective therapy, using play as an educational medium is providing a form of direction to the therapy that runs counter to Axline's philosophy. Clearly, CBPT is not used solely to educate the child. However, the use of play to teach skills or alternative behaviors is one aspect of CBPT. Often, educating the child takes place in CBPT as a model, such as a puppet, behaves in such a way that teaches the child. For example, CBPT as used with sexually abused children has many facets. One is to teach the child skills that may help prevent future maltreatment. Although it is the adult's role to ensure the child's safety, the sexually abused child can be taught to turn to appropriate adults if ever again placed in an abusive situation (see Chapter 11).

Praise

Axline (1947) contended that praise was not acceptable. She felt that praise communicated that the therapist did not accept the child as he or she is, but rather that the therapist wanted the child to be a certain way. In contrast, praise is a critical component of CBPT because it helps children feel good about themselves. Praise also communicates to the child which behaviors are appropriate and which ones are not.

Interpretations/Connections

Axline considered interpretations or connections important but contended that they not be made until the child introduced them. The relationship between therapist and child was used to provide a corrective emotional experience for the child. The therapist demonstrated unconditional acceptance rather than interpretation of symbolic play. By contrast, in psychoanalytic play therapy, the ultimate tool is interpretation. Melanie Klein felt that play was a substitute for verbalization, and that the therapist's role was to interpret the child's play. Anna Freud placed less emphasis on play as the equivalent of the child's verbalizations but instead stressed play as the means by which the therapeutic relationship is built. Anna Freud allowed the child to "work through" resistances before offering interpretations. Although the Freudian and Kleinian schools differ in this regard, there is still an emphasis on interpretation. In this respect, CBPT is actually more similar to psychoanalytically oriented treatment, in which the therapist brings the conflict into verbal expression *for* the child.

SUMMARY OF SIMILARITIES AND DIFFERENCES

Cognitive-Behavioral Play Therapy is similar to other play therapies in its reliance on a positive therapeutic relationship between therapist and child. Good rapport and trust are critical elements in engaging the child in treatment. Similarly, play activities as a means of communicating between therapist and child are universal to play therapies. In establishing the therapeutic relationship and in interacting with the child via play, play therapists communicate to the child that therapy is a safe place.

Differences among various play therapies are a bit more complex. Whereas CBPT is based on establishing goals, more traditional play therapies do not impose such direction on a child. Even the act of therapist selection of play materials and activities, an important aspect of CBPT, is considered countertherapeutic in more traditional play therapies. CBPT at times is educational in that it may teach the child a particular skill. In contrast, traditional approaches contend that play therapy should not be used as a form of education. Similarly, CBPT builds on the child's strengths by using praise and reinforcement appropriately, whereas more traditional therapies consider such an approach as potentially communicating nonacceptance of the child. Finally, in the area of interpretations, whereas Axline felt that interpretations must come first from the child, CBPT is more like the psychoanalytic approach in helping bring the child's conflict into verbal expression.

MAJOR CONTRIBUTIONS OF COGNITIVE-BEHAVIORAL PLAY THERAPY

Incorporating elements of cognitive, behavioral, and more traditional play therapies, CBPT reaches young preschool-age children. The emotional and behavioral difficulties of children at this age are often ignored or treated in ways that do not help the child gain self-mastery and self-esteem. In CBPT, the child is viewed as an active participant in change. This underlying philosophy of CBPT is considered critical to its potential efficacy.

The major contributions of CBPT appear to be threefold:

1. Cognitive and behavioral interventions are incorporated into a play therapy paradigm in a systematic and goal-oriented manner.
2. CBPT takes into account developmental, and in particular cognitive-developmental, factors in assessment and treatment planning.
3. CBPT is empirically based, both in its use of experimentally tested approaches and in its support of an empirical evaluation of treatment effectiveness.

4

Behavioral Interventions

Behavioral interventions with preschoolers often teach the adults in the child's life to use a specific program with the child. Although behavioral approaches have been used directly in treatment with young children, these interventions tend to employ play as a medium through which such strategies are applied. A review of the literature suggests that a specific field of behavioral play therapy per se does not exist.

In part this may be because behavior therapists in general have failed to integrate developmental, clinical, and behavioral understandings in their work with young children (Harris and Ferrari 1983). Despite the need for integration of these fields, several theoretical models have had an important influence on the wide array of behavioral interventions used with children today. These models—classical conditioning, operant conditioning, and social learning theory—will be reviewed and discussed in terms of their contributions to play therapy.

CLASSICAL (RESPONDENT) CONDITIONING

In classical conditioning, a previously neutral stimulus eventually comes to elicit autonomic or reflexive responses. One of the most important clinical examples of classical conditioning is *systematic desensitization*. In systematic desensitization, anxiety or fear can be reduced by replacing a maladaptive response with an adaptive one (Wolpe 1958, 1982). The foundation of systematic desensitization is to break the association between a particular stimulus and the anxiety or fear response that it usually elicits. This is accomplished by presenting the stimulus and then preventing the anxiety from occurring. Stimuli can be presented by having the individual imagine them or by actually using real life exposure (in vivo systematic desensitization).

One means of preventing anxiety is through muscle relaxation. The rationale is based on the premise that the body reacts to anxiety with muscle tension, which in turn increases thoughts that contribute to anxiety. Deep muscle relaxation reduces this tension and is therefore incompatible with anxiety (Jacobson 1938). Muscle relaxation training is used frequently, although other adaptive alternatives to fear and anxiety can be taught. Children may be helped to engage in relaxing activities. These can be used in addition to, or in place of, specific relaxation skills training. Play activities that are enjoyable and counter to anxiety can be used.

Play therapy provides an ideal situation for breaking the association between a stimulus and its maladaptive response. Some theorists consider play itself to have curative properties. Difficult events are actively brought into play by the child, and the "play version" changes as the child acts and reenacts the situation. Thus, as the child plays out a situation in order to gain mastery over it, the play itself may resemble a desensitization paradigm. For example, with hospitalized children, play may desensitize the threat of stress from hospital procedures (D'Antonio 1984) or help children regain control lost from the experience of being a patient (Brunskill 1984).

A case example will help to illustrate the use of systematic desensitization in play therapy. Jim, a 5-year-old boy, exhibited a fear of closed spaces. He had once been accidentally locked in a bathroom when his younger sister had closed the door. Although Jim's mother tried to comfort him through the door, it was several hours before the lock could be removed and Jim released. After this incident, he refused to stay in any room unless the door remained open. His problem came to the attention of professionals when Jim would not allow his pediatrician to examine him with the door closed. His intense screaming, and the description by his mother of related problems (e.g., refusal to go into elevators), prompted the pediatrician to refer Jim and his parents to a child psychologist.

Jim was treated by a simple systematic desensitization paradigm (see Table 4–1). Playing with certain toys appeared to be relaxing and thus incompatible with Jim's anxiety. When involved in play, he could stay in a room with the door ajar for increasingly greater periods of time.

TABLE 4–1
Systematic Desensitization Hierarchy for 5-Year-Old Afraid of Being in a Room with a Closed Door

Large room, therapist in room
1. Playing with toys; door open
2. Playing with toys; door half closed
3. Playing with toys; door open 1 inch
4. Playing with toys; door closed but not shut tight
5. Playing with toys; door closed

Small room, therapist in room
6. Playing with toys; door open
7. Playing with toys; door half closed
8. Playing with toys; door open 1 inch
9. Playing with toys; door closed but not shut tight
10. Playing with toys; door closed

Small room, therapist not in room
11. Playing with toys; door open
12. Playing with toys; door half closed
13. Playing with toys; door open 1 inch
14. Playing with toys; door closed but not shut tight for 10 seconds
15. Playing with toys; door closed but not shut tight for 30 seconds
16. Playing with toys; door closed but not shut tight for 1 minute
17. Playing with toys; door closed for 10 seconds
18. Playing with toys; door closed for 30 seconds
19. Playing with toys; door closed for 1 minute
20. Playing with toys; door closed for 2 minutes

Elevator, with therapist
21. Standing in elevator with doors held open
22. Standing in elevator with doors closed, and exiting on same floor (reopening door immediately)
23. Riding elevator to next floor

Graduated stages in the hierarchy were presented, as Jim was instructed to play and make simple, positive self-statements (see Chapter 5). The positive statements consisted largely of affirmations that he would be all right and *could* stay in the room with the door closed. The therapist provided positive feedback (e.g., "That was great," "Good job") after successful completion of increasingly difficult items. When he showed discomfort, there was a return to the previous step, with added intermediate steps to facilitate his progress. Jim seemed to derive satisfaction as he continued to overcome his fear. The combination of play, self-statements, and praise from the therapist and his mother for his accomplishments allowed Jim to overcome his fear of closed doors.

In summary, interventions based on classical conditioning can be integrated into play therapy. Much of this work has been done with systematic desensitization. Using Jim as an example, one can see that it is possible to help a young child overcome fear through systematically introducing play and self-statements that are incompatible with anxiety.

OPERANT CONDITIONING

In the second behavioral model, operant conditioning, behavior can be influenced by environmental events. Behaviors that are changed or maintained by their consequences are called operants, because they operate on or influence the environment. Environmental influences provide consequences that strengthen or weaken the behavior. Positive consequences increase the frequency of behaviors by reinforcing them, whereas negative consequences decrease the frequency of behaviors. Thus, all operant approaches involve the manipulation of environmental events that precede or follow the targeted behavior (Skinner 1938).

Contingency management is a general term describing any operant technique that modifies a behavior by controlling its consequences. Management programs are frequently set up by therapists in collaboration with parents to monitor the child's behavior outside the therapy session. However, contingency management programs can be set up within the play therapy session for specific behaviors that take place in therapy (e.g., awarding stars for playing with a toy appropriately) or for behaviors that take place outside (e.g., awarding points to be turned in for a specific reward for the encopretic child who has not soiled).

The most common type of contingency management is *positive reinforcement*, which is often used in combination with other procedures. Most commonly, positive reinforcement involves a social reinforcer, such as praising a child for something he or she has done, or providing material reinforcers, such as stickers. However, other types of positive reinforcement involve activities, tokens, or covert reinforcement (e.g., imaginal positive thoughts, positive self-reinforcement). Positive reinforcement occurs in a wide variety of play therapies, including interventions that are not considered to be behavioral. The therapist's praise or other reinforcement of the child communicates to the child which of his or her behaviors are appropriate. In this way, the therapist conveys a powerful message to the child and consequently may influence the child's behavior.

Positive reinforcement is used frequently in play therapy, although it is rarely the sole intervention. Therapists use praise routinely with children (e.g., for playing quietly in the waiting area when their parents are being seen, for pictures that they have drawn, or for schoolwork that they bring to show the therapist). Simply by encouraging the child to explore certain topics rather than others, the therapist may be reinforcing a particular direction for therapy. If a particular problem is the focus of treatment, the therapist may use praise as the child exhibits mastery over the problem. Positive reinforcement is a powerful technique, and therefore it is important for the therapist to exercise good clinical judgement in its use.

When offered without consideration of the child's overall situation, use of positive reinforcement can have adverse effects. Merely reinforcing a child for exhibiting specific behaviors does not necessarily deal comprehensively with the behavior. For example, one can praise a child for playing appropriately and *not* throwing toys. However, if the child is throwing toys because of some environmental circumstance, one must also deal with factors that are encouraging and maintaining the behavior. Merely helping the child to stop throwing toys may not be sufficient if the natural environment will not support the change.

To use positive reinforcement, the behavior that one wishes to encourage must already occur. Unfortunately, it is not always the case that children do the things we want them to do. In many instances, the child has some of the skills necessary but is either unable or unwilling to exhibit the desired behavior. Rather than waiting for the complete behavior to occur, it is possible to help the child take steps in that direction and exhibit some of the behaviors that make up the more complete behavior. *Shaping* is the process of reinforcing successive approximations to a desired response. In shaping, positive reinforcement is given for a behavior that is not the desired response but is close to it. Then closer and closer steps to the desired response are rewarded. This process is at the core of skill acquisition (e.g., learning to read and write). Imagine the young child learning to read without any positive feedback along the way!

An example of shaping takes place at the end of the play therapy session with the child who refuses to clean up the toys. The therapist may help the child and provide immediate labeling and positive feedback (e.g., "I like the way you are picking up the toys") as the child begins to comply with the task. The therapist then encourages efforts toward the expected task (i.e., picking up all the toys) by shaping related tasks along the way (e.g., putting one crayon in the box, moving a few blocks towards the storage area).

Shaping is important in the acquisition of any skill; learning appropriate behaviors and verbal expressions of feelings is no exception. In helping the child with verbal self-expression, the therapist may shape successive approximations to an appropriate expression of feelings. For example, the child begins by hitting the punching bag with little understanding. Gradually, the therapist can reinforce the child for efforts to describe in words that she is hitting the punching bag because she is angry; that she is angry because she doesn't like her new baby sister; and that she sometimes wishes that she could hit her sister. Since hitting her sister is not acceptable, the child must understand that it is more appropriate for her to express her feelings in words.

This type of shaping of expression of feelings takes time. It often begins with the therapist's hypotheses about the child's feelings. Because the child may not verbally label these feelings directly, the therapist develops hypotheses based on the child's behavior, expressions, and related verbalizations. As these feelings become clearer with time, the therapist helps the child express them in words rather than through inappropriate action.

Sometimes a child has some of the requisite skills for a behavior but only exhibits the behavior in certain circumstances or with certain people. A child may be able to share toys and play appropriately in therapy but misbehave terribly in the day-care setting. In such situations, the therapist may become a *discriminative stimulus* for behaving. The child might learn to use some of these positive skills in a group therapy setting with the same therapist. If the child is still not ready to use these skills in the day-care setting, it may be helpful for the therapist to spend some time with the child at school. In addition to the teacher's using good child management skills in the classroom, the presence of the therapist may aid the child in using positive behaviors learned in therapy. Obviously, this is costly, and the therapist would need to be gradually eased away from the classroom. Such a technique is a form of *stimulus fading*, where the discriminative stimulus (therapist) is gradually faded.

Extinction is the process by which reinforcement is withheld from behavior that was previously reinforced. The result of extinction is a decrease in the frequency of that behavior. Extinction itself does not teach new behaviors, so it is frequently used in conjunction with a reinforcement program. In this way a child can be reinforced for learning a new behavior at the same time that another behavior is being extinguished.

One important way in which this is done is through *differential reinforcement of other behavior* (DRO). This involves the reinforcement of behaviors that are different from or incompatible with the maladaptive behavior. The main premise is that the unacceptable behavior cannot occur if a competing, more desirable behavior is taking place. This technique is often used in combination with extinction procedures, where problematic behavior is extinguished and alternative, positive behavior is reinforced.

Differential reinforcement of other behavior is most effective when there is a clear alternative that is incompatible with the identified problem behavior. One is reminded of the pediatrician who has his patients chew gum when giving them injections, because of the impossibility of crying and chewing at the same time (Karoly and Harris 1986). An example in therapy is the child who tries to break toys during the session. Reinforcing that child for appropriately playing with the toys rather than breaking them, is an example of DRO.

When a child has maladaptive behaviors, it is important to look at the environment to see what is reinforcing and therefore maintaining these behaviors. Frequently, it is attention from a significant adult that maintains a child's maladaptive behavior. Removing that attention and providing the child attention for more appropriate behaviors can promote more adaptive behaviors.

Sometimes children need to be removed from reinforcers that are maintaining their responses. This may literally mean removing the child from whatever is reinforcing the behavior in the immediate environment. One technique for this is *time-out*, which is more frequently used in the natural environment, such as school or home, but may be used within the play therapy session as well. Although, technically, time-out means time away from reinforcement, it has come to mean removing the child from a desirable environment to a less attractive one.

Time-out may be used in play therapy when a child does not follow a preestablished rule, such as No Breaking Toys in the Therapy Session. In that situation there may be a time-out from therapy, where the child is removed from the situation for a brief period. This might involve moving the child to a part of the therapy room where there are no toys. During the time-out period, the child would not have access to the reinforcing aspects of therapy (e.g., the therapist's positive attention).

Time-out is considered effective because it keeps the child from whatever is reinforcing the maladaptive behaviors. The duration of the time-out interval is not considered to be the crucial variable because increasing the amount of time in time-out does not add to its efficacy. Of course, even a very brief time in time-out during the therapy session has the *disadvantage* of removing the child from the opportunity of interacting with the therapist in the session. Thus, time-out in treatment should be used sparingly and for maladaptive behaviors that cannot be dealt with in other ways. It is important that the child understands what *is* acceptable, and that positive reinforcement is forthcoming for such adaptive, appropriate behaviors. When time-out is used, it should be needed less frequently over the course of therapy as the child learns more appropriate responses.

Often, individuals have learned persistent maladaptive avoidance behaviors. These behaviors may persist long after they serve any usefulness for the individual. *Response prevention* is a technique by which the individual is exposed to an anxiety-provoking stimulus but is not permitted to make typical avoidance responses. Response prevention is used most frequently with persistent compulsions in adults. Because the outcome data on response prevention is mixed and the technique can be

aversive, it is used only when alternative, non-anxiety-inducing interventions have been ineffective.

Although response prevention is rarely used with children, it is
mentioned here because a form of this technique can be used in an
effective, nonaversive way with young children. Consider the young
child who is learning toileting skills. A common fear for many children
aged 2–4 is that they will be "flushed down the toilet" if they sit on it.
Children have many fantasies about what happens to their bowel movements (and to them) when the toilet is flushed. Most children get over
this fear naturally. Part of what happens is that they learn that they do not
get flushed down the toilet. In other words, their worst fears do not
become reality, and eventually they are no longer afraid.

For some children this fear does not subside, and a "toilet phobia"
may persist. The encopretic child to be discussed in Chapter 7 exhibited
such a toilet phobia. One technique used in the play therapy with this
5-year-old child was a form of response prevention. In this case, a toy
bear sat on a "make-believe" toilet. The boy, in acting out his fears, kept
trying to make the bear get "flushed down the toilet." The therapist, in
an effort to show the bear (and the child) that it could sit on the toilet
without being flushed away, had the animal stay on the toilet without
negative consequence. Thus, the bear was exposed to the feared situation
(i.e., sitting on the toilet) and was taught alternatives to the maladaptive
fear (i.e., sitting calmly rather than falling in).

A variety of techniques based on operant conditioning have been
incorporated into play therapy. Many of these techniques are used in
treatments that are primarily behavioral. However, many of these techniques are accepted by therapists of various orientations and are used in
therapies that are not necessarily considered behavioral.

SOCIAL LEARNING THEORY

The third behavioral model, social learning theory, rests on the assumption that behaviors are learned and modified through observational
learning, which takes place in a social context. One of the most common
types of social learning is that which occurs through modeling, or

observing the behavior of others. Extensive research shows that modeling is an effective way to acquire, strengthen, and weaken behaviors. In many situations, learning through modeling can be more efficient and effective than learning through shaping and direct reinforcement.

Because of the limited nature of the young child's cognitive and verbal abilities, modeling is an important component of play therapy. Puppets and dolls are readily available for the therapist to use as models for the child in treatment. Research supports the strength of modeling techniques with children's fears and anxieties. However, modeling has been used to treat a wide variety of other clinical problems, such as social isolation (Evers and Schwarz 1973, O'Connor 1969), impulsivity (Kendall and Braswell 1985), antisocial behavior (Sarason and Ganzer 1973), and poor self-help skills (Matson 1982).

Modeling designed to enhance the child's skills might involve either coping or mastery models. In the former, the model may display less than ideal behavior and then gradually become more proficient. Essentially this is akin to shaping the model toward the desired goal and may demonstrate for the child the steps toward the goal. It may also provide the child the opportunity to observe someone being permitted to make mistakes on the way to an eventual successful experience.

An example is the use of a coping model in therapy with a child whose social skills are limited. The model (e.g., a puppet) may make "mistakes" in interaction with others and develop better social skills as it learns from these interactions. The child then observes the model in its efforts to learn more appropriate ways of interacting, and the child may learn from exposure to the puppet's attempts.

The opposite is true with mastery models. In these situations the model exhibits a "flawless" performance from the beginning. To continue with the previous example of social skills, the mastery model would portray "perfect" social interaction for the child. This models the desired behavior for the child but does not allow the child to observe the gradual efforts towards mastery as evidenced in the coping model. It is not surprising that several studies support the idea that coping models are more effective than mastery models in facilitating desired changes (e.g., Bandura 1969, Meichenbaum 1971).

The fact that behaviors are modeled for the child does not ensure that the child will imitate them. Modeled behaviors may be imitated by the child or ignored. Sometimes the child will reject the modeled behaviors. In any case, the child's reaction to models in therapy is important and provides the therapist with clues about the child. For example, the socially awkward child may push away an appropriately interacting model, express anger at the model's successes, or even try to show the model how to do it a different way. Table 4-2 provides examples of the use of modeling in play therapy.

It is important to note that in all types of modeling, more than behavior is modeled. The child is also exposed to cues and situations surrounding the model's behavior. Thus, the child can witness environmental cues that may facilitate the model's behavior, as well as the model's attitude and verbalizations.

Modeling can also be covert, where the individual imagines a model performing certain behaviors rather than actually observing them. This

TABLE 4-2
Examples of Modeling in Play Therapy.

Behavioral Technique Modeled via Puppet	Vignette
Shaping/Positive Reinforcement	Child is afraid to go to school. Therapist helps puppet go near the school building, visit the school, and gradually stay in the classroom (shaping). The puppet receives encouragement and positive feedback (reinforcement) from therapist as it makes closer and closer approaches to being in school.
Shaping Socially Appropriate Expression of Feelings	Child makes doll hit the father whenever he comes to visit. Therapist knows that the child is angry with her father because he visits infrequently. Therapist has the doll turn her hitting into verbal expression, "I am mad at you, Daddy, because you don't visit."
Differential Reinforcement of Other Behavior (DRO)	Child makes the puppet slap another puppet. Therapist knows that the nursery school teacher is concerned that the child deals with her anger by hitting other children. The puppet's slapping is ignored (extinction). When appropriate behavior (e.g., shaking hands) is shown, the puppet is praised.

technique is used frequently in child therapy when the therapist tells the child a story in which a protagonist (model) exhibits some particular behavior or emotions. Often this takes the form of, "I once knew a boy who . . . " or "Sometimes kids tell me that . . . ." In this way, the therapist can convey some information to the child without directly talking about the child's own behavior.

Research on modeling was developed within a social learning framework and has been historically linked with behavior therapy. However, early explanations of modeling relied on the cognitive components of observational learning (Bandura 1969). Bandura considered attention, retention, motor reproduction, incentive, and motivation as major factors in learning through observation. Much of this early work laid the groundwork for later cognitive-behavioral interventions.

Another important intervention within a social learning framework is *behavioral rehearsal*, which provides an opportunity to help children master difficult situations and learn more adaptive skills. By rehearsing, new behaviors are observed and then practiced by the client. The goal is for the child to learn to modify maladaptive ways of responding via role-playing a variety of responses. In behavioral rehearsal, the therapist can provide immediate concrete feedback, followed by continued rehearsal of problem situations.

Older children can rehearse new skills (e.g., acting properly with a sibling, talking to a parent about a difficult topic). With young children, the therapist can model more adaptive responses via puppets, and coach the puppets. In this way coping strategies are modeled for the child. Shaping and positive reinforcement can be incorporated into the role-playing activity, and the child can rehearse new skills.

Interventions based on social learning theory, such as modeling, are often an integral part of play therapy regardless of the therapist's basic theoretical orientation. For example, modeling is used by all but the most nondirective therapists to demonstrate alternatives for the child. Similarly, behavioral rehearsal provides the child with an opportunity to practice new skills in an effort to develop more adaptive ways of responding.

GENERALIZATION IN BEHAVIOR THERAPY

One paradox of behavioral interventions is that they have the power to effect change in specific behaviors but often do so at the expense of generalization of treatment gains over time (see Karoly and Harris 1986). Clearly, one goal of treatment is for the individual to exhibit and maintain adaptive behavior in the natural environment after treatment has been terminated. This may be particularly problematic with children. In adults, generalization may occur in part because of the individual's purposeful efforts to generalize newly learned skills to different settings. However, without the child's awareness of the need to use new skills in various settings, or efforts by significant adults to help the child do so, generalization can be quite difficult for children.

A number of procedures are considered to enhance the likelihood of children's generalization of new skills across settings. First, it is important for the therapy to deal specifically with the transfer of desirable behaviors to natural settings and not leave this process to chance (Baer et al. 1968). That this is frequently not done may contribute to relapse rates. Play therapy lends itself well to planning for situations where generalization and maintenance may be problems. For example, if a child's behavior is most problematic at school, the therapist can set up a schoollike setting with puppets and have the puppets model appropriate school behaviors. Role-playing various possible activities and having the child observe these provides models of adaptive responses for the child. The therapist must see that such situations are incorporated into the treatment, so as to promote maintenance of treatment gains.

Second, reinforcement should come from many people and not from the therapist alone. Parents, teachers, baby–sitters, and all adults in the child's life should provide the child with appropriate reinforcement and positive feedback. Third, reinforcement should be provided to the child in many settings. The child needs this feedback in a variety of natural environments, not just from one (e.g., home, school). This is important because the behavior is likely to change only in the settings where it is being handled appropriately. The newly learned adaptive behaviors should be encouraged and reinforced by a variety of individuals across settings in order for these behaviors to be maintained.

Finally, any procedure that enhances self-control of behavior is likely to promote changes that are more durable and generalized. Providing a means to self-monitor and exhibit control offers the child a sense of mastery over problem behavior. The inclusion of cognitive change strategies, introduced in the next chapter, may provide the child with skills that enhance the behavioral interventions and help maintain changed behavior.

5

Cognitive
Interventions

Cognitive therapy as an approach to treatment has evolved over the last 20 to 30 years. Pioneering efforts by Aaron Beck with cognitive treatment of depression (Beck 1963) and by Albert Ellis with interventions to counter irrational, neurotic thinking (Ellis 1962) set the stage. Currently, the cognitive therapy model is used to treat a wide variety of clinical problems and populations, with an array of applications and approaches.

Cognitive therapy with children is one product of this growing field, although admittedly, it has been referred to as the "new kid on the block" (DiGiuseppe 1981). Cognitive approaches have been used in work with adolescent and younger school-age children, although only limited work has been reported on cognitive interventions with preschoolers.

This situation may in part be explained by the same criticism leveled at behavior therapists, namely that cognitive therapists have failed to integrate developmental and clinical understandings in their work with young children. A further, and significant, problem is the integration of cognitive-developmental considerations. The assumption that the cognitive capabilities of preschoolers are incompatible with a cognitive therapy approach has hindered further work in this area.

The basic model of cognitive therapy as it is applied to adult populations will be considered next. Cognitive approaches to adolescents and children will be reviewed and discussed in terms of their potential contributions to play therapy.

COGNITIVE THERAPY

Cognitive therapy is based on the cognitive model of emotional disorders, which involves the interplay among cognition, emotion, behavior, and physiology (Beck and Emery 1985). This model holds that behavior is mediated through verbal processes; disturbed behavior is considered to be an expression of irrational thinking.

The major premises of cognitive therapy are threefold: First, thoughts influence both the individual's emotions and behaviors in response to events. Second, perceptions and interpretations of events are shaped by the individual's beliefs and assumptions. Third, errors in logic, or "cognitive distortions," are prevalent in individuals experiencing psychological difficulties (Beck 1976). These cognitions are unspoken, and often unrecognized, assumptions made by the individual.

Cognitive therapy is designed to be brief, time-limited, and directive. Therapy is focused on specific and concrete goals and is contingent upon a strong therapeutic relationship. The core of the cognitive approach is described as "collaborative empiricism" (Beck et al. 1979). In work with adults, the therapist and client assume an equal share of responsibility for resolving the client's problems. The client is considered to be the expert on the idiosyncratic, personal meanings attached to events. The therapist "coaches" the client and structures the treatment, thereby minimizing the resistance that often accompanies more directive approaches. Collaboratively, the therapist and client identify the client's cognitions; test the validity of these thoughts, beliefs, and assumptions; and make needed changes in behavior and thought.

Cognitive therapy focuses on beliefs, such as expectations, evaluations, and attributions of causality. These beliefs, or assumptions, are considered to be hypotheses rather than fact. This allows individuals to more objectively examine their assumptions. Cognitive therapy also looks at patterns of thinking, or schemata (Beck 1964, 1972). Schemata are considered to be the underlying structures that organize one's experience and form the basis of one's beliefs. These are the themes that capture an individual's view of upsetting experiences (e.g., "If I do not do well in school, my parents will be angry at me"). Referred to as "core beliefs," they are thought to represent the core of the cognitive disturbance.

The cognitive model is based on the interplay between verbal processes and behavior. Building on this model, cognitive therapy is largely verbally based, with the client working together with the therapist to identify cognitions and test the validity of personal thoughts, assumptions, and beliefs. The nature of cognitive therapy as it is conceptualized with adults assumes a basic level of verbal and cognitive ability on the part of the client. Its use with less verbally oriented individuals raises some interesting issues. The appropriateness of cognitive therapy for children whose verbal abilities are more limited will be considered next.

IS COGNITIVE THERAPY APPROPRIATE FOR USE WITH CHILDREN AND ADOLESCENTS?

Cognitive therapies with adults assume that the individual has the cognitive capacity to differentiate between thinking that is rational and irrational; logical and illogical. The individual may need help in identifying and labeling such thoughts. However, once delineated, the inconsistencies can potentially be understood by the client. Such assumptions cannot necessarily be made with children. In fact, what appears irrational to an adult can be construed as very rational by a young child.

Fraiburg (1959) provides an excellent example of the extraordinarily magical world of the young child. David, a 2½-year-old child, was being prepared for a trip to Europe with his parents. He was a bright and verbal child, and his parents spoke with him about all the interesting things that they would do in Europe. David knew what a plane was, and seemed interested in the trip until he stopped asking questions and seemed upset. His parents were unable to determine what was troubling David, until one day when he acknowledged, " I can't go to Yurp! I don't know how to fly yet!" Clearly, David believed that his all-powerful parents did in fact know how to fly, that he too would one day learn to fly, and that it is the person, not the airplane, that flies (pp. 121–122).

Fraiburg referred to the preschool period as "the magic years," because magic best described the preschooler's irrational problem solving and resistance to logical thinking. Therefore, cognitive therapy with children must deal with the *child's* perspective of what is rational, not the adult's. For this reason, cognitive therapy with children focuses largely on absences in thinking rather than on distortions per se. Treatment helps develop adaptive cognitions, rather than replacing maladaptive ones.

COGNITIVE THERAPY WITH CHILDREN AND ADOLESCENTS

Cognitive therapy with children is receiving increasing attention and has recently been applied to diverse populations, including impulsive (Kendall and Braswell 1985); depressed (Emery et al. 1983); and encopretic (Knell and Moore 1990) children. Another growing application is the use of cognitive-behavioral principles for preventive purposes with non-clinical populations (e.g., Botvin and Tortu 1988). Whereas the principles of cognitive therapy can be communicated directly to adults, they may need to be communicated to children in less direct ways. To do this effectively, the therapist must be alert to developmental issues and alter therapeutic strategies accordingly. DiGiuseppe (1981) contends that each therapy technique should be seen as part of a continuum of procedures for use with children of different cognitive abilities. With this in mind, we turn to the application of cognitive-behavioral interventions with children and adolescents.

Specific cognitive-behavioral interventions will be discussed first as they are used with adults, adolescents, and school-age children; then, when appropriate, how they can be applied in working with preschoolers.

SPECIFIC CLINICAL INTERVENTIONS

Behavioral Methods

Behavioral methods in cognitive therapy focus on altering behaviors: decreasing maladaptive responses and increasing adaptive responses.

Such behavioral methods may be used singly, or may be combined with cognitive interventions. Behavioral interventions are often used to prepare an individual so that the benefits of cognitive therapy may be maximized. Whether used in conjunction with cognitive interventions or alone, behavioral methods provide powerful tools for change.

Self-monitoring

Self-monitoring refers to clients' observations and recording of information about certain aspects of their behavior. For example, an adolescent may be asked to keep a record of situations in which she feels rejected by her friends, how long the feelings last, and what makes these feelings change.

The monitoring of activities and moods can serve several purposes. Self-monitoring may be the only means of obtaining some information from the natural environment. Subjective reactions to such events can also be obtained. When used initially in assessment, self-monitoring serves as a baseline for later comparisons, and it is then useful throughout therapy. Hypotheses can be tested using self-monitoring, which may provide more accurate data than could be recalled. It also serves as a jumping-off point for discussion in therapy (DeRubeis and Beck 1988), providing structured information about the client's experiences.

As an assessment tool, self-monitoring has been criticized for its reactive effects (e.g., Nelson 1977). That is, it may produce changes in the target behavior. Such reactivity may have positive implications when self-monitoring is used for intervention purposes. Also, individuals may have difficulty accurately observing and reporting on their own behavior, or may selectively attend to one aspect of their behavior (Roth and Rehm 1980). Despite such limitations, appropriately structured self-monitoring tasks may offer important clinical information that cannot be obtained in other ways.

Self-monitoring can be used accurately by children as young as 4 or 5 years old (Fixsen et al. 1972, Risley and Hart 1968). It is especially useful if the child is asked to monitor activities or events, such as the number of times homework was completed or chores were finished. Usually, with young children, it is important for parents to help at home with this task rather than to expect such monitoring to be done independently. If it is explained carefully and simply, however, the child can be expected to understand the task and complete it with supervision. Figure 5–1 shows the self-monitoring of a 6-year-old child who was practicing a simplified relaxation exercise at home. Although her parents helped remind her when it was time to practice, she easily filled out this chart after each relaxation session at home.

For school-age children, self-monitoring of mood is much more difficult than monitoring of activities or events. When monitoring feelings, it is most useful to simplify the scales and to anchor specific feelings

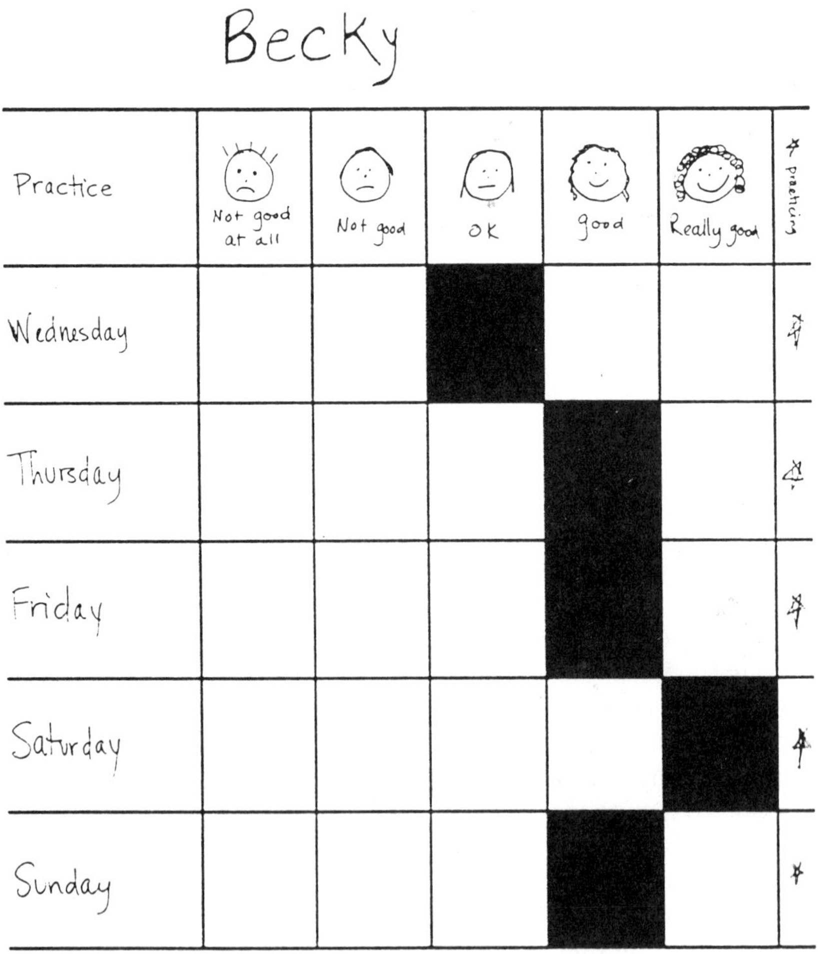

FIGURE 5–1.   Self-monitoring of Relaxation Exercises by a 6-year-old Girl.

to concrete examples. Older children can understand 10-point scales, with zero representing "the worst you ever felt in your whole life," and 10 standing for "the best you ever felt in your whole life" (Emery et al. 1983). Preschoolers are more inclined to have all-or-nothing thinking about feelings and to lack understanding of the complexities of their moods. Scales used with young children may need to be very concrete. Alternative scales for monitoring mood with young children include those anchored to faces (Garber 1982, cited in Emery et al. 1983) and to simple-feelings words (Barden et al. 1980). With very young children, faces depicting specific moods (e.g., mad, happy, sad) usually work best and can be understood by most children. It is often helpful to devise scales which progress in a "worst to best" order, such as sad faces increasingly getting happier. Scales should not include more than three or four options. Parents can monitor the accuracy of these perceptions by helping clarify the child's feeling (e.g., "How did you feel when you lost your doll? You were crying. Which picture looks like how you felt?").

Activity Scheduling

In this intervention, originally used with depressed adults, specific tasks are planned for, and then implemented, by the client. The rationale was that depressed individuals neither engage in nor expect to enjoy activities; the lack of pleasant activities subsequently contributes to their continued depressive affect (Lewinsohn 1974, 1975). One intervention with depressed individuals is to develop a list of pleasurable activities and then ensure that the client engages in some of them.

Scheduling specific activities with clients may increase the probability that they will participate in these activities. With adults, activities are agreed upon mutually between the client and therapist. By anticipating interferences with scheduled activities, the therapist and client can discuss any obstacles in advance and plan to avoid them.

Planned activities for children and adolescents may reduce time spent in passive or ruminative activities. This can be particularly useful for depressed, withdrawn, or very anxious children. These children may avoid activities because they do not expect to enjoy them, or because they perceive themselves as a failure when they try. When pressure is removed and the child is encouraged only to attempt the activity, many realize that they can have fun, despite expectations that they will not. Even if they do not enjoy the activity, they can still be reinforced for their efforts.

When activity scheduling is used with young children, it is best done with parent and child cooperating together. Although parent involvement is critical, it is equally important that the child have an active sense of control in activities planned. Providing the child with choices and control can be useful, particularly for the preschooler who is struggling with issues of autonomy. This can be especially important for withdrawn or sad children or children who are struggling with parents over control (e.g., regarding eating, toileting).

Systematic planning should provide the child with as much sense of control as possible. Providing "no-choice choices" can help preschoolers feel some input in their lives. An example of a "no-choice choice" is given to the child when the parent asks, "Do you want to play with the ball outside or the trucks in the basement?" This clearly communicates that the child is expected to play, but in this example the child maintains control over the toy and place.

For this to be effective, the parent must provide a limited range of acceptable options. The choice, "Do you want to play with the ball outside or go to the amusement park?" is a false one, if going to an amusement park is not truly an option. Further, it is important that the child maintain the sense of control in making the choice. If the child's choice is countered by the parent's efforts to encourage, or insist on, the alternate option, the child's sense of accomplishment in making a choice is lost.

It is important that the child feel a sense of competence at the assigned tasks, and that significant adults provide contingent reinforcement for activities well done. Reinforcement should not always be based on the final product but should also involve positive feedback for the child's efforts and perseverance. Such positive reinforcement can also enhance the child's mood. To ensure successful experiences, tasks can be broken down into small steps, thus reducing the difficulty of the activity and providing reinforcement for successive approximations to the completed activity.

Cognitive Methods

Whereas the behavioral methods used in cognitive-behavioral therapy usually involve an alteration in activity, cognitive methods deal with changes in cognition. This is an important distinction, because cognitive theories suggest that changes in affect *and* behavior occur as a result of changes in thinking.

In conducting cognitive therapy with children, the therapist must teach the child to identify, modify, and/or build cognitions. Self-report, frequently used with adults, is problematic as a tool for eliciting cognitions from children, so other methods must take its place. The therapist should be flexible and be able to gather information from many sources, such as the child's play and spontaneous verbalizations, as well as from parents, teachers, and other significant adults.

Recording Dysfunctional Thoughts

Cognitive therapists frequently ask clients to self-monitor their thoughts. A variety of methods are used, such as writing in a log book (e.g, Rehm 1982) or talking into a tape recorder (Craighead et al. 1979). Most frequently, self-monitoring is done through the *Daily Record of Dysfunctional Thoughts* (Beck et al. 1979). On this "thought sheet," the client monitors stimuli, emotional responses, and cognitions.

Although children can be encouraged to record their thoughts in a diary or notebook, or verbally into a tape recorder, the use of a *Daily Record of Dysfunctional Thoughts* is fairly limited with children. This type of recording is not only complex conceptually, it requires a level of writing not usually present until later childhood. However, parents may be instrumental in reminding the child to record simple thoughts at prearranged times, or after particular incidents.

For preschoolers, such recording of dysfunctional thoughts is more often a monitoring that is done by parents of the child rather than by children themselves. More accurately, then, such monitoring is a recording of dysfunctional statements made by the child rather than a recording of thoughts per se. The astute parent will listen for such comments not only in direct communication with the child but also via the child's play. Although overheard and repeated by the parent instead of being directly reported by the child, these comments can be invaluable in providing clues to the preschooler's perceptions.

An example of how this can be done is highlighted by the case of 5-year-old Mark, whose divorced parents had fiercely battled over custody and visitation issues. Mark frequently played with puppets, and in this play the daddy would steal the children away from the mommy and then drop them back at her house as he pleased. In the child's play, the father was always referred to as "super dad." Mark would often comment on how "stupid" the boy puppet was, and how much the father puppet must hate the son. The mother's recording of her observations of such play was invaluable to the therapist in understanding Mark's perceptions of himself and his difficult family situation.

Cognitive Change Strategies

With adults, a key component in changing faulty cognitions is through hypothesis testing. Thoughts, beliefs, assumptions, and expectations are treated as hypotheses to be tested scientifically. Often referred to as "irrational beliefs," these problem areas are identified and "experiments" designed to test these thoughts. This examination typically involves a three-pronged approach: Look at the evidence, explore the alternatives, and examine the consequences.

Although most adolescents have the cognitive capabilities to use similar cognitive change strategies, the nature of adolescence presents some unique challenges for the therapist. Among these are family interactions and parental cognitions that may interfere, bodily changes, sexual feelings, and peer interactions that may exacerbate and distort cognition (see Bedrosian 1981 for a more complete review of these issues). The clinician sensitive to these developmental issues will find that cognitive change strategies work well with adolescents.

With children, especially those at the concrete operational stage, these strategies present different challenges. Because children's cognitive abilities are more limited than those of adolescents, the hypothesis testing inherent in this approach is problematic. Children may have difficulty exploring situations, providing alternative explanations, and understanding consequences. In addition, the young child's thinking may appear to be irrational to an adult, but may be very real to the child. Thus children do have the capacity to misinterpret and distort reality; their inferences may be consistent with *their* perceptions of reality, although these perceptions are not necessarily accurate.

Children's reactions to the break-up of their parents' marriage provide an example of inaccurate, although personally consistent, perceptions. Parental divorce is often viewed by children as their fault, or at least due in part to some behavior on their part. The child makes assumptions such as "Daddy is leaving because I am a bad kid," or "If my behavior were better, Mommy wouldn't have left." If pushed to provide an alternative explanation (such as "Mommy and Daddy fight a lot; Daddy is leaving because he and Mommy don't get along"), the child may remain stuck with the previous, more personal explanation.

Therefore, helping children with changing cognitions dictates that the child will need assistance from adults in generating alternative explanations, testing them, and altering beliefs (Emery et al. 1983). Preschool-age children will need even greater assistance in implementing cognitive change strategies. To challenge one's beliefs, it is necessary to distance oneself from the beliefs, something that is very difficult for preschool-age children to do. Additionally, the child needs an "accumulated history of events" in order to understand the ramifications of certain situations (Kendall 1991). Learning takes place in part from experience, and the very young child still has limited experiences on which to build. At this age, thought and reality are not always separate. However, play does provide an arena to help the preschooler bridge the gap between beliefs and reality, and to build experiences that may help the child.

Play allows the child to reenact problem situations and potentially to gain mastery over events and circumstances. The therapist can assist in this mastery by providing the "experiments" in the play situations, and by assisting the child in looking at the evidence, exploring the alternatives, and examining the consequences. For example, the therapist may structure some of the play with the child to reflect alternative scenarios, so that the child then experiences different reactions and consequences for the same situation.

Changing cognitions through play therapy may be highlighted by the case of 5-year-old Mark, presented earlier in this chapter. Mark's mother was able to provide information through her recording of the child's play and conversations at home. Additionally, the therapist could observe Mark and form hypotheses about the meaning of his play. In spontaneous play, Mark would repeatedly have the daddy puppet steal the children and return them to the mommy puppet. The therapist could use this play to help understand Mark's sense of confusion, frustration, and fear about the family situation. Mark's labeling of the dad as "super dad" also provided information about the child's perceptions that his father had certain magical powers. The therapist could use Mark's play to help him see that he was indeed safe at home with his mother and would not be hurt by his father. Given Mark's interest in the puppets, the therapist used them to reenact alternative scenes for Mark. Scenes were enacted that verbalized the puppet's confusion and fears about his dad, ways that he could feel better about himself, as well as the fact that he could be safe.

Coping Self-statements

The way an individual interprets events, not the events per se, affects the person's ability to cope. The cognitive therapists believe this, but no one may have said it better than Epictetus in the first century C.E. when he stated "I am upset, not by events, but rather by the way I view them." When one believes negative self-thoughts, maladaptive physiological reactions may follow. These negative experiences may then prompt continued negative self-statements, which may in turn lead to poor decisions. This feedback loop is illustrated by the child who predicts he will not win a part in the school play, supported by his negative self-statements (e.g., "My acting is not very good"), which lead to physiological reactions, such as shaking and sweaty palms.

Cognitive therapists work with adults to help them develop more adaptive self-statements. One approach is Meichenbaum's (1985) stress inoculation training, which in part helps the individual develop positive coping statements. These statements prompt more adaptive coping responses. Meichenbaum contends that these self-statements should be specific and related to issues of competence and a sense of control. He offers examples such as "I can meet this challenge," "Relax, I'm in control," "I handled it pretty well" (pp. 72–73). Such statements are merely provided as examples; it is important that self-statements are specifically relevant for each individual.

Clients of all ages can be helped to develop such coping self-statements. However, treatment strategies must be modified based on the age and cognitive level of the individual. Whereas using these interventions with older children and adolescents may be quite similar to using them with adults, the teaching of coping self-statements must be modified when working with young children. Children in the preoperational stage of cognitive development may benefit most from learning simple statements about themselves. Often in the form of self-affirmation, these modified self-statements can be used with children as young as 2½ to 3 years old. Obviously, at this young age the self-statements are very simple, both linguistically and conceptually. The words can be as simple as "I can sit," or "Good sitting." Such self-statements contain a component of self-reward (e.g., the message "I am doing a good job"). This can be thought of as "the little engine that could" approach, reflecting Walter Piper's (1950) story for children, where the engine gets up the hill while repeatedly saying "I think I can, I think I can."

Positive self-statements can be modeled by the parent for the child. For example, the young child loves hearing praise for accomplishments. Praise such as "good boy" or applauding the child are often effective, but even more helpful is specific verbal labeling of what the child has done well (e.g., "Good girl, you picked up the toys"). Turning these into self-statements does not always happen spontaneously; parents must learn to prompt positive self-affirmative comments from their children. In addition, children's positive self-comments are often short-lived and situation-specific, and thus it is important both to teach generalization as well as to ensure that parents reinforce the positive message for the child. For some parents this concept is a difficult one, in that they *expect* good behavior from their child and do not feel that such behavior needs to be praised. It is important for parents to understand that children will not internalize positive feelings unless taught the value of their actions. One way children learn the positive value of what they do is through specific labeling with positive feedback for their behavior.

Such positive self-statements were illustrated in therapy with Jim, the 5-year-old child who was fearful of closed doors after accidentally being locked in a bathroom (discussed in Chapter 4). A systematic desensitization paradigm was used with Jim, and he was able to tolerate being in a room as the door was gradually closed. While he was learning to stay and deal with his fear, he played in ways that alleviated his anxiety, and learned to make simple positive self-statements, such as "I can stay in this room," "I feel good playing in here," and "I feel good, I am brave."

Bibliotherapy

Although not technically a cognitive intervention, bibliotherapy is being used increasingly as an adjunct to therapy. The dramatic increase of self-help literature for adults has provided a medium to help individuals question their irrational beliefs and consider their options. Many of these books are specifically based on cognitive theory (e.g., Beck 1988, Burns 1980). Often, they attempt to introduce the concepts of cognitive therapy and help readers apply these ideas to their lives in an effort to alleviate problems.

The use of bibliotherapy with children may have a somewhat different focus. Rather than specifically teaching concepts and suggesting ways of using these in one's life, children's books provide more of a storytelling approach. Children's literature has always had messages and morals, but only recently has there been a proliferation of stories about children with specific problems or those dealing with traumatic events (e.g., divorce, death, moving). In such stories, a particular message is conveyed more indirectly, with the hope that the listener will learn something through the characters in the book. Essentially, the story models for the listener ways of coping with life events. Books and other written materials (and videotapes, too) are a positive addition to cognitive interventions. Many such books are written specifically for the preschool population and are highly useful in play therapy with young children.

Often, bibliotherapy with preschoolers does not depend on published materials but is created specifically for the child. A short-term intervention with 2½-year-old Billy highlights the creative use of bibliotherapy in treatment. Over a 6-month period, Billy and his family had experienced numerous fires in abandoned houses in their neighborhood. Just before Billy was seen in a mental health setting, the garage of the house next door had burned. Before the fire was put out, Billy had been carried from his bed in the middle of the night. Billy's language was limited, and the family was having great difficulty helping him understand that everything was going to be all right. He became upset when he heard any kind of siren or saw a fire truck. It was also difficult for him to fall asleep at night.

The therapist wrote a brief story about a child who experienced similar fires near his home. The story ended with the boy learning that he and his family could be safe. In the story, the child felt safe when he went to bed at night, could talk about his feelings and tell his family about his fears. Billy was asked to draw some pictures to go with the story, and given his age, his drawing ability was limited; however, by doing so he was able to personalize the story. The therapist read the story to the child over the course of several sessions. A copy of the story was sent home with the parents, and they read it to Billy every night before he went to sleep. Such an individualized approach proved useful for this child and was presented to him in a modality (story) that was understandable and with which he could interact, by providing his own "illustrations."

CONCLUSION

In summary, although cognitive therapy with children and adolescents has received increasing attention, there are still only a limited number of examples in the literature of cognitive play therapy with preschool-age children. Despite the paucity of literature, certain cognitive interventions can be applied with very young children if these interventions are presented appropriately. Self-monitoring and activity scheduling have been successfully used with preschoolers, although both interventions may need to include a significant component of parent involvement to ensure a positive outcome. Cognitive interventions can also be used with preschoolers to help them modify their thoughts and learn more adaptive coping skills. Particularly useful with young children are coping self-statements and bibliotherapy. Clearly, for these interventions to be effective their presentation must be relatively simple, concrete, and not verbally complex.

6

Assessment

Although it is possible to begin play therapy with a child without any type of assessment process, most therapists will consider the first few sessions as part of an intake or evaluation period. The nature of this assessment may range from informal observation to formal interviews or testing. Whereas more nondirective therapies may not include a specific assessment period, others rely heavily on information obtained during an initial evaluation. For example, with more structured, directive play therapy, a complete assessment is necessary before beginning. The therapist should have information about the child's current functioning, level of development, and presenting problems. Additionally, a sense of the child's perspective of the problem areas is important. In order to develop a treatment plan with specific goals, the therapist needs to understand the situation from the parents' perspective as well as the child's. Assessment does not always take place during one discrete period, but often continues after the initial evaluation as part of the entire treatment process.

In this chapter we will begin by considering some basic principles that are considered critical in the assessment of young children. After discussion of more traditional psychological assessment, including standardized measures of child functioning through parent-report measures and individually administered tests, nonstandardized assessment measures will be considered. Play assessments, both structured and unstructured, as well as issues in interviewing are presented. The implications for these issues in assessment within a cognitive-behavioral play therapy framework are discussed and highlighted with a case example.

PRINCIPLES IN THE ASSESSMENT OF YOUNG CHILDREN

Assessment of the child for therapy should be approached from the perspective of normal development. If psychopathology or problems in development are considered to be "normal development gone awry" (Wenar 1982), then to understand problem behaviors one must first understand normal development. If normal child development with its ranges and individual differences is used as a backdrop, the difficulties a given child presents can be seen in sharper relief.

Information from the parents provides the foundation for further assessment. The parent interview may be the primary source of information, owing to the child's difficulty in self-expression and the fact that referral is usually initiated based on parental concern about the child. The parent interview should clarify and operationally define any specific concerns. For example, rather than simply describing concerns regarding their child as being "out of control" or having "tantrums," the parents should be asked to give examples of specific behaviors, including antecedents and consequences. Additionally, the therapist should gather information regarding what efforts the parents have made to deal with the child's behavior. A complete developmental history will provide not only information regarding key areas of development but also a glimpse into the parents' expectations and perceptions of the child's difficulties (Braswell and Kendall 1988).

Assessment information should be obtained from multiple sources. Children behave differently in different environments and with different people. If information about the child is gathered from only one source, it is not possible to really understand how the child behaves in the other settings in which he or she functions. This is particularly problematic if the therapist only gathers information from the parents, but the child spends time with other caretakers (e.g., day-care provider, baby-sitter) who are not interviewed.

Assessment information should be obtained from the child. Typically, the descriptions children give of their problems are not considered necessary or useful. To the extent that clinicians seek reliable and valid information, the child interview may not be helpful. However, the therapist who disregards this information from the child ignores the importance of the child's perceptions. Because these perceptions may have a mediating influence on the child's behavior and, ultimately, on the effectiveness of treatment, it is important to consider this information in treatment planning (Bierman 1983). Without the child's input, a valuable source of data is lost.

Assessment should include evaluation of readiness for treatment. Assessment includes more than an evaluation of the presenting problems. It is important to assess the child's and/or parents' ability to engage in therapy, as well as the parents' ability to support the child's treatment.

If these principles are considered in planning and carrying out an assessment, the chances of obtaining useful information are maximized. Next we will consider some of the specific measures used in assessment of young children.

PARENT-REPORT MEASURES OF CHILD DEVELOPMENT AND BEHAVIOR

A number of parent-report measures are used in assessing young children. These measures can be completed fairly easily and quickly by the parent and can provide the clinician with valuable information. Because these measures have norms, they provide a background of normal development against which to view the child's individual development.

The following measures are by no means exhaustive. They merely represent several measures that are frequently used and considered to be both reliable and valid.

Child Behavior Checklist (CBCL)

The Child Behavior Checklist (CBCL), developed by Achenbach and Edelbrock (1983) for children between ages 4 and 16, is a widely used, well-standardized checklist for assessing children's symptoms. Both age- and gender-appropriate norms are available. A special form exists for use with children from 2 to 3 years old. The scale includes a measure of social competence and behavior problems; the latter provides a profile of the child's behavior relative to the normative group. Summary scores representing internalizing and externalizing problems can be calculated. Because the scale is filled out by a significant adult in the child's life (usually a parent), it is a measure of the parent's *perception* of the child. The CBCL is carefully constructed and is considered valid both for screening for problems in children and for measuring treatment effectiveness.

Minnesota Child Development Inventory (MCDI)

The Minnesota Child Development Inventory (MCDI), developed by Ireton and Thwing (1972), is a 320-item, yes–no inventory of child development for children aged 1–6 years. Based on parent (or other significant adult) report, the inventory provides a measure of development on six separate scales based on parent perception of the child's development. The scores are plotted on a profile that gives the child's developmental status relative to a normative sample.

If the parents are considered to be reliable informants, this inventory can provide an overview of the child's developmental level without conducting extensive testing of the child. It can also be used as a screening measure to determine whether individual developmental/intellectual evaluation of the child is indicated. If testing is administered, the MCDI can be used as a means of contrasting parent perception of the child's abilities with the child's measured functioning.

INDIVIDUALLY ADMINISTERED INTELLIGENCE AND PERSONALITY MEASURES

Among traditional psychological tests are a number of intellectual and projective techniques that can be used with preschool-age children. Such measures, however, are frequently not employed by play therapists of a variety of orientations, although they have considerable potential for providing important clinical information about the child. Tests of cognitive/intellectual development offer information about the child's cognitive abilities and may provide some information regarding the child's capacity to benefit from more verbally oriented therapies. Projective tests may offer information about the child's conflicts, coping styles, style of organizing information, and view of the world. A complete review of such measures is beyond the scope of this chapter; the reader is referred to Sattler (1988) for an extensive discussion of traditional psychological assessment of children.

Although much of this information can also be gathered from observation over time and from other sources, formal testing often provides a stepping-off point that is critical in treatment planning. In many cases it is helpful to gather such information at the onset of treatment. This is particularly true for preschoolers, because many young children referred for therapy have developmental lags of some kind. Because they are not yet of school age, these children are not under the watchful eye of a teacher who can use classmates as a comparison group.

The child's overall test-taking behaviors and response style can provide information that adds to specific test results. Interpretations based on behavior in testing situations is subjective and open to much interclinician variability. However, when tests are given in a standardized way, hypotheses about a child's test-taking behavior are liable to less subjectivity than if such interpretations were being made about a child in a free play setting.

Projective Measures

Projective techniques are relatively unstructured tasks consisting of rather vague and ambiguous stimuli presented with only brief, general instructions. These techniques are based on the projective hypothesis, which states that the way in which an individual perceives and interprets the test materials or "structures" the situation is a "projection" of his or her personality (Frank 1939). Thus, the individual's thought processes, feelings, needs, anxieties, conflicts, and motivations will be reflected by responses to the task. The theoretical rationale of projective techniques is questionable, as are the psychometric properties of most projective tests (Anastasi 1982). Nonetheless, they are extremely popular with clinicians and continue to be considered a valuable clinical tool.

Projective tests are not typically used by cognitive-behaviorally oriented therapists. However, they should not simply be disregarded because of their original development by psychodynamically oriented theorists. Certain projective tests may provide the very young child structure that may be similar to the structure provided by dolls and puppets. Projective techniques with very young children may provide concrete, pictorial representations to which the child can respond. In contrast with an interview, the more structured projective test material may offer the child a less ambiguous array of stimuli than is provided by merely responding to the interviewer's questions. This would be particularly true for projective tests, such as several of the apperception tests, which represent pictures that are within the child's repertoire of experiences.

Apperception Tests

Thematic Apperception Test/Children's Apperception Test.
Two of the most popular projective tests used with children are the Thematic Apperception Test (TAT) (Murray 1943) and the Children's Apperception Test (CAT) (Bellak and Bellak 1949). Despite the widespread use of these techniques, their utility has been limited by a number of factors. Many children have difficulty with the TAT because the cards primarily use adult figures (twenty-nine of thirty-one cards depict only adults). By contrast, the CAT was developed to provide pictures that would be more relevant for young children. However, the CAT cards depict anthropomorphized animal figures, which are often not taken seriously by any but the very youngest children. Often, children are able only to identify and label the animal and the activity presented, without providing any further information. Because the animals are depicted in "humanlike" activities, they may seem silly to many children. Older children may also feel infantilized by the nature of the pictures. A set of human figures (CAT-H) exists and substitutes humans for the animals in the CAT. However, these pictures are still problematic for many children.

Another limitation of the aforementioned apperception pictures is that the nature of the stimulus figures, not the child's unique personality, may be the primary determinant of the child's responses (e.g., McArthur 1976). Children may not respond to cards that depict unfamiliar, unrealistic, or unambiguous situations (McArthur and Roberts 1982). Finally, the interpretation of the TAT and CAT is highly subjective, owing to the lack of a standardized system of scoring.

Roberts Apperception Test for Children.   The Roberts Apperception Test for Children (RATC) (McArthur and Roberts 1982), designed for children ages 6 through 15, can be used with 3- to 5-year-olds, although no norms are available for the younger age group. Unlike the TAT, the RATC has norms for youngsters between 6 and 15 years old. Despite the lack of norms for this young population (3–5 years old), it is still useful for several reasons. Children are depicted in all sixteen of the stimulus cards, in which everyday interpersonal events are represented. It portrays situations such as parent–child, sibling, and peer relationships, as well as school issues and situations involving aggression and mastery. There are separate sets of cards for white and black children, although at this time there are no norms for black children.

Sentence Completion Tests

The Sentence Completion Test, a projective technique, can provide valuable information about the individual's thoughts, perceptions, assumptions, and underlying beliefs. Although there are many versions of this task, they are usually not standardized. The typical Sentence Completion Test allows the individual to complete sentence stems, such as "I get upset when . . . " or "My mother. . . . " If they are able to do so, older children or adults usually write in their responses, whereas younger children respond orally. The traditional Sentence Completion Test is usually not used with children under age 5 or 6, because of their difficulty in comprehending the expectations and therefore responding in a coherent manner.

Puppet Sentence Completion Task.   The Puppet Sentence Completion Test was developed to make the traditional Sentence Completion Test more accessible for preschool-age children (Knell 1992). It is modeled after the traditional Sentence Completion Test which is used with older children, adolescents, and adults. The puppet version employs three puppets, two controlled by the therapist and one by the child. The task consists of two parts: one in which the sentence completion activity is modeled for the child by the therapist's two puppets, and the second part in which the child completes sentences. The therapist begins the second part only when it is clear that the child understands the task (see Table 6–1).

TABLE 6–1
Puppet Sentence Completion Test (Knell 1992)

Directions: The therapist should let the child choose a puppet. After the child has chosen a puppet, the therapist chooses two puppets. If the child so wishes, the therapist can let the child pick the puppets for the therapist.
The following code is used in the directions:
Puppet A—Therapist's
Puppet B—Therapist's
Puppet C—Child's

Part I
Directions: Puppet A states the sentence stem. Puppet B quickly responds. The therapist then turns to Puppet C (held by the child) for a response. The therapist supplies answers for Puppet B. Move to Part II as soon as it is clear that the child understands the task by providing a response for Puppet C.

Puppet A: My name is _____ .
             [turn to Puppet B:] My name is _____ .
             [turn to Puppet C:] My name is _____ .

Puppet A: My favorite ice cream is:
             [Puppet B:] ____Chocolate ice cream__ .
             [Puppet C:] _____ .

Puppet A: I am:
             [Puppet B:] ____4 years old_____ .
             [Puppet C:] _____ .

Puppet A: My favorite toy is:
             [Puppet B:] ____my teddy bear____ .
             [Puppet C:] _____ .

Puppet A: My favorite color is:
             [Puppet B:] ____blue_____ .
             [Puppet C:] _____ .

If the child does not understand the task, go back through and have Puppet B prompt the child to help Puppet C give a response. Continue until task is clearly understood by the child. Do not go on to Part II until it is clear that the child understands the task. If the child does not seem to understand what is expected in Part I, Part II will probably not be understood.

Note: Some children catch on quite quickly and do not seem to like the repetition necessary in Part I. For these children, it is permissible to go directly to Part II. Although it is preferable to write down the child's responses immediately, because the therapist has a puppet on each hand it may be necessary to record responses immediately following the administration of Part I.

(continued)

TABLE 6–1 (*continued*)

Part II

Directions: In Part II, Puppet A states the sentence stem. The sentence is stated directly to Puppet C. The response made by the child (Puppet C) should be written in the blank immediately. Some children will give two responses, one for the puppet and one for themselves. Both responses should be noted.

1. My favorite food is _____ .
2. I love to _____ .
3. Outside I play with _____ .
4. Mommy is _____ .
5. Daddy is _____ .
6. My favorite TV show is _____ .
7. (*If applicable*) My brother's name is _____ .
8. (*If applicable*) My sister's name is _____ .
9. I like to pretend to be _____ .
10. If I were bigger I would _____ .
11. At night when I sleep I _____ .
12. I am afraid of _____ .
13. I hate _____ .
14. The best secret is _____ .
15. The worst secret is _____ .
16. Mommy is nice when _____ .
17. Daddy is nice when _____ .
18. Daddy is mean when _____ .
19. Mommy is mean when _____ .
20. I am happiest when _____ .
21. I am saddest when _____ .
22. I get scared when _____ .
23. My biggest problem is _____ .
24. The worst thing about me is _____ .
25. With my hands I like to touch _____ .
26. With my hands I don't like to touch _____ .
27. Someone I don't like to touch me is _____ .
28. Someone I like to touch me is _____ .
29. My body is _____ .
30. I don't like to be touched on my _____ .
31. A secret I am not supposed to tell is _____ .
32. I am the maddest when _____ .
33. I am the happiest when _____ .
34. I like to pretend to be _____ .

The Puppet Sentence Completion Test is structured to facilitate the child's understanding of what is expected. It is more developmentally suited to the preschooler for two reasons. First, the task itself is not begun until it is clear that the child understands the directions. The directions are conveyed via modeling with the puppets, and the child's responses to the preliminary section of the task indicate to the therapist whether or not the child understands what is expected. Second, the child has the opportunity to complete the stem either by means of the puppet or without the puppet as a prompt. For some children, the use of the puppet provides a tool that makes the task easier because they do not need to directly tell the therapist how they feel. For others, modeling with the puppet explains the task to them, at which point they are comfortable responding freely to the task without the puppets. In either case, the task is introduced with puppets, which are familiar to and enjoyed by most children.

Because there is no standardized Sentence Completion Test, any sentence stems can be used with the Puppet Sentence Completion Test. This is helpful because particular sentence stems may elicit information about certain areas. For example, stems such as "The worst secret is . . . " or "When I am in bed I think about . . . " may provide structure for the sexually abused child to convey information that would be difficult to reveal in an interview. Stems such as "When my mommy and daddy stopped living together . . . " may be useful with children experiencing the divorce of their parents. Ideally, a set of common stems might be used with all preschool-age children. Special stems, unique to their life situation or presenting problems, can be added for specific populations (e.g., children of divorced parents, children who have been sexually abused).

Preliminary use of this instrument suggests that it can be understood by children as young as 3 years of age. Many children understand the task quite quickly and are able to move past the first part. When children refuse to respond to items or provide "silly" answers, this may provide useful information about the child. For example, Richard, a boy aged 4½ who had been sexually abused by a baby-sitter, responded to several items, as follows:

> My favorite toy is: fire truck.
> My favorite food is: spaghetti.

With my hands I don't like to touch: <u>dirty things.</u>
I am afraid of: <u>ghosts.</u>

However, he refused to answer, or gave silly, garbled, nonword answers to sentence stems such as:

Mommy is:
I am happiest when:
A secret I am not supposed to tell is:

Although one reasonable hypothesis is that the child did not understand the more complex sentences (such as "A secret I am not supposed to tell is . . . "), this appears unlikely, given his above-average receptive language skills and the fact that he could appropriately respond to equally complex stems (e.g., "With my hands I don't like to touch . . . ").

Feeling Scales/Drawings

Various authors have written about the use of drawings to depict feelings in assessment and treatment of young children (e.g., Bierman 1983, Harter 1977, 1983, Hughes and Baker 1990). By providing concrete referents, such as pictures depicting people with various facial expressions ("feeling faces"), children may be able to provide information about their own feelings.

For example, a preschooler may not respond to questions such as "How do you feel about your new sister?" However, if the child is offered pictures with faces depicting simple emotions (e.g., sad, happy, angry), she may be able to point to the picture that most closely describes her feelings. Another option is to give her pictures of a family with a new baby; she may be able to respond more appropriately to the picture than to a question. There are numerous ways these pictures can be used. If the clinician asks the child to look at feeling faces, the child can be asked to point to the one that describes how she felt when her new sister was brought home. Or, after viewing a family picture with mother, father, girl, and baby, the child may be asked to describe the picture and tell what she is feeling.

Numerous variations exist. For example, a child may be given a feeling face and asked to tell a story about the face, tell about something that makes him or her feel that way, or in some verbal or nonverbal way convey to the therapist thoughts about particular feelings. Techniques utilizing concrete referents such as feeling faces may also be used to assess responses to a particular task (e.g., feelings after doing a relaxation exercise). Even young children can be shown pictures and asked to "rate" personal feelings. This technique is used often, for example, having a child point out feelings after a visit with a noncustodial parent, or how a sibling might feel during a family fight. Many children who are quite verbal still have difficulty with words denoting emotions.

As discussed previously, the preschool child has difficulty understanding the existence of contradictory feelings. This all-or-nothing thinking offers children a very limited view of their own emotions, an issue addressed by Harter (1977) through the use of drawings depicting conflicting views. With a 6-year-old patient, Harter used a simple drawing depicting the smart and dumb parts of a person, to show that sometimes an individual can feel smart and sometimes dumb. She continued this theme with other feelings and conflicts, such as happy/sad; good/bad; and talk/don't talk (Harter 1977).

These approaches are especially useful with less verbal children. The case example of a 4-year-old child fearful of separating from her parents, presented later in this chapter, provides one example of how this may be done. There is also an example of the use of pictures and feeling faces with an elective mute 6-year-old in Chapter 8. She used these concrete representations to nonverbally show her feelings.

PLAY ASSESSMENT

In the clinical literature, play has been primarily viewed as a treatment, rather than assessment, technique. Between 1930 and 1960, when play therapy was popular, little was written about the clinical use of play as an assessment technique. However, during the same time, in the developmental literature, much attention was focused on the description and classification of play from a normal, developmental perspective. Although much of this work predated the use of play for assessment purposes in the clinical setting, it has only recently been integrated into the clinical literature. When play was used diagnostically, the child's reaction to the unstructured play environment was often used to generate hypotheses about the child's functioning.

Some of the most systematic work in the developmental field was done by Parton (1932), who studied the normal social development of play. She noted six categories of play: unoccupied behavior; solitary independent play; onlooker behavior; parallel activity; associative play; and cooperative play. The Parton scale, widely known by developmentalists, is used commonly in research but rarely in clinical work. Although this understanding of the development of play is important, it really does not speak to the clinical insights that may be gained from watching a child play.

Other, more clinical attempts to systematically assess play included Lowenfeld's "Miniature World Technique" (1939, 1950), in which the child constructed a world out of miniature toys. The child built a "world" out of these toys, and the result was used by the therapist for interpretation. Other similar techniques include Buhler's (1951a, 1951b) World Test and the Erica method developed by Bratt and Harding (Sjolund 1982, cited in Schaefer et al. 1991). The materials in the Erica method consist of 360 miniature toys, coded into twelve categories (e.g., aggressive, active, peaceful). The assessment takes place over three sessions, with the child's construction photographed and a record form completed at the end of each session. Finally, a diagnostic formulation consisting of developmental, milieu, somatic/psychosomatic, and psychopathological diagnoses is derived. Both the World Test and the Erica method have standardized procedures, equipment, and methods for interpretation. However, neither is used frequently in this country, although the Erica method is quite popular in Scandinavian countries.

Despite the development of such measures, play assessments are typically informal and lack any methodological rigor. They may provide the therapist with a wealth of information about the child, albeit not in a systematic fashion. There are no standardized play interviews that confirm a particular diagnosis or elicit specific symptoms. However, play interviews can be used to support parent report or can suggest a different direction from one based on the problem as described by the parent. Commonly they are used in a somewhat "projective" manner, as a way for the clinician to observe and understand how the child views the world as conveyed through play.

The variety of information that can be obtained from the play interview is endless. However, these types of assessment are bound to be subjective inasmuch as the information is understood by therapists in a manner consistent with their theoretical orientation. However, regardless of orientation, therapists often develop a list of areas to assess when observing and interacting with a child in play. (See Sattler 1988 for a discussion of areas to assess with young children.)

ASSESSMENT INTERVIEW

Children under the age of 5 years are typically not interviewed as part of the assessment process. In fact, the child's own description of the presenting problem is usually not considered either a necessary or useful part of the assessment. Such direct information from the child is often considered inaccurate, unreliable, and unnecessary, because more useful information can be obtained from the parents. Although it is wise not to consider the clinical interview of the child as the major source of data, the interview can provide one avenue to understanding cognitive and affective variables that might be mediating other difficulties (Bierman 1983). At the very least, it offers the clinician a unique perspective of the child's view.

In addition to cognitive limitations that make young children difficult to interview effectively, many young children do not have the context within which to place the assessment experience. Whereas school-age children may be more accustomed to talking with adults outside their families, many preschool-age children have never had such an experience. Even for preschoolers in alternative-to-home-care settings, such as day care, the numbers of adults with whom they interact on a regular basis may be fairly limited. This lack of experience in interacting with strangers, coupled with the uniqueness of the clinical setting, may prompt timidity in interacting with a therapist, even for children who are normally not shy or reserved.

Developmentally Sensitive Interviewing

Interviewing preschoolers is possible if one is aware of the cognitive-developmental characteristics of youngsters at this age and conducts the interview accordingly. According to Hughes and Baker (1990), the cardinal prerequisite of developmentally sensitive child interviewing is *flexibility*. Such flexibility is determined in part by the child's developmental level, the purpose of the interview, the relationship between child and interviewer, the setting, and the interpersonal styles of both child and interviewer.

Interviews are largely a combination of verbal questioning and play observation and assessment. Standard verbal interview techniques will not be effective with young children, and interviewers must adjust their techniques according to the developmental level of the child. The child may need concrete referents, options, and structure in order to understand the interviewer and respond appropriately. Bierman (1983) presents an excellent overview of the ways in which a developmentally sensitive interview can be conducted with a preschool-age child.

CLINICAL ASSESSMENT IN COGNITIVE-BEHAVIORAL THERAPY WITH ADULTS

With adults, cognitive therapists obtain basic clinical data, as well as specific information about the client's thoughts, feelings, beliefs, and underlying assumptions. Although information is obtained in the initial clinical interviews, assessment in cognitive therapy is an ongoing process. The areas of cognition that are of interest include self-statements, attributions, expectations, self-efficacy expectations, irrational beliefs, basic assumptions, schemata, mental images, and current concerns (Freeman et al. 1990). Such information may be gathered from interview as well as from observation in the natural environment, self-monitoring, thought sampling, self-report measures, and traditional psychological tests. Most widely used with adults are the clinical interview and self-monitoring measures.

A wide array of assessment procedures has been developed to assess specific presenting problems in adults, such as depression and anxiety—for example, the Beck Depression Inventory (BDI) (Beck 1978), and the State form of the State-Trait Anxiety Inventory (Speilberger et al. 1970). Many of these measures are of the self-report type, where the individual is presented with a predetermined set of items to rate along some specific dimension. Such measures assume that the cognitions being measured are within the client's awareness, and that the individual will respond honestly. Although the client may be influenced by a wish to respond in a certain way, these measures are commonly used in clinical practice and can provide the clinician with a rich source of data.

CLINICAL ASSESSMENT IN COGNITIVE-BEHAVIORAL THERAPY WITH CHILDREN AND ADOLESCENTS

In contrast with the assessment of the adult client, cognitive-behavioral assessment of children takes place with the parents or significant others as well as with the child. In many instances it is the adults closest to the child who can provide information that may contribute to an understanding of the child's feelings, beliefs, and concerns. The observant parent may note comments or behaviors of the child, which, when reported to the therapist, provide information that would be difficult for the young child to convey directly.

For example, Anna was a 4½-year-old girl who seemed to be struggling with a number of major life changes she and her family had experienced. Within the course of approximately 6 months, a third child was born, the family moved, she began a new preschool program, and her grandfather died. One night, a friend of the mother's joined the family for dinner. The children were aware that after dinner their mother and her friend were going out and they were to stay home with their father. Anna began screaming and crying at the dinner table: she did not want her mother's friend to be at the table, she did not want to eat, she didn't like the way everyone was "looking" at her. Anna's mother was aware that none of these statements contained what was truly bothering Anna. The mother pointed out to Anna that perhaps the child was upset because she wanted to spend time with her mother rather than having her mother go out. When the parents later discussed this situation with the therapist, the information showed how Anna was dealing with her feelings. At that time, Anna was not able to say directly what she was feeling, and although she could convey it through her doll play, the mother's example was explicit and clear and related to a real-life situation that needed to be handled by the family.

A number of measures exist to assess specific problems in children (e.g., Children's Depression Inventory [CDI], Kovacs 1985; State-Trait Anxiety Inventory for Children [STAIC], Spielberger 1973). Many of these measures rely on the child's self-report and therefore are only used with school-age children, who are better able to verbally represent their feelings.

Self-report assessment would provide valuable information about the child's perceptions, attributions, and expectations. However, the direct assessment of these constructs in young children is quite difficult and rarely obtained via self-report measures. Thus, direct assessment of the child is often more inferential than with adults. Understanding the child's cognitions and beliefs comes through observation and interaction: play assessment, developmentally sensitive interviewing, and self-report measures utilizing feeling faces and other concrete referents. Taken alone, direct assessment may not provide a complete picture of the child's situation, but by using it in combination with parent report, one may come closer to understanding the child's perspective.

DIAGNOSTIC CLASSIFICATION SYSTEM

Assessment is often undertaken in order to understand whether a child's behavior is in any way pathological. As noted earlier, epidemiological and large-scale surveys have found that a large number of problematic behaviors occur in preschoolers. Rather than suggesting that the incidence of psychopathology is high in this age group, these studies appear to indicate that certain behaviors considered to be pathological are common in the general population. Further, in context, such behaviors are considered to be normal and not reflective of serious psychopathology. Children often present with such behaviors but outgrow them in time.

It appears that the current, most commonly used diagnostic classification system, *DSM-III-R* (1987), does not provide adequate guidelines for the behavior problems of young children. Except in extreme cases, or in profound developmental or emotional difficulties such as mental retardation or autism, the classification system has very serious limitations for use with preschoolers. For children under age 5, the diagnostic labels may have implications about prognosis, etiology, or treatment that are not appropriate (Campbell 1990). Additionally, less extreme difficulties are not adequately addressed by such classification systems. The diagnostic labels that are commonly and appropriately used with pre-schoolers are Adjustment Disorder, Attention Deficit Disorder, Oppositional Disorder, Avoidant Disorder, and Separation Anxiety Disorder. The potential for overdiagnosis is great. There are few clear criteria for age-appropriate behaviors as compared with those that meet criteria for a particular diagnosis. Further, no guidelines exist for understanding a child's adaptive response to a traumatic life event in the context of a temporary detour from normal development, as opposed to a more long-standing, psychopathological reaction. Our ability to understand "normal development gone awry" in the typical preschool-age child is often not enhanced by an understanding of psychopathology as characterized by *DSM-III-R*.

CASE EXAMPLE

Ashley, a 4½-year-old African-American child, was brought for an assessment by her parents. At the time of referral, she did not want to attend nursery school and had severe tantrums when her parents left her at school.

Parent Interview

The parents were interviewed, and the following history was obtained. Ashley was currently in nursery school for the first time, having previously been cared for by a baby-sitter in the family home. Her 5-year-old sister was attending kindergarten at the same center, but in a different building. This was the first time that Ashley had been separated from her sister, to whom she was very attached. Developmental milestones were reportedly normal. The child had essentially toilet-trained herself in order to keep up with her older sister.

Two significant stressors emerged from the interview with the parents. The father had recently been released from a brief jail sentence for driving while intoxicated. During this time, a close friend of the family had been killed. Although the child was not able to verbalize to her parents her feelings about these two incidents, it appeared that they were affecting her functioning, and most specifically increasing her fears of separation from her parents. An additional important stressor was the fact that both parents worked. When the child had to be removed from the school setting because of her out-of-control tantrums, her father would take her to his job with him. This arrangement, although problematic for the father, provided Ashley with much attention from her dad, as well as the comfort of knowing that she was with one of her parents, and therefore, she and they were "safe."

Standardized Testing

The mother completed the Child Behavior Checklist (CBCL). The mother's completed CBCL and scored profile are shown in Figures 6–1 and 6–2, respectively. Ashley's profile is in the clinical range, with her internalizing scale higher than externalizing. Both internalizing and externalizing scales were in the clinical range. Based on her mother's perception, Ashley is described as a clingy, shy, moody, withdrawn child, who is stubborn and has a temper. Her endorsement of items is consistent with the information obtained in the interview with the parents. The fact that the CBCL is in the clinical range suggests that mother's report of Ashley's current behavior compared with that of other girls her age is clinically significant. Although the behaviors described are not atypical for pre-schoolers, the extent of Ashley's current behavior cannot be considered to be merely age-appropriate.

The completed CBCL itself points to additional information, beyond what is provided by the profile. In filling out the form, the mother wrote in quite a bit of extra information. She mentions her own childhood, her experience with her older children, and her perceptions of Ashley's difficulties. By viewing the form, one gets a better sense of the serious concerns that this mother has for her daughter, and of the mother's own anxieties about the situation.

Play Interview with Child

Ashley and her 5-year-old sister, Beth, were brought to the first appointment by their parents. Ashley presented in the waiting room as timid and afraid, hanging on to her sister's jacket and peering out at the examiner in a most reluctant way. She agreed to enter the clinician's office only if accompanied by Beth. Her sister was clearly the more assertive and

CHILD BEHAVIOR CHECKLIST FOR AGES 4-16

CHILD'S NAME Ashley

PARENTS' USUAL TYPE OF WORK, even if not working now. *(Please be specific — for example, auto mechanic, high school teacher, homemaker, laborer, lathe operator, shoe salesman, army sergeant.)*

SEX ☐ Boy ☒ Girl
AGE 4
ETHNIC GROUP OR RACE Black

FATHER'S TYPE OF WORK _____

TODAY'S DATE
Mo _____ Date _____ Yr _____
CHILD'S BIRTHDATE
Mo _____ Date _____ Yr _____

MOTHER'S TYPE OF WORK _____

GRADE IN SCHOOL

THIS FORM FILLED OUT BY

☒ Mother (name): _____

☐ Father (name): _____

NOT ATTENDING SCHOOL ☑

Please fill out this form to reflect *your* view of the child's behavior even if other people might not agree. Feel free to write additional comments beside each item and in the space provided on page 2.

☐ Other – name & relationship to child: _____

I. Please list the sports your child most likes to take part in. For example: swimming, baseball, skating, skate boarding, bike riding, fishing, etc.

☐ None

	Compared to other children of the same age, about how much time does he/she spend in each?				Compared to other children of the same age, how well does he/she do each one?			
	Don't Know	Less Than Average	Average	More Than Average	Don't Know	Below Average	Average	Above Average
a. _____	☐	☐	☐	☐	☐	☐	☐	☐
b. _____	☐	☐	☐	☐	☐	☐	☐	☐
c. _____	☐	☐	☐	☐	☐	☐	☐	☐

II. Please list your child's favorite hobbies, activities, and games, other than sports. For example: stamps, dolls, books, piano, crafts, singing, etc. (Do **not** include listening to radio or TV.)

☐ None

	Compared to other children of the same age, about how much time does he/she spend in each?				Compared to other children of the same age, how well does he/she do each one?			
	Don't Know	Less Than Average	Average	More Than Average	Don't Know	Below Average	Average	Above Average
a. Dolls	☐	☐	☒	☐	☐	☐	☒	☐
b. Drawing	☐	☐	☒	☐	☐	☒	☐	☐
c. _____	☐	☐	☐	☐	☐	☐	☐	☐

III. Please list any organizations, clubs, teams, or groups your child belongs to.

☐ None

	Compared to other children of the same age, how active is he/she in each?			
	Don't Know	Less Active	Average	More Active
a. _____	☐	☐	☐	☐
b. _____	☐	☐	☐	☐
c. _____	☐	☐	☐	☐

IV. Please list any jobs or chores your child has. For example: paper route, babysitting, making bed, etc. (Include **both** paid and unpaid jobs and chores.)

☐ None

	Compared to other children of the same age, how well does he/she carry them out?			
	Don't Know	Below Average	Average	Above Average
a. _____	☐	☐	☐	☐
b. _____	☐	☐	☐	☐
c. _____	☐	☐	☐	☐

I did not have close siblings. My older 2 children are 5 years apart -- different sexes and wanted different things. My experience does not take into account an understanding of how one can idolize another. Am I too harsh in my judgment of Ashley seeming to adore Beth? Possibly -- I just don't have a concept but the latest problem with school has alarmed me.

Figure 6–1. Child Behavior Checklist for Ashley (aged 4½) as Completed by Mother.

(continued)

V.

1. About how many close friends does your child have? ☒ None ☐ 1 ☐ 2 or 3 ☐ 4 or more
(Do not include brothers & sisters) Has not made true friendship bond with anyone other than Beth
(sister, age 5)

2. About how many times a week does your child do things with friends outside of regular school hours?
(Do not include brothers & sisters) Outside play with neighbors with Beth included. ☐ Less than 1 ☐ 1 or 2 ☒ 3 or more

VI. Compared to other children of his/her age, how well does your child:

		Worse	About Average	Better	
a.	Get along with his/her brothers & sisters?	☐	☐ Lisa age 15	☒ Beth age 5	☐ Has no brothers or sisters
b.	Get along with other children?	☒	☐	☐	
c.	Behave with his/her parents?	☐	☒ favors father	☐	
d.	Play and work by himself/herself?	☐	☐	☒	

VII.

1. For ages 6 and older—performance in academic subjects: (If child is not being taught, please give reason)

	Failing	Below average	Average	Above average
a. Reading, English, or Language Arts	☐	☐	☐	☐
b. History or Social Studies	☐	☐	☐	☐
c. Arithmetic or Math	☐	☐	☐	☐
d. Science	☐	☐	☐	☐
e. _____	☐	☐	☐	☐
f. _____	☐	☐	☐	☐
g. _____	☐	☐	☐	☐

Other academic subjects—for example: computer courses, foreign language, business. Do not include gym, shop, driver's ed., etc.

2. Is your child in a special class or special school? ☐ No ☐ Yes—what kind of class or school?

3. Has your child repeated a grade? ☐ No ☐ Yes—grade and reason

4. Has your child had any academic or other problems in school? ☐ No ☐ Yes—please describe

When did these problems start?

Have these problems ended? ☐ No ☐ Yes—when?

Does your child have any illness, physical disability, or mental handicap? ☒ No ☐ Yes—please describe
Unsure-possible dyslexia is a concern. Pediatrician told me in Aug — too early to test — Need second opinion.

What concerns you most about your child? When drawing, she draws away from herself (upside down)
I feel she is immature. I often can't reason with her & convince her to make a logical conclusion. She is stubborn. She refuses to accept idea of liking school or making new friends. I realize my next statement seems to negate immaturity but I feel she is. She does not have a "mind of her own" at times — wants exact same food or drink Beth does

Please describe the best things about your child: She is responsible. She puts her belongings away after use. She takes care of her needs and gets things for herself. If she is not fearful of our absence due to work, she will get dressed during summer or weekends without prodding by parent.

Figure 6-1 (*continued*)

109

Below is a list of items that describe children. For each item that describes your child **now or within the past 3 months**, please circle the **2** if the item is **very true** or **often true** of your child. Circle the **1** if the item is **somewhat** or **sometimes true** of your child. If the item is **not true** of your child, circle the **0**. Please answer all items as well as you can, even if some do not seem to apply to your child.

0 = Not True (as far as you know)   1 = Somewhat or Sometimes True   2 = Very True or Often True

(Left margin handwritten note, read vertically): Allows Beth to make choices for both. Will come in from outdoor play for exact same snack or drink same choice. Both has only a few thought of it first. Both has

0 1 ②	1.	Acts too young for his/her age
⓪ 1 2	2.	Allergy (describe): _____
⓪ 1 ②	3.	Argues a lot
⓪ 1 2	4.	Asthma
⓪ 1 2	5.	Behaves like opposite sex
⓪ 1 2	6.	Bowel movements outside toilet
⓪ 1 2	7.	Bragging, boasting
0 ① 2	8.	Can't concentrate, can't pay attention for long
0 1 ②	9.	Can't get his/her mind off certain thoughts; obsessions (describe): Refusal of acceptance of our choices for her care. Even with sitter. Says she wants to stay home alone.
0 ① 2	10.	Can't sit still, restless, or hyperactive
0 1 ②	11.	Clings to adults or too dependent
⓪ 1 2	12.	Complains of loneliness
0 1 2	13.	Confused or seems to be in a fog
⓪ ① ②	14.	Cries a lot
⓪ 1 2	15.	Cruel to animals
0 Ⓧ ②	16.	Cruelty, bullying, or meanness to others
0 Ⓧ ②	17.	Day-dreams or gets lost in his/her thoughts
⓪ 1 2	18.	Deliberately harms self or attempts suicide
0 ① 2	19.	Demands a lot of attention
⓪ 1 2	20.	Destroys his/her own things
⓪ 1 2	21.	Destroys things belonging to his/her family or other children
0 ① 2	22.	Disobedient at home
0 1 2	23.	Disobedient at school N/A
0 1 ②	24.	Doesn't eat well (enough—irregular appetite)
0 1 ②	25.	Doesn't get along with other children
0 Ⓧ ②	26.	Doesn't seem to feel guilty after misbehaving
0 1 ②	27.	Easily jealous
⓪ 1 2	28.	Eats or drinks things that are not food— **don't** include sweets (describe): _____
0 ① 2	29.	Fears certain animals, situations, or places, other than school (describe): and needs security of taking small toy to hold on to when leaving home
0 1 ②	30.	Fears going to school (when she was going to day care)

⓪ 1 2	31.	Fears he/she might think or do something bad
⓪ 1 2	32.	Feels he/she has to be perfect
0 ① 2	33.	Feels or complains that no one loves him/her
⓪ 1 2	34.	Feels others are out to get him/her
Ⓧ ① 2	35.	Feels worthless or inferior
⓪ 1 2	36.	Gets hurt a lot, accident-prone
0 ① 2	37.	Gets in many fights
⓪ 1 2	38.	Gets teased a lot
⓪ 1 2	39.	Hangs around with children who get in trouble
⓪ 1 2	40.	Hears sounds or voices that aren't there (describe): _____
⓪ 1 2	41.	Impulsive or acts without thinking
0 ① 2	42.	Likes to be alone
⓪ 1 2	43.	Lying or cheating
0 ① 2	44.	Bites fingernails (used to 3 months ago)
0 ① 2	45.	~~Nervous~~, highstrung, or tense
⓪ 1 2	46.	Nervous movements or twitching (describe): _____
⓪ 1 2	47.	Nightmares
⓪ 1 2	48.	Not liked by other children
0 ① 2	49.	Constipated, doesn't move bowels (used to)
0 ① 2	50.	Too fearful or anxious
⓪ 1 2	51.	Feels dizzy
⓪ 1 2	52.	Feels too guilty — just the opposite does not seem to care
⓪ 1 2	53.	Overeating
⓪ 1 2	54.	Overtired
⓪ 1 2	55.	Overweight
	56.	Physical problems without known medical cause:
⓪ 1 2	a.	Aches or pains
Ⓧ 1 2	b.	Headaches
⓪ 1 2	c.	Nausea, feels sick
⓪ 1 2	d.	Problems with eyes (describe):
⓪ 1 2	e.	Rashes or other skin problems
⓪ 1 2	f.	Stomachaches or cramps
⓪ 1 2	g.	Vomiting, throwing up
Ⓧ 1 2	h.	Other (describe): _____

Figure 6–1 *(continued)*

110

0 = Not True (as far as you know)			1 = Somewhat or Sometimes True		2 = Very True or Often True		

0	①	2	57.	Physically attacks people	0	1	②	84. Strange behavior (describe): _____
0	①	2	58.	Picks <u>nose</u>, skin, or other parts of body (describe): _____				*Strange mad faces.*
				_____	⓪	1	2	85. Strange ideas (describe):
⓪	1	2	59.	Plays with own sex parts in public				_____
⓪	1	2	60.	Plays with own sex parts too much	0	1	②	86. Stubborn, sullen, or irritable
⓪	1	2	61.	Poor school work N/A	0	1	②	87. Sudden changes in mood or feelings
⓪	1	2	62.	Poorly coordinated or clumsy	0	1	②	88. Sulks a lot
0	①	2	63.	Prefers playing with older children	0	①	2	89. Suspicious
⓪	1	2	64.	Prefers playing with younger children	⓪	1	2	90. Swearing or obscene language
⓪	1	2	65.	Refuses to talk	⓪	1	2	91. Talks about killing self
0	1	②	66.	Repeats certain acts over and over; compulsions (describe): <u>closes door</u> <u>over and over after self.</u>	0	①	2	92. Talks or walks in sleep (describe): <u>Sits up and talks or cries</u> <u>average 4x per month</u>
				Does not actually do	⓪	1	2	93. Talks too much
0	①	2	67.	Runs away from home (Says She's going to) lately-never thought of it before	0	①	2	94. Teases a lot
0	1	②	68.	Screams a lot				
0	①	2	69.	Secretive, keeps things to self	0	1	②	95. Temper tantrums or hot temper
⓪	1	2	70.	Sees things that aren't there (describe):	⓪	1	2	96. Thinks about sex too much
				_____	0	1	②	97. Threatens people
				_____	⓪	1	2	98. Thumb-sucking
					⓪	1	2	99. Too concerned with neatness or cleanliness
ⓧ	①	2	71.	Self-conscious or easily embarrassed	⓪	1	2	100. Trouble sleeping (describe):
⓪	1	2	72.	Sets fires				
⓪	1	2	73.	Sexual problems (describe):	0	1	2	101. Truancy, skips school N/A
				_____	⓪	1	2	102. Underactive, slow moving, or lacks energy
				_____	0	1	②	103. Unhappy, sad, or depressed
0	①	2	74.	Showing off or clowning	⓪	1	2	104. Unusually loud
0	1	②	75.	Shy or timid	⓪	1	2	105. Uses alcohol or drugs for nonmedical purposes (describe):
⓪	1	2	76.	Sleeps less than most children				_____
⓪	1	2	77.	Sleeps more than most children during day and/or night (describe): _____	⓪	1	2	106. Vandalism
				_____	⓪	1	2	107. Wets self during the day
					⓪	1	2	108. Wets the bed
⓪	1	2	78.	Smears or plays with bowel movements	0	1	②	109. Whining
⓪	1	2	79.	Speech problem (describe): _____	⓪	1	2	110. Wishes to be of opposite sex
				_____	0	1	②	111. Withdrawn, doesn't get involved with others
0	1	②	80.	Stares blankly	0	1	②	112. Worrying
⓪	1	2	81.	Steals at home				113. Please write in any problems your child has that were not listed above: <u>Demands a certain eating utensil +</u> <u>will not change mind when reasoned with.</u>
⓪	1	2	82.	Steals outside the home				
0	1	②	83.	Stores up things he/she doesn't need (describe): <u>Saves junk. + especially</u> <u>small items.</u>	0	1	②	— *Often stubborn*
					0	1	②	— *Moods change frequently*

Figure 6–1.   *(continued)*

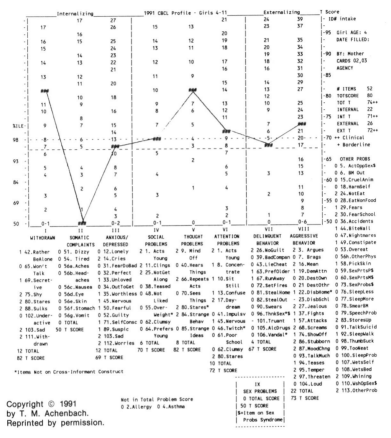

Figure 6–2. Child Behavior Checklist Profile for Ashley (aged 4½)

talkative of the two children. With little prompting, Beth told the therapist that Ashley did not like to go to school. Ashley answered many questions by saying "I don't know," although she was better able to respond if her sister was asked the same question first. In those situations it was not always clear whether she was simply repeating her sister's responses or saying what she wanted. The two girls played with the doll house and puppets while they talked with the therapist, and Ashley was able to say that she hated to take naps and therefore did not like school.

Ashley's parents brought her alone to the second appointment. She appeared less timid and shy, and willingly went with the therapist to the office. The therapist attempted to engage her in puppet play around the theme of going to school, to which she responded, "I don't like school. I don't want to talk about it." She did, however, communicate verbally to some extent, and expressed herself quite well through pictures and faces. She was able to draw pictures and then dictate stories to the therapist about her drawings. She could also tell stories in response to "feeling faces" (e.g., sad, mean, scared) drawn and labeled for her by the therapist. Figure 6–3 contains several of her pictures and the stories she told, transcribed by the

(feeling face drawn by therapist) Mean face. Mommy and Daddy go to store. Linda slaps me.

(feeling face drawn by therapist) Beth. Scared face. People run out in dark and leave me.

(feeling face drawn by therapist) Bethie and Linda ran out in the dark. I see a monster running in dark from me. They're gonna get me. I want them to come back. I'm crying and crying for my Mommy and my Daddy. The end.

(picture drawn by Ashley) Mommy and Daddy go to work when it is a school day. I don't like them going there. They go to work. I have to stay at babysitter long.

Figure 6–3.   Pictures and Stories from Ashley (aged 4½).

therapist as Ashley spoke. Several of the themes that emerged involved separation issues, fear of being left alone and fear of the dark. Although seemingly unable to directly tell the therapist how she felt, she responded well to the use of feeling faces and pictures.

Discussion

This case highlights some important points about assessment with preschool-age children. First, information from the parents in this case was highly valuable, particularly in providing data about the significant stressors the family had experienced, and the parents' perception of the child's difficulties going to school. Equally critical was information about the parents, particularly the mother's anxieties and concerns about this child and her own parenting of the child. This information was gathered from the interview, as well as from the mother's comments on the CBCL. This assessment involved multiple sources, including the parents, school staff, the child, and even her 5-year-old sister. Play observation and interviewing with both Ashley and her sister, and then with Ashley alone, provided much information not only regarding how 5-year-old Beth saw Ashley, but also how the two girls interacted. Ashley's attachment to Beth, and her difficulty in exhibiting her own personality, were made evident in the first clinical interview held with both girls together. However, Ashley's ability to respond to the clinician without her sister was also clear during the second appointment without Beth.

The play and interview assessment of Ashley included some techniques that were effective in acquiring information (e.g., faces, storytelling) and others that were not (e.g., puppet play around school issues). In following the child's lead during the assessment period, a direction was established for assessing her in a developmentally sensitive way. This assessment also highlighted the child's ability to participate in play with the therapist, an activity that could be meaningful and potentially therapeutic.

PART III

CLINICAL
APPLICATIONS

Child therapists typically see preschoolers who present with a wide variety of problems. Although these difficulties may be quite serious, they are usually relatively minor. The less serious difficulties are rarely indicative of psychopathology but may still be extremely challenging for parents and children alike. Distinguishing psychopathological conditions from normal developmental reactions can be a complex task. The reader is referred to the chapter on assessment (Chapter 6), as well as to literature devoted to this issue (e.g., Schwartz and Johnson 1985, Campbell 1990).

Behavior problems occur at a high rate among normal, non-clinic-referred children (see Campbell 1990 for a review). Problem behaviors tend to decrease with age, suggesting that they may resolve without specific therapeutic interventions. Schwartz and Johnson (1985) contend that such problems are considered developmental in nature because they are common, less severe than those seen in pathological conditions, and often transient. Finally, they are often seen in specific problem behaviors rather than in symptom constellations. Schroeder and Gordon (1991) report that up to 50 percent of children may exhibit at least one specific, transient problem behavior, with 5–15 percent exhibiting clusters of behaviors. They note that less than 1 percent of children present with severe psychological disorders. Nonetheless, such problems can be of great concern to parents who may report them to pediatricians during regular office visits. Reassurance and placing the child's behavior in a developmental perspective may be helpful for some families. The astute pediatrician decides regularly when reassurance and simple suggestions may be helpful, and when mental health referral is indicated. Even though certain problems are common, frequent, and transient in nature, psychological interventions are often warranted.

Common problems in preschoolers are often directly related to developmental tasks and transitions. The ways in which parents manage the child during these early, formative years can in large measure determine whether the problems will be transient or of ongoing concern. Further, how the child learns to cope will play an important role. In fact, one of the major goals of parenting young children is to facilitate the child's ability to gain control over normal developmental tasks such as fears, toileting, and developing appropriate social relationships. Additionally, parents may need to help the child cope with life events and circumstances such as death, divorce, or the birth of a sibling. Much of the treatment literature focuses on teaching the parents of preschoolers to modify their approach to parenting. These interventions may ignore the importance for the child of learning alternative, adaptive styles of coping with difficulties.

Cognitive-Behavioral Play Therapy (CBPT) focuses on the child and his or her ability to learn more adaptive coping skills. In cognitive therapies, by definition, the client is an active participant in treatment. In some respects it is difficult for children, particularly those in the preoperational stage of development, to truly be active participants in the "collaborative empiricism" of cognitive therapy. If we define collaboration with children as we do with adults, the clinician may not feel that the child is truly collaborating. Within their capabilities, however, the preschool-age child can participate in treatment, work with the therapist on specific areas, and feel "a part" of the treatment. The balance that the therapist strikes between being directive and following the child's lead will help define how the child and therapist collaborate in the child's treatment. Children in such a situation may construe positive change as coming in part from their own efforts, not just from those of their parents.

The chapters in this section explore the ways in which CBPT can be conducted in a developmentally sensitive way with preschool-age children. Each chapter covers a different presenting problem or diagnosis. Background information, including the current state of understanding of the problem or disorder, is presented. Assessment and treatment concerns are highlighted, and implications for CBPT are discussed. Application of specific cognitive-behavioral interventions are considered. Finally, case material is presented that highlights the problem under consideration and describes CBPT approaches to treatment.

In order to provide a wide spectrum of examples of the practical application of CBPT, the five chapters in this section span a variety of concerns. Chapter 7 covers toileting issues, and in particular the diagnoses of enuresis and encopresis in young children. The use of CBPT is highlighted in treatment of an almost 5-year-old child with primary encopresis. Chapter 8 considers speech and language problems, and in particular the diagnosis of elective mutism. Elective mutism is a fairly rare disorder, and treatment of the young child who is silent presents many interesting challenges for the therapist. Cognitive-Behavioral Play Therapy of a 6-year-old elective mute child is presented and discussed. Chapter 9 addresses the issue of divorce and its effect on young children. A case example of the treatment of an almost 6-year-old child considers the way in which CBPT can assist the child in developing adaptive coping strategies as he continues to deal with feelings regarding the divorce. Chapter 10 considers the problem of fears and phobias. Although fears are very common in young children, when they become extreme and debilitating, treatment may be indicated. Two cases of CBPT with childhood fears are presented and discussed. The younger of the two children discussed, one month short of 2½, is perhaps the youngest documented case of successful CBPT. Chapter 11 discusses the problems experienced by sexually abused children. The implications for CBPT with sexually abused children are considered in the context of vignettes from treatment of young children.

7

Cognitive-Behavioral Play Therapy with Children with Elimination Problems

Toilet training is one of the more difficult tasks of childhood, although most children gain control of eliminative functions within the expected age range and without serious problems. When a child is resistant to the training process or has frequent accidents, one considers the diagnoses of enuresis (discharge of urine into bed or clothes) or encopresis (passage of feces into inappropriate places). Both disorders are categorized by whether they occur at night (nocturnal) or during the day (diurnal), as well as whether they are persistent (primary) or if control has been achieved for a period of at least one year and then lost (secondary).

ENURESIS

There is some debate about the age at which a child who wets is considered to be enuretic. According to *DSM-III-R* (1987), enuresis is not diagnosed until a child who is at least 5 years old exhibits repeated voiding of urine into clothing or bedding at least two times per month. Some consider that the age criterion should be lowered to 3 or 4 years, since most 5-year-old children have been successfully toilet trained for several years. Nonetheless, wetting is common in preschool-age and early school-age children, with as many as 15–20 percent of 5–year-olds still experiencing nocturnal enuresis (Perlmutter 1985). The percentages of children with enuresis decrease systematically with age, with approximately 5 percent of children exhibiting enuresis at 10 years, and less than 2 percent at 12–14 years (Doleys 1983). Nocturnal enuresis is much more prevalent than diurnal enuresis, with the majority of cases of enuretic children over the age of 5 years wetting at night rather than during the day.

Considerable debate exists regarding the etiology of enuresis, although varying theories have been proposed. The assumption that enuresis is a symptom of psychological disturbance, perhaps as a result of underlying conflict, anxiety, or stress, has not been supported by research (Schaefer 1979). In general, when there is psychological disturbance in enuretic children, it is usually related to stressful life situations (e.g., divorce, birth of a sibling), rather than to more severe forms of psychopathology (Douglas 1973). Furthermore, such psychological difficulties may be more prevalent in secondary enuresis, where the child exhibits continence and then begins wetting again. Other theories supporting organic, maturational, or learning factors have been advanced, and these tend to have more credence for primary enuretics. Research findings regarding decreased bladder capacity and sleep disturbances in enuretic children are equivocal (Doleys 1983). The exact cause of enuresis is unknown, although the evidence supports the notion that primary enuresis reflects maturational delays in developing urinary continence. Psychological explanations may be more appropriate for secondary enuresis, which is much less frequent and constitutes only approximately 15 percent of all reported cases of the disorder (de Jonge 1973).

Most children with primary enuresis do not have significant emotional or behavioral problems, although the consequences of wetting may interfere with adequate peer interaction and lower a child's self-esteem. Such problems may be evident even if the wetting does not occur in the presence of peers. Children may be teased because peers know that they wet the bed, or because they attend school with an odor from wetting the previous night. In other situations, children are reluctant to attend overnight parties or trips, for fear that others will know they are bed wetters. Still other children may participate in these overnight activities, and their secret may be revealed if they are unable to stay dry.

Given these common peer difficulties, enuretic children may experience psychological difficulties secondary to their wetting. In addition to peer difficulties, significant family issues may result from the child's enuresis. Often, families will have made a variety of attempts to deal with their child's wetting, with varying degrees of success. Among those reported are restriction of fluids after dinner, having the child urinate before going to bed, and awakening the child periodically throughout the night to urinate. The result of these efforts, particularly when they are unsuccessful, often adds to the family's frustration level, and at times may increase the belief that the child is not trying hard enough. Thus, both peer and family issues may potentially have a negative effect on the enuretic child's self-esteem.

ENCOPRESIS

Encopresis refers to fecal incontinence at least one time per month in children 4 years of age and older (*DSM-III-R* 1987). By definition, encopresis is nonorganically based, and therefore organic conditions resulting in fecal incontinence must be ruled out before encopresis is diagnosed. In addition to the distinction between primary and secondary encopresis, it is important to note whether the child has retentive encopresis, where there is constipation, lack of elimination, and eventually fecal impaction, or nonretentive encopresis, where feces are not retained in the intestines and there is soiling.

Few epidemiological studies of encopresis exist. Estimates of its occurrence range from 1.5–7.5 percent of children, although the upper range is drastically lowered (less than 3 percent) when referring to children over the age of 4 years (Doleys 1983). More than 50 percent of the cases are of secondary encopresis, which suggests that the child is capable of bowel continence (Walker et al. 1988), and has demonstrated such ability for at least 1 year.

The major psychological theories of encopresis involve psychodynamic and behavioral perspectives. Psychodynamic theories viewed encopresis as a symptom of some unconscious conflict or a result of significant psychopathology, early/inappropriate toilet training, mother–child conflict, or significant family disturbance (e.g., Lehman 1944). In contrast, behavioral models explain encopresis based on inadequate or inappropriate learning as factors in the development and maintenance of the disorder.

Inappropriate, inadequate, or aversive toilet training experiences are used by both psychodynamic and behavioral theorists to explain encopresis. During the preschool years, it is not uncommon for children to have fears associated with toileting. Some children respond to training by crying, clinging to a parent, or refusing to go near the toilet. These fears are usually seen in toddlers (18 months and older) and are focused on fears of the toilet, or more specifically, fears of falling into the toilet. Young children may fear that they will be flushed down the toilet along with their bowel movements. Such fears are common, are not necessarily secondary to a traumatic toileting experience, and typically subside as there is growing understanding that the bowel movement gets flushed down the toilet but that the child is safe. A toilet phobia may exist when this type of fear persists and interferes with the child's ability to use the toilet (Doleys 1983).

In some cases, inappropriate or coercive toilet training methods are used, and the child's fears may be based on these experiences. If the child is punished or ridiculed for accidents, a resistance to using the toilet may develop. In some instances the child associates the toilet with harsh discipline or parental coercion to eliminate in the toilet, and may avoid it altogether. Other children have had an incident that resulted in a frightening or painful bowel movement, which they associate with any subsequent bowel movements. It is difficult for these children to understand that the earlier experience will not necessarily be repeated each time they eliminate in the toilet. In these situations it is important to understand the development of the fear, and in particular the environmental context that may be maintaining the child's fears.

Finally, some children have experienced insufficient or inadequate toilet learning. If toilet training has not been a priority for the family, the child's lack of appropriate toileting may be the result of incomplete understanding of what is expected. This is commonly seen in seriously neglected children whose parents may not place any priority on appropriate toileting. When, for example, toileting is expected of the child in a foster home, the earlier experience may confuse and/or frighten the child.

ASSESSMENT

Assessment of the child with elimination problems should include information from clinical interview, behavioral data, and assessment of the child. In addition to a complete history of the problem, the therapist seeks information about other problems the child might have, family issues, and any previous treatment. Specific information about the child's toileting habits is important and is often obtained by having the parents keep baseline data for several weeks after the first appointment. Differentiating among the different types of elimination disorders for both enuresis and encopresis (e.g., retentive vs. nonretentive encopresis) is important. A medical evaluation is always indicated if it has not already been performed in order to rule out any organic problems that might be causing, or contributing to, the child's elimination difficulties. An ongoing working relationship with the child's pediatrician may be helpful in some cases in which a combination of psychological and medical interventions is indicated. Finally, one aspect of a comprehensive evaluation should include an assessment of family issues as well as the parents' motivation for treatment.

There is a great deal of literature regarding the indirect assessment, via the parents, of the child's elimination disorders (e.g., Fielding and Doleys 1988). Much less has been written about direct assessment of the young enuretic or encopretic child. In interview, preschoolers with toileting difficulties may not respond to direct questions about their elimination difficulties. Further, they may be reluctant to directly bring such concerns into their play when they are being observed. However, their play may revolve around activities that represent their perceptions about toileting (e.g., making clay balls that resemble bowel movements and having them magically disappear). Such symbolic representation is important, but cognitive-behavioral assessment usually deals with the problem more directly. Thus, the therapist may need to structure the assessment such that specific information regarding the child's perceptions about toileting can be gathered. For example, the therapist may introduce a doll or puppet with toileting difficulties (using the child's language about these functions) to assess how the child responds.

TREATMENT

Problems in elimination may be difficult for children and parents, and at times resistant to intervention. Many children have experienced multiple home remedies and medical interventions before psychological intervention is recommended. Mental health interventions have typically fallen into one of three broad categories: traditional insight–oriented therapy (including verbal and/or play techniques), behavioral treatments, and the use of mechanical devices. Many interventions reflect a combination of two or more general approaches. Often, interventions ignore factors such as child and parent compliance, the child's role in toileting, and the need to acquire specific toileting skills and maintain these skills once acquired.

Treatment of Enuresis

Enuresis is the presenting complaint for many children, and the pediatrician's first task is to rule out any organic explanation for the incontinence. The incidence of organic urinary incontinence is very low, with estimates of 1–3 percent (Forsythe and Redmond 1974). Because organic causes are so uncommon, as soon as laboratory results are available the family is typically reassured that nothing is medically wrong.

Professionals may be reluctant to treat younger enuretic children who have never exhibited urinary continence, because the disorder usually remits with age. In fact, the spontaneous remission rate is approximately 15 percent per year for untreated enuretic children from ages 5–19 years (Forsythe and Redmond 1974). For many children the treatment of choice is no treatment at all, and many pediatricians respond with a wait-and-see attitude or some basic instructions in toileting. Nonetheless, because most enuretic children do not have significant psychological difficulties, referrals to mental health professionals are often made on the basis of the family's discomfort level with the wetting, as opposed to the pediatrician's specific concern about the child. Often, mental health referrals are not made until the child is older, and the enuresis has become more problematic for child and family. By this time, secondary psychological difficulties may be compounding the situation, although once the enuresis is cleared, these other difficulties frequently abate (Schroder and Gordon 1991). Although the wait-and-see attitude for younger children may be appropriate, treatment for the school-age enuretic is often warranted.

Traditional psychodynamic psychotherapy alone has not proven effective in treating enuresis, although many behavioral interventions have been associated with success. Examples of behavioral techniques that have proven effective include simply having the child keep records of accidents, or reinforcing the child for maintaining a dry bed (Doleys 1983). Such simple interventions may be useful as a first step for children who have not been treated previously, or they may be used in conjunction with other interventions (Walker et al. 1988). Some children will need more intensive interventions than simple record keeping and positive reinforcement. Overall, behavioral approaches are associated with the highest cure rates and lowest relapse rates (Foxman et al. 1986).

One behavioral intervention commonly used is the urine alarm (bell-and-pad method). Originally developed by Mowrer and Mowrer (1938), this procedure did not gain popularity until 30 years after its development. The urine-sensitive pad placed under the child is connected to a bell/buzzer or light. When the child urinates, the alarm is activated, awakening the child, who is taught to go to the bathroom to finish urinating. The urine alarm is one of the most effective forms of treatment, with successful elimination of wetting occurring in 70–90 percent of cases. A further benefit is that the child may experience a sense of mastery following a successful intervention. Unfortunately, relapse rates are relatively high, although they have been decreased by the addition of overlearning procedures. An intensive, effective program, Dry Bed Training (DBT), developed by Azrin and colleagues (1974), incorporates the urine alarm system into a comprehensive program including overlearning as well as other techniques such as reinforcement for inhibiting urination, practice, and nighttime awakening. Studies suggest that DBT may be significantly better than the urine alarm used alone (see Walker et al. 1988 review). Overall, programs that include the urine alarm system as part of a more comprehensive intervention appear to have the greatest success rates.

Pharmacological interventions have been used with enuretic children, with imipramine (Tofranil), a tricyclic antidepressant, the most popular. Although many children show a positive response to imipramine, only a small percentage of children cease wetting completely while on the medication (see review by Stewart 1975). Additionally, negative side effects have been noted and there is a high relapse rate when drugs are withdrawn. These facts suggest that imipramine is not the treatment of choice for most enuretic children.

Treatment of Encopresis

For encopresis, treatment approaches have involved medical procedures, psychotherapy, hypnosis, biofeedback, and behavioral programs, as well as treatments that combine several of these interventions. Pediatricians often focus on bowel cleansing and training of normal habits, often with the assistance of purgatives (e.g., laxatives, enemas), stool softeners, and/or dietary manipulations. These basic pediatric interventions may be more successful in younger children, although more severe cases tend to require more psychological interventions. Unfortunately, such physical interventions may focus extensive attention on the child's gastrointestinal functioning.

With regard to psychological interventions, traditional psychodynamic psychotherapy alone has not proven effective in treating encopresis (e.g., Achenbach and Lewis 1971). However, the highest treatment success rates have been reported for comprehensive behavioral treatments (Werry 1986a). These programs focus on the contingencies for toileting and soiling. The primary focus of the behavioral interventions has been the contingent positive reinforcement of appropriate defecation (e.g., Ayllon et al. 1975). Additional components, such as mild punishment (e.g., Edelman 1971), extinction (e.g., Conger 1970), and biofeedback (e.g., Kohlenberg 1973), have been employed. Several programs use a combination of reinforcement and punishment techniques in combination with medical procedures (e.g., Azrin and Foxx 1974, Doleys and Arnold 1975, Wright and Walker 1976).

A growing body of the behavioral literature on encopresis addresses treatments that use parent-implemented interventions, with minimal contact between therapist and child (Siegel 1983). Most striking, and perhaps most problematic, is the level of resistance and noncompliance frequently seen in children with elimination problems when their parents are implementing behavioral interventions. The need for children to change their own behavior and to be active participants in treatment is important, and too often ignored.

INDICATIONS FOR COGNITIVE-BEHAVIORAL TREATMENT OF ELIMINATION PROBLEMS

Issues of control are often evident in children with elimination problems. The emphasis by parents on toileting is conveyed in some way to the child. Unlike other areas of life, elimination is totally under the child's control. Youngsters may not have a say in any other aspect of the day, including what they wear, eat, or play with, but ultimately the parent cannot "make them" eliminate. Typically, children are entering their most negative stage ("the terrible twos") at about the same time they are learning toileting skills. Regarding toileting, Weisberger (1987) states that the child "not only has the final say about whether he will or not, he has the ultimate weapon" (p. 26).

In addition to the control issues, toileting presents the child with an opportunity to gain mastery over a significant developmental task. According to Weisberger (1987), "Toilet training that encourages the child's will as he himself faces alternatives (and very real consequences) helps strengthen that will in a realistic way. So while he ultimately yields to societal pressure for cleanliness, he is not submitting because he has been threatened or bribed but because he is helped to confront the reality of the reality. He cooperates because he sees the connection between what he does and what follows. . . . He learns he can do it. And the process is all" (pp. 46–47). If the child learns appropriate toileting skills, the parent may convey a sense of pleasure to the child. As children internalize their parents' pleasure, they gradually develop their own sense of pleasure and accomplishment in staying clean and using the toilet.

Given the importance of control and mastery in children with elimination problems, the sense of active participation conveyed in Cognitive-Behavioral Play Therapy (CBPT) may be of particular importance in treatment. When parent-implemented behavioral programs are used to treat elimination problems, it is often difficult to ensure that the *child* wants to change the soiling or wetting being treated. As parents change contingencies for the child, a change in motivation or cooperation on the part of the child may be needed to ensure success. However, many parent-implemented programs do not address the need for the child's sense of mastery to be increased, and some may fail based on the child's lack of involvement in treatment. This is particularly true with primary encopresis, which appears to be more often the result of inadequate training and learning, than with enuresis, which may have more physiological etiologies that are not yet completely understood.

We turn now to a case example of the use of CBPT with a young encopretic child. The case will be described, along with a discussion of the assessment, treatment, therapy outcome, and follow-up. Finally, the cognitive-behavioral facets of the treatment and the role it may have played in the child's growing sense of mastery will be considered.

CASE EXAMPLE[1]

Terry was an almost 5½-year-old Caucasian boy, who presented with primary functional nonretentive encopresis. He was the firstborn, and most quiet and passive, of a set of male triplets. He had repeatedly told his parents that he did not want to be like his brothers, and according to parental report became upset when people could not tell them apart. An intellectual evaluation completed by the school psychologist indicated he was in the average range of intelligence (Stanford-Binet IQ = 103), although he did have developmental expressive and articulation language disorders. After a medical work-up revealed no organic etiology for the soiling, Terry's pediatrician referred the family to a child psychologist. Terry had no other known medical or psychological conditions.

Assessment with Parents

In the initial interview, Terry's parents reported that he soiled several times daily, and if not changed by an adult, Terry would remain in soiled pants. No history of constipation was reported. The child had been minimally responsive to medical interventions (e.g., diet modifications) intended to alleviate the soiling. All efforts to train Terry to use the toilet for bowel movements were unsuccessful, although he successfully had been trained to use the toilet for urination at age 3 years. The parents felt that Terry was not afraid of using the toilet, based on their observations and his comments. However, he had told them that he did not want to learn to use the toilet and be "like his brothers," both of whom were completely toilet trained.

The parents were asked to keep records of Terry's toileting/soiling for 12 days. During this collection of baseline data, the parents checked Terry's pants for evidence of soiling at four specific times (12:30 P.M., 3:30 P.M., 6:30 P.M., and bedtime). Soiling was defined as evidence of any fecal material or fresh discoloration of the underpants. The parents were in-

---

[1]This case was originally described in detail in Knell, S. M., and Moore, D. M. (1990). Cognitive behavioral play therapy in the treatment of encopresis. *Journal of Clinical Child Psychology* 19:55–60.

structed to remain neutral in interacting with him while checking his pants, and merely explained to him that they needed to see "if his pants were clean or soiled." Any soiling that occurred during these intervals was recorded at the prescribed times (see Figure 7–1).

Assessment with Child

Assessment with Terry consisted of structured play sessions in which the topic of soiling was introduced through a toy bear who "pooped his pants" (Terry's words as described to the therapist by his parents). The therapist made note of Terry's reactions to the toy bear and the information Terry brought spontaneously into the play situation. In reality, assessment took place throughout the course of treatment as Terry brought to the sessions new information that was used to understand his

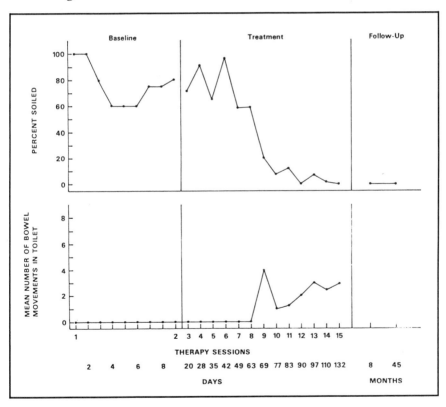

Figure 7–1. Percent Soiled and Mean Number of Bowel Movements in Toilet as a Function of Treatment for Encopretic 5-Year-Old

perceptions about his soiling. Because of limitations in his expressive language, Terry was not directly interviewed. With the exception of the intelligence measures given independently, no other specific testing was done.

Treatment

The therapist used CBPT with the child and concurrently worked with the parents in the behavioral management of the child's encopresis. The child and parents were seen on a weekly basis with the parental work taking half the session and the child's therapy the other half. These sessions were set up with the parents seen first, so that information from home could be used in the child's therapy.

Cognitive-Behavioral Play Therapy

Individual CBPT was initiated after the collection of baseline data. Initially, much of the time was spent with the child playing spontaneously. His struggles with toileting and competition with his brothers could be seen in his play. Structured, directive behavioral interventions were incorporated into a more traditional, nondirective play therapy approach. The therapist systematically took specific themes from the child's play and structured cognitive-behavioral interventions to address these issues. In particular, the therapist utilized a toy bear that soiled its pants and did not use the toilet.

The therapist created structured situations with the bear that were yoked to the child's contingency management program and were designed to be approximately one step ahead of the child's program. Thus, for example, the bear went through a "contingency management program" in the sessions, where he received stars and praise for appropriate toileting and dry pants. Gradually, the child began competing with the bear, comparing numbers of stars and expressing his wish to "beat the bear."

What follows is a description of several themes in Terry's play and the various cognitive-behavioral interventions and their implementation in his treatment. Sample vignettes illustrating the techniques can be found in Tables 7–1 and 7–2.

Fear of Toilet.   According to his parents, Terry had denied fear or anxiety associated with toilet use such as is often evident in children as they learn toileting skills. However, in sessions he repeatedly made a stuffed

TABLE 7-1
Examples of Behavioral Techniques in Cognitive-Behavioral Play Therapy with Encopretic 5-Year-Old Child.

Behavioral Technique	Play Situation	Therapist Intervention
Shaping	Child plays with bear near toilet	Therapist has bear gradually approach toilet, sit on toilet, make bowel movement in toilet
Exposure and response prevention	Child repeatedly has bear get flushed down toilet	Therapist has bear sit on toilet without getting flushed down
Positive reinforcement	Bear keeps pants clean and uses toilet	Bear receives praise and stickers for clean pants and toilet use
Shaping socially appropriate expression of feelings	Child, "I want to punch bear's face."	Therapist rephrases, "You're mad because . . . "

TABLE 7-2
Examples of Cognitive Techniques in Cognitive-Behavioral Play Therapy with Encopretic 5-Year-Old.

Cognitive Technique	Play Situation	Therapist Intervention
Identifying (irrational) beliefs	Child has bear repeatedly fall into toilet	Therapist notes child's repetition of bear being flushed down toilet
Changing (irrational) beliefs	Child has bear repeatedly fall into toilet	Therapist says to bear, "You won't fall in and get flushed down the toilet."
Positive self-statements	Bear uses toilet	Therapist says for bear, "I feel good when I use the toilet."

bear fall into the toilet and be "flushed away." Clearly, Terry had some concerns about using the toilet that had not been evident to his parents. Although he could not express these directly or specifically, his play indicated that he feared falling into the toilet and was concerned that he, along with his bowel movements, could be flushed down the toilet. The repetition of this theme through the bear suggested this was a concern that Terry had not resolved.

First, the therapist acknowledged the child's perceptions by identifying the child's belief that the bear *and* the bowel movement could get flushed down the toilet. The *identification of an irrational belief* thus consisted of the restatement of the belief. Although the literature refers to these as irrational beliefs, the terminology may be inaccurate and misleading for young children. For Terry, as with other young children, the belief that he could be flushed down the toilet was very real. Although an adult understands that one cannot get flushed down the toilet, this was a genuine possibility as far as Terry was concerned.

Despite Terry's continuing to enact the bear getting flushed down the toilet, the therapist gradually had the bear get closer and closer to sitting on the toilet without falling in. Thus, the therapist would have the bear come close to the toilet and then sit on it briefly, with the final goal of the bear sitting on the toilet for a period of time. Such closer and closer steps to sitting on the toilet were an effort to *shape* the bear's behavior. Thus, the bear made closer and closer approximations to the desired behavior.

Finally, the therapist had the bear sit on the toilet without, of course, getting flushed down it. Sitting on the toilet without being flushed was a form of *exposure* and *response prevention.* That is, the bear was presented with the toilet (exposure), but kept from the expected consequence of falling in (response prevention). While the bear was sitting on the toilet, the therapist was verbalizing for the bear that it would not get flushed away. For example, "You won't fall in and get flushed down the toilet. It's safe to sit on the toilet." Thus, the therapist was *changing the (irrational) belief* of falling into the toilet, by providing evidence to counter the child's belief.

Increasing Child's Sense of Mastery of Toileting.

Terry had made clear that he did not wish to use the toilet, in part because he did not want to be like his brothers. This distinction Terry made between himself and his brothers seemed to stem in part from his lack of a separate identity and sense of positive self-image. In addition to his apparent lack of interest, it appeared that Terry did not feel he could master toilet use.

The bear received *positive reinforcement* in the form of praise and stickers for both appropriate toilet use and dry, nonsoiled pants. The therapist indicated how the bear had done and rewarded the bear with stickers at the beginning of the play therapy session. In an effort to yoke the treatment of the bear to that of the child, the therapist kept the bear only a brief step ahead of the child. The bear and child were both reinforced verbally for their efforts. Thus, Terry was always aware of the bear's "progress" as well as his own.

While repeating statements to counter irrational beliefs, the therapist also repeated positive self-statements for the bear. Included were statements intended to reinforce positive, adaptive functioning and thoughts (e.g., "I will feel good when I use the toilet"). Thus, the bear modeled positive self-statements that would enhance a feeling of mastery and competence as a result of appropriate toilet use.

Facilitating Appropriate Expression of Feelings. Terry appeared to have a difficult time expressing his feelings in words. He would hit the bear or pretend to make the bear "poop" all over the office. However, he could not express his anger or frustration in words. The therapist used the bear to show how the animal could express its feelings about using the toilet. This was accomplished by the bear putting feelings into words. Thus, the bear verbalized anger rather than acting it out through activities and self-statements (e.g., "I'm mad but I can say I'm mad. I don't need to poop in my pants to show it").

Behavioral Management

The behavioral management program implemented by the parents began at the same time as the CBPT with the child. This intervention consisted primarily of a sticker program in which the child was reinforced for nonsoiled pants and appropriate toilet use. Parents continued to check for soiling at the specified times. The child would receive a sticker for any time period in which he had not soiled, and for appropriate toilet use. To encourage toilet use, Terry was placed on the toilet for 10 minutes three times per day at approximately ½ hour after each meal. When he was soiled, the parents gently reminded him that he needed to clean himself and change his underpants. He was taught to do this in such a way that he needed minimal assistance from a parent. He would take his dirty underwear and place it in a pail of soapy water, which was kept in the bathroom. Then he would put on new underwear, which he got from an easily accessible shelf in the bathroom.

By week 8, the child's soiling had decreased. By this time he appeared to be comfortable sitting but had still had not had a bowel movement on the toilet. Because the soiling had decreased without a concomitant increase in toilet use, there was concern over the possibility of fecal impaction.

To increase appropriate use of the toilet and to avoid fecal impaction, Terry was told that he should continue to try to make a bowel movement in the toilet. However, if he had not been able to do that in the next 3 days, he would be given some "medicine" to "help him" use the toilet if he could not do so on his own. Therefore, Terry could avoid receiving an enema if he exhibited any appropriate toilet use by the third day. Given his history of medical interventions and other issues associated with use of such an aversive procedure, this was presented to him as calmly and neutrally as possible by the parents. They seemed capable of presenting the enema to Terry without further traumatizing him. They understood that the use of an enema could be a frightening experience for a child and were instructed in how to present it in a way that would minimize his fear.

Terry did not use the toilet, so it was necessary to give him an enema. Because of his continued lack of appropriate toileting, three enemas were used over the course of 9 days. The child made a bowel movement in the toilet after each of the enemas, representing the first three times he had ever used the toilet for a bowel movement. He apparently responded well to the enema and was quite happy after each bowel movement in the toilet. The parents provided a lot of immediate praise for these bowel movements in the toilet and in addition to the social reinforcement of praise, they gave him tangible reinforcements (i.e., small toys) after the first two bowel movements in the toilet. Toys were not given to the child for any further toilet use.

Earlier, the therapist had instructed the parents to develop a "friends who care" list of those who would be happy to hear of Terry's toilet use. This technique, developed by Azrin and Foxx (1974), provides the child with positive social reinforcement from a number of people. After these first three bowel movements, many of the friends and relatives on the list were called, and as prearranged by the parents, they praised the child's efforts. According to his parents, Terry was quite pleased with this attention. Interestingly, at Terry's request, the therapist as well as the bear were on the list of "friends who care." Unable to complete a telephone call to the bear, Terry was content to wait until the next session, and immediately tell the bear about his accomplishment upon entering the office!

The "friends who care" technique was also used in the play therapy, with the bear developing a list of individuals to call when it used the toilet appropriately. The bear's list consisted of parents and animals friends, and other toys and puppets in the therapy office. Needless to say, Terry's name was also on the bear's list.

Results

Treatment consisted of fifteen sessions, which took place over the course of 132 days. The results are depicted in Figure 7–1.

Soiling

At baseline, the child was soiled 77 percent of the time. The soiling continued to decrease until he had only three soiling accidents between sessions twelve and fourteen (representing a 20-day time span). Terry had no incidents of soiling after the fourteenth session (110 days after treatment began).

Toilet Use

During baseline and during the first eight sessions (63 days), Terry did not use the toilet for bowel movements. After the enemas were administered, Terry used the toilet as described above. After the twelfth session, he used the toilet spontaneously and regularly for bowel movements. Throughout the course of treatment, Terry continued to use the toilet appropriately.

Follow-up

Terry was monitored, via contact with his parents, for 45 months after treatment termination. Appropriate toileting without soiling accidents was reported through 8- and 45-month follow-up. Parental report at follow-up indicated that they had not experienced any other psychological or medical problems with the child.

Discussion

This foregoing case represents the successful treatment of primary, nonretentive encopresis in an almost 5½-year-old boy, utilizing CBPT and behavioral management approaches. The behavioral management was similar to other treatment approaches previously described in the literature (e.g., Wright and Walker 1976). Unique to the intervention was the CBPT with the child, which was designed to address issues that could not be addressed in the parent-implemented behavioral program.

This treatment provided several examples of how the individual work with the child addressed issues that could not have been addressed through behavioral treatment alone. One example of this was the child's expressed desire not to be like his brothers. His difficulty in maintaining a separate, unique identity seemed, in part, to be manifested in his soiling. Whereas the parents reported that the other two boys had begun to develop "identities" (e.g., a collection of a particular kind of toys), Terry's identity appeared to be that he "pooped." The behavior gave him a way to be different, and in that sense, an identity.

Cognitive-Behavioral Play Therapy could address such cognitive self-perceptions and self-statements. The competition with the brothers took place, in part, symbolically in Terry's interaction with the bear. In fact, his efforts to be more successful than the bear may have helped Terry achieve more control over his toileting. In that sense, his success provided him with an identity as a child who *could* master the use of the toilet, rather than as a child who soiled his pants.

Three limitations of the treatment of the present case are noteworthy. First, it is possible to construe data collection during the establishment of a baseline as a type of intervention. As part of the baseline, the parents checked the child's pants four times daily and recorded the child's soiling, thus attending to the soiling on a regular basis. Although there was certainly more parental attention as they checked Terry's soiling, a stable baseline was achieved. Thus, increased parental attention was not sufficient for the treatment of encopresis because no significant changes were noted in soiling or toileting until the implementation of *specific* interventions.

Second, clear demonstration of which factors contributed to change is not possible, in that one cannot ferret out the relative contributions of behavioral management and CBPT in the successful treatment of this child. Given the concomitant interventions of CBPT and behavioral management, the results could be explained on the basis of either treatment or on the basis of the combined treatments.

Finally, there is no way of ruling out maturation as an explanation for the child's learning appropriate toileting. However, given the dramatic changes in the child's encopresis during treatment, and his lack of responsiveness to all previous medical interventions, it seems unlikely that maturation alone would explain the changes.

Thus, alternative explanations of the successful elimination of Terry's encopresis do not seem likely, and the positive outcome appears to be based on the treatment provided. Unfortunately, it is not possible to determine which components of the treatment were responsible.

CONCLUSIONS

Currently, most interventions with encopretic preschoolers have focused on behavioral management *of* the child, without addressing the child's cognitions/feelings. Although many behavioral treatments of encopresis are successful without such components, these cognitive interventions might directly address the child's distortions and misperceptions about the presenting problem. Through CBPT, Terry could directly identify his anger and potentially modify the cognitive distortions associated with it. For example, he learned that he could successfully use the toilet and keep his pants clean and that he did not need to soil in order to be different from his brothers. He also overcame his fear of sitting on the toilet. Obviously, the present case cannot address whether or not CBPT would be useful for other encopretic children. With Terry, it is likely that his developmental level and perceptions of his soiling were influential factors. Additionally, his language disorder may also have made aspects of the play (e.g., symbolic modeling) more useful to him then a predominately verbal approach. Certainly, his relatively young age, the lack of learning of appropriate toileting, and the fact that he had no other psychological difficulties were all positive factors. Cognitive-Behavioral Play Therapy might have been much more problematic with an older child with other psychological difficulties who had previously had toileting skills but did not continue to use them.

Encopresis is a complex, multi-faceted disorder with differential treatment possibly required for different types of encopresis (Doleys 1983). The applicability of CBPT alone in the treatment of encopretic children is unknown. It is highly likely that because of the nature of this problem, CBPT should be conducted in combination with behavior management programs. It would also be helpful to delineate further which child/family variables would be most amenable to a CBPT approach, behavioral interventions, or a combination of the two. Does adding a cognitive component enhance the efficacy of more behaviorally based programs? Conversely, are there situations in which a cognitive play component either detracts from or does not add to parent-focused interventions?

Cognitive-Behavioral Play Therapy may be indicated when parents cannot implement management programs. For example, if the problem is too aversive to the parent (e.g., Knell and Moore 1988) or if the parent–child relationship has inhibited development of the child's self-mastery (Klonoff et al. 1984, Klonoff and Moore 1986), the child's direct involvement may be necessary. Specificity is needed regarding the various conditions and treatments that have been successful with these variables.

In this case, better measurements of the child's perceptions about his soiling might have been useful. The therapist's understanding of Terry's perceptions was largely based on inferences drawn from observation of his play and from information provided by the parents. A more direct measure of his perceptions might have been possible, although the limitations in Terry's language skills may have been problematic.

8

Cognitive-Behavioral Play Therapy with Children with Speech and Language Problems

OVERVIEW OF THE PROBLEM

During the first 3 years of life, a child moves from being a newborn without language to being a fairly sophisticated listener and speaker. The accomplishments in language development during these early years occur at a rapid rate, as the child develops vocabulary and articulatory competence while learning the syntactic and pragmatic rules of his or her native language. There is a wide variability in the rate with which a child meets language milestones. Guidelines exist for determining when a child has a significant language problem, and when language development may be somewhat delayed but not seriously so (e.g., Lillywhite et al. 1970). The nature of language development is such that children exhibit difficulties in its acquisition at various times. However, when such difficulties are serious and persistent, a speech or language disorder may be present.

Estimates of the incidence of speech and language disorders vary, although these problems may affect as many as 10 percent of school-age children (*DSM-III-R* 1987). Developmental language disorders are classified according to whether the child's language is delayed because of difficulty in receptive, expressive, or articulation abilities. In addition to these three general areas, several other types of speech and language problems exist, including speech dysfluencies (cluttering, stuttering). Language delays in children are not uncommon and are often associated with more general delays in cognitive development. Because such language problems may be explained by the presence of another disorder, such as mental retardation or a pervasive developmental disorder such as autism, these disorders must be ruled out as a cause of the language delay. Language difficulties are often associated with behavioral problems (Cantwell et al. 1979). With any of the language disorders, social difficulties may be present, although these children usually wish to communicate and interact with peers. However, their speech difficulties may make social interaction problematic. For example, they may be teased and/or ignored by peers and siblings. Additional behavioral problems may be related to the family difficulties that result from problems in communication between family members and the language-disordered child.

Treatment for children with a language disorder typically involves a speech/language-based intervention. Because of commonly associated emotional or behavioral problems, psychological interventions may also be warranted. Such mental health interventions are often overlooked if the speech and language difficulties are the focus of concern. Conversely, many children with behavior problems referred for mental health treatment have speech and language difficulties that are obscured by their behavior problems (Cohen et al. 1989).

ELECTIVE MUTISM

Whereas developmental language disorders are predominantly speech/language based with psychological sequelae, elective mutism is a psychological disorder that manifests itself via a language disorder. Children with elective mutism refuse to talk in one or more major social situations, despite an ability to comprehend and speak. Excessive shyness, social isolation, school refusal, and noncompliance may be present. Many authors note the need to differentiate elective mute children from those with "reluctant speech" (Williamson et al. 1977b). The speech refusal of these children is less persistent and pervasive than that of the elective mute child; thus reluctant speech is considered to be a less severe form of elective mutism. This distinction may have important implications in treatment planning. Interventions for children with reluctant speech may build on situations in which the child is already speaking. Because elective mute children speak in few, if any, situations, treating their silence usually requires more work in building a basic foundation in speaking.

Few reports exist regarding the incidence of elective mutism, although it is considered to be rare. Clinic studies have indicated that fewer than 1 percent of clinic-referred school-age children are diagnosed as elective mute, with most cases reported when the child starts school (Labbe and Williamson 1984). Although little is known about elective mutism left untreated, it is considered to become more intractable over time, with few reports of spontaneous remission (Hayden 1980). Most frequently identified etiological factors are traumatic events and/or a family environment that either models or suppresses speech. Maternal overprotection is often noted, but it is unclear if this is an etiological factor or a response to the child's behavior.

Because elective mutism is rare, much of the knowledge about the disorder and its treatment comes from individual case reports or small samples without control groups. It is believed that most elective mute children fall into one of two categories. Children in the first group are described as immature, withdrawn, shy, and manipulative. The second group of elective mute children are described as tense and anxious. Elective mute children are often very dependent on parents, especially their mothers. Regardless of the etiology, these are children whose normal development has gone awry; their behavior would only be considered normal during the much earlier phase of "stranger anxiety" seen in the infant under 1 year of age (Lesser-Katz 1986).

Elective mute children may give the impression of a language disorder. However, the child typically speaks normally with someone, often the mother. Wright (1968) describes associated speech and language problems in only 20 percent of cases of elective mutism. Some of these cases involve only minor speech articulation difficulties. Rutter (1977) suggested that some elective mute children avoid speaking in order to cope with the teasing they receive because of their speech dysfluencies. Others (e.g., Wright 1968) conceptualize elective mutism as the child's way to control the environment through silence. Rosenberg and Lindblad (1978) contend that elective mute children are determined to maintain their symptom of muteness. A higher incidence of other behavioral problems, including elimination problems, has also been noted in elective mute children (Kolvin and Fundudis 1981).

ASSESSMENT

Information from the elective mute child's parents and significant others in the child's life is critical to the evaluation process. In addition to an overall developmental history, the therapist will want to gather detailed information about the child's language development. The history should include clear, detailed information regarding the situations in which the child speaks, and those in which the child is silent. As part of this data gathering, the therapist should seek patterns that may clarify the variables underlying the child's mutism (e.g., consistent variables regarding to whom the child speaks or in what situations). Parents may also provide information that clarifies the child's perceptions regarding the mutism. For example, elective mute children who speak to their parents often convey information regarding their silence. In describing such conversations, the parents provide information the child might not directly convey to the therapist. This information often becomes an integral part of the treatment process.

Direct assessment of the elective mute child obviously presents some unique challenges. The young elective mute child who does not speak to the therapist may nonetheless respond through pictures, play, and visual cues (e.g., smiling, eye contact). Therefore, much of the direct evaluation will be based on the child's nonverbal behavior, including interaction with play materials, as well as an assessment of the interaction with parents and the therapist.

TREATMENT

There is consensus within the treatment literature from a variety of theoretical orientations that direct attempts to force the child to speak will be ineffective. A gradual and supportive progression from nonverbal to verbal play characterizes most treatments. Early approaches to treating elective mutism were largely concerned with dynamic issues in personality rather than with the removal of the symptom of mutism (Labbe and Williamson 1984). The psychoanalytic literature often emphasizes the meaning of the silence and the ways in which the symptom synthesizes conflicts from different developmental levels. Psychoanalytic treatment often did not involve any verbal communication by the child, and in some cases therapy was conducted for over 2 years without the child ever speaking (Chethik 1973). Such cases were not necessarily considered "failures" because the child ultimately did not speak. Rather, because treatment was primarily concerned with modification of personality dynamics, the measurement of treatment success involved a great deal more than whether or not the child spoke. Thus, psychoanalytically oriented therapists felt that they could help elective mute children whether the children talked or not.

Since the mid-1960s, behavioral approaches to the problem have rejected this orientation and have focused on efforts to help the elective mute individual talk (see Labbe and Williamson 1984 for a review). The behavioral literature on elective mutism supports direct efforts to increase the individual's speech production. This does not appear to be construed as an attempt to force the child to speak, but rather as an effort to encourage or facilitate talking. A number of behavioral approaches have been employed, with many reported cases using a combination of interventions. Contingency management utilizing positive reinforcement of verbal behavior and extinction of nonverbal behavior has been used in a large number of successful cases (e.g., Baumeister and Jamail 1975, Struaghan et al. 1965, Williamson et al. 1977b). This approach may be more effective with reluctant speech, where the child's occasional talking provides an opportunity to increase speech production. In contrast, it is difficult to reinforce the elective mute child who will not talk in the presence of the therapist. For the child who will speak in certain environments or with certain individuals, stimulus fading has been used to gradually change the stimuli controlling speech (e.g., Richards and Hansen 1978, Wulbert et al. 1977). In these treatments, new situations become discriminative stimuli for speaking. Thus, over time the child learns to speak in response to new and different situations or stimuli.

Other behavioral approaches rely on techniques to initiate the child's response. These techniques may be necessary if contingency management or stimulus fading techniques cannot be used. These response initiation procedures include shaping (e.g., Williamson et al. 1977a); response cost (e.g., Sanok and Striefel 1979); escape avoidance (e.g., Piersel and Kratochwill 1981); and reinforcement sampling (e.g., Williamson et al. 1977a).

Indications for Cognitive-Behavioral Treatment of Elective Mutism

By definition, elective mute children have chosen not to speak despite their ability to do so. Treatment for children who refuse to speak is a complex issue in that the child is capable of talking, but for whatever reason will not. Treatments focused on "pressuring" the child to speak are often abysmal failures. If leaving these children alone were effective, this route might be appropriate. However, there is little evidence that elective mutism gets better without treatment. Therefore, treatment approaches must involve the child in a way that encourages the individual's own wish to speak.

As the toddler develops increasingly complex linguistic skills, the motivation to communicate is inextricably linked with the reinforcement most children receive from their parents for talking. Speaking, like elimination, is entirely under a child's control. Normally the child gains satisfaction and a sense of mastery from communicating and is encouraged to continue. However, in some situations speaking is not reinforcing. In fact, for some children silence becomes more rewarding than talking. Thus, these children may gain control of their environment by remaining silent. Active participation in treatment is important in a disorder in which the main symptom, speech refusal, is entirely under the child's control. Elective mute children have control over their silence; therefore, to change, they must take control over their speaking. Cognitive-Behavioral Play Therapy (CBPT) for elective mute children may be particularly appropriate because it provides the opportunity to be part of the change, to feel a sense of mastery and control over talking, and to learn more adaptive responses to situations that may elicit silence.

The following case employed CBPT with a young elective mute child. Assessment and treatment issues as well as therapy outcome and follow-up will be considered. The cognitive-behavioral focus of the treatment, and its role in the development of the child's mastery of her difficulties, will be presented.

CASE EXAMPLE

Chrissy was a 6-year-old Caucasian girl who presented with elective mutism. She spoke only with a few selected children and her parents. She refused to speak to all other adults except for two individuals whom she had known for over 1 year: the mother of one of her friends and a college student in the neighborhood.

Chrissy had a speech dysfluency, diagnosed when she was 3 years old. Her parents reported that shortly after her third birthday, she had been pressured by a preschool teacher to stop stuttering. At about the same time, she was teased excessively by her peers when she spoke, and subsequently stopped talking in most settings. There had been many attempts to get Chrissy to talk, including a number of speech therapy programs in which she refused to speak. In one language stimulation program in which Chrissy was enrolled when she was almost 5, a number of approaches were used, including reinforcement and ignoring. Chrissy took turns and initially appeared interested, but she quickly became bored and fidgety and did not speak throughout the course of the program. A second attempt at speech/language intervention occurred shortly before Chrissy's sixth birthday when she was placed in speech therapy with another child with an expressive language disorder. Again, Chrissy participated nonverbally but did not talk.

At 5 years, Chrissy was age-appropriate and eligible for kindergarten but was kept in nursery school for an extra year. Her parents hoped that this period before school entry might give her time to mature and become more willing to talk. Chrissy started kindergarten shortly after her sixth birthday. She seemed comfortable at school, told her parents how much she enjoyed it, and seemed quite excited about school activities. However, she only spoke to other children when it appeared that no adults were watching. As soon as a teacher, principal, or other adult came into view, she stopped speaking. She was an active participant at school; for example, she would take toys in to "Show and Tell," but would only "show" and not "tell." She demonstrated her acquired school skills at home (e.g., alphabet, numbers) to her parents, but her teacher had no way to assess what Chrissy was learning. After several months in kindergarten, she began to mouth words when her classmates were reciting or singing, but would not speak, and would not move her mouth when it appeared that an adult was watching. School personnel were very concerned about Chrissy, and were considering placement in a special classroom for severely behavior disordered children.

Chrissy was a clever and nonverbally communicative child. Frequently she could communicate her wishes and needs without speaking, and much of the time people were able to guess what she wanted. Her efforts to communicate nonverbally were often quite creative. For example, in mid-December after her sixth birthday, Chrissy asked her parents to help her prepare a "wish list" for Christmas. She dictated the items to her parents and insisted that they write down her name, address, and telephone number at the top. Several days later, the family took Chrissy to a mall so that she could see Santa Claus. The parents observed with anticipation, wondering if and how Chrissy would communicate with him. Was Santa considered an "adult"? Would Chrissy talk to him, or would she remain silent? When she reached the front of the line, Chrissy took out the list from her pocket and handed it to Santa Claus. Because she had insisted on having her name, address, and telephone number on the top of the list, it appeared that Chrissy felt that she did not need to talk with Santa because he had all the vital information. Her parents had not realized that Chrissy had the list with her, nor that she had anticipated her visit with Santa when she asked them to help her with her Christmas list.

Assessment with Parents

A Child Behavior Checklist (CBCL) (Achenbach and Edelbrock 1983), filled out by Chrissy's parents at the initial interview, yielded a nonclinical profile. In fact, the only items endorsed as "somewhat or sometimes true" were: acts too young for her age; can't concentrate, pay attention for long; can't sit still, restless, or hyperactive; disobedient at home; doesn't eat well; fears certain animals (dogs); refuses to talk; and speech problem (dysfluency). Only one item, wets the bed, was endorsed as "very true or often true." Even with these endorsed items, the profile was flat, suggesting that according to her parents' report, Chrissy did not present with any major psychopathology, despite the serious concerns about her mutism.

In reviewing the child's records and interviewing the parents, the therapist learned that many adults had attempted to get Chrissy to talk. This included friends, relatives, and professionals with whom the family came in contact. It was the parents' impression that Chrissy was aware of this. She seemed sensitive to attempts to "trick" her into talking, and her response was always to be uncooperative with these efforts.

Chrissy was an only child. Her parents saw her as shy but not withdrawn. Her mother reported that she too had been a shy child and had a history of speech dysfluency. The mother was the primary caretaker and had been home with Chrissy since her birth. The child had never been in the care of baby-sitters or other caretakers for any period of time. The parents denied knowledge of any stress or trauma in the child's life. They denied any other difficulties with the exception of bed wetting, which occurred practically every night. Because of the wetting, Chrissy wore diapers at night, but underwear without difficulty during the day. At the time of the assessment, the parents wished to defer any treatment of Chrissy's enuresis.

Assessment with Child

Assessment via observation of Chrissy's play was conducted for the first three sessions. Specific therapeutic interventions were not introduced until the fourth session. After her initial hesitation at the first session, Chrissy engaged readily with the materials in the office. She appeared enthusiastic and interested in drawing and toys. No effort was made to interview her or formally test her in any way. The therapist did not want to communicate to Chrissy that she would be expected to talk. This period of assessment was used to understand Chrissy better through her play, as well as to communicate to her what the therapy experience would be like.

Treatment

Chrissy was seen for a total of thirty-three sessions, which included the first three assessment sessions, over the course of 1 year. Sessions were held weekly for the first 5 months, bimonthly for the next 3 months, and then monthly for the last 4 months. The therapist saw the parents regularly (usually at every second session with the child) to offer support and obtain information about Chrissy. The parents were encouraged not to question her or engage her in conversation about her refusal to speak. If she brought up the topic of speaking, they were asked to remain neutral and matter-of-fact in response to her comments.

In a conference with the teacher and principal, it was also agreed that the school would approach Chrissy's silence by ignoring it. Although they were not entirely comfortable with this approach, they were willing to deal with her in this way for a trial period.

Cognitive-Behavioral Play Therapy sessions were structured and involved the use of several puppets with a variety of presentations. Different puppets presented with a variety of "problems," including talking. One of the puppets (Mouse) wanted to make some new friends. Another puppet (Frog) talked all the time, and a third (Tiger) did not talk. Behavioral and cognitive techniques were employed to help all of the puppets with their difficulties so that the primary focus would not be on the issue of not talking. (See Tables 8-1 and 8-2 for sample vignettes depicting specific behavioral and cognitive approaches, respectively.) The therapist gradually *shaped* the behaviors of each of the puppets in the desired

TABLE 8-1
Examples of Behavioral Techniques in Cognitive-Behavioral Play Therapy with 6-Year-Old Elective Mute Child.

Behavioral Technique	Therapist Intervention
Shaping behavior	Puppet reinforced for gradual steps toward talking (e.g., moving lips, whispering, playing kazoo)
Shaping socially appropriate expression of feelings	Pointing to feeling faces, expressing feelings nonverbally, labeling feelings with words
Positive reinforcement	Puppet receives praise and stickers for talking

TABLE 8-2
Examples of Cognitive Techniques in Cognitive-Behavioral Play Therapy with 6-Year-Old Elective Mute Child.

Cognitive Technique	Therapist Intervention
Identifying (irrational) beliefs	Therapist says to puppet: "Maybe you're afraid when you talk at school that everyone will make a fuss."
Changing (irrational) beliefs	Therapist says for puppet: "It would be OK to talk." "It would make me happy not to have to be quiet."
Positive self-statements	Therapist verbalizes for puppet: "It's hard to start talking, but it will get easier after I start."

direction. For example, the puppet who wanted to make friends learned better peer interaction; the puppet who talked too much became quieter; and the puppet who did not talk began to speak. The therapist *reinforced* the puppets individually for their efforts. Each puppet could then "verbalize" beliefs about why it had the particular difficulty, and these beliefs were challenged by the therapist (*countering [irrational] beliefs*). The socially appropriate expression of feelings was also shaped gradually as the puppets learned to put their feelings into words rather than acting those feelings out. Positive self-statements were also modeled by the puppets.

Although Chrissy did not speak at first, it was quite evident that she was listening to what was being said. She interacted actively with the animal puppets (e.g., smiling, hugging) and watched intently when the therapist engaged the puppets in play and conversation.

Course of Treatment

Below are a series of vignettes highlighting the major themes and progress made in treatment (see Figure 8–1). Any "comments" made by the puppets were verbalized by the therapist, unless indicated otherwise. When conversations appear in quotes, they are from actual (taped) transcripts of the sessions.

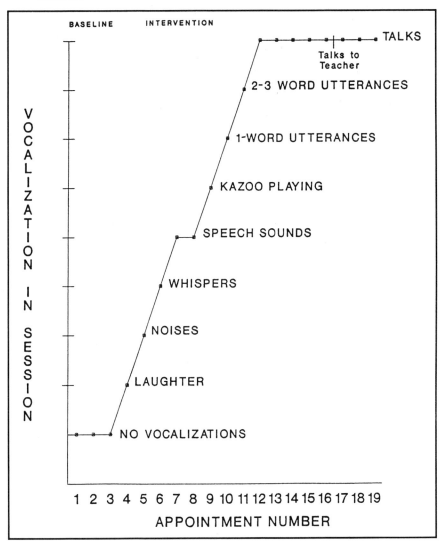

Figure 8–1.   Progression of Talking for Elective Mute 6-Year-Old over the Course of Treatment.

Session 4.   Chrissy was overheard talking to her parents in the waiting room but stopped mid-sentence as soon as the therapist entered. She eagerly accompanied the therapist to the office. Although the puppets had been available to the child during the first three assessment sessions, the therapist "formally" introduced them to Chrissy at the fourth session. The therapist introduced the tiger as "shy" and not interested in talking. At first the mouse tried to get Tiger to talk, physically opening and closing her mouth, but then the therapist said, "She's not ready, she will talk when she is ready." Chrissy laughed in response to this scene.

Session 5.   The frog kept singing and talking, and was told by one of the other puppets that he "talks too much." Chrissy interacted with the puppets and mouthed words, but did not speak. The therapist used stickers, and gave one to Chrissy for the picture she drew, one to Tiger for talking, and one to Frog for not talking. The puppets played with the toy phone, each taking turns calling their moms, and Chrissy took the phone and made noises, but did not actually speak.

Session 6.   Frog asked Chrissy what she was going to draw, and she whispered to the therapist "mom." She nonverbally expressed anger at Frog by her facial expressions, physical efforts to make him close his mouth, and destruction of a paper belonging to the puppet. The therapist drew several "feeling faces" (mad, sad, happy), identified them with verbal labels, and wondered out loud how Chrissy felt about Frog when he talked so much. Chrissy pointed to the mad face. When the therapist expressed the importance of letting people know when you are mad or upset with them, Chrissy made an angry-looking face at Frog and whispered in his ear. Chrissy used noises and guttural sounds while pretending to talk on the telephone. She set up a scene where the therapist was to answer the telephone. The therapist waited until the "ringing" noise Chrissy was making became more audible before "recognizing" that the telephone was ringing and answering it.

Following this session, the parents reported that Chrissy's speech appeared more fluent to them, and some of the dysfluencies evident in the past seemed to have lessened. The therapist encouraged them to praise her for the fluency of her speech.

Session 7.   In response to Frog when he was talking excessively, Chrissy said "Shhhh."

Session 8.   In talking on the telephone to her mom, Tiger said that she hoped no one would make a fuss when she talks. Frog made noises (e.g., sh, amm, hmmm), and Chrissy made louder and louder imitations of the noises. She began banging blocks and appeared angry. The therapist commented on expressing feelings like anger.

The parents noted this week that Chrissy was aware of a school conference they had with her teacher. She asked about it, and according to her mother, seemed afraid of what was said. Later that evening at bedtime, Chrissy said to her mother, "It's hard to be quiet all the time." Her mother asked her about that, and she responded, "Never mind, I was talking to my puppy."

Session 9. Chrissy played a kazoo in imitation of the therapist and the puppets. In playing with the dollhouse, she made noises for the alarm clock, for snoring, and to indicate that the dolls were getting dressed. She used intonation but no real words when talking on the telephone, clearly indicating the turn-taking of a telephone conversation without any dialogue.

Session 10. Chrissy made noises as she walked around the office. The therapist indicated that the teacher told her about the students' pet, a rabbit, and the therapist wondered aloud about the rabbit's name. Chrissy whispered "Bunny," and the therapist wrote the name next to Chrissy's picture of the rabbit. Throughout the rest of the session she played the kazoo, used the telephone with some intonation, whispered without spoken words, and pointed to feeling faces/words.

Session 11. In the waiting room, the parents mentioned that Chrissy might want to tell the therapist where she was going after the session. As child and therapist entered the office, the therapist noted that she wondered where Chrissy was going. Chrissy responded with "Ho Ho." The therapist acted puzzled and kept repeating "Ho Ho, I wonder where you are going." Chrissy did not respond. She picked up a cat/duck two-sided puppet, and the therapist said, "This side is a cat, but I wonder what this side is," to which Chrissy responded "Quack, quack." The therapist, continuing to appear puzzled about "Ho Ho," repeated the phrase a few times, to which Chrissy responded, seemingly in frustration, "Santa Claus." The therapist commented on how exciting it would be to see Santa, and then wondered aloud what Chrissy wanted for Christmas, and in a very strained voice Chrissy said "Bouncing babies." The session continued with Chrissy talking in mostly two-word utterances, for example saying "Tie boots" after she demonstrated her proficiency with tying her shoelaces. At the end of the session, she had a conversation, over the telephone with Frog.

Frog (*therapist speaking for Frog*): May I speak to Chrissy, please?
Chrissy: This is Chrissy.
Frog: Can you come over to play?
Chrissy: Yes.
Frog: Bring a toy with you.
Chrissy: Bring blocks.
[*This conversation was repeated three times.*]

Session 12.   Chrissy entered the office, turned off the lights—although it was bright in the room because of the sunlight through the windows— and began talking. She talked about Christmas, what presents she wanted, and what she thought about seeing Santa Claus. Her play centered around themes of Christmas as she and the puppets wrapped presents and decorated the tree. The therapist let Chrissy know how interesting the conversation was, and how happy she was that Chrissy was so excited about Christmas. The therapist's praise was specifically about the content of Chrissy's conversation, not the fact that she was talking. Chrissy received stickers for the conversation, as well as for showing the therapist that she could tie her shoelaces. At the end of the session, when Chrissy and the therapist walked into the waiting room, Chrissy's parents were not there. Chrissy was in mid-sentence when they walked in, and she abruptly stopped talking to the therapist, as if she did not want her parents to know that she had spoken to the therapist.

Session 13.   Chrissy was talkative during the session, starting off by introducing Frog to Puppy, a stuffed animal she had brought with her. She indicated that the animal wanted a sticker, and with the therapist tried to figure out what the puppy could do to earn a sticker. She decided that Puppy could sing a Christmas song, which Chrissy sang all the way through. She got angry at Frog, taking him first to the police, then to Santa (seemingly the ultimate authority). The therapist indicated that Tiger was still not talking, and the following conversation ensued:

Chrissy: Make her talk.
Therapist: I can't make her talk; she'll talk when she is ready.
Chrissy: (*to Tiger*) When are you gonna talk?
Tiger: [*moves lips, uses distorted, unrecognizable voice*]
Chrissy: NO, use your regular voice like mine and yours [*pointing to therapist*].
Therapist: Tiger is at school, and the teacher is asking her to say her ABCs and 123s.

Chrissy: I talked at school to a b-b-boy, a bad boy. He tells bad jokes. [*pause*] Tiger, talk. Say one.
Tiger: One.
Chrissy: Two.
Tiger: Two.
Chrissy: Three.
Tiger: Three.

The therapist gave Chrissy a sticker for helping Tiger talk, and Tiger got a sticker for talking.

Session 14. Chrissy reminded the therapist that Tiger talked the previous week, and the therapist reminded Tiger that she will be going back to school next week when her vacation is over. Again, Chrissy would not talk to the therapist in front of her parents, although she did show them the puppets. The therapist indicated that next week Chrissy and the therapist and her parents will play a game together at the end of the session.

Session 15. Chrissy was excited about the game she will be playing with her parents and the therapist, and asked several questions about it. She asked about Tiger, regarding whether or not she went back to school and if she was talking there.

Therapist: Chrissy, Tiger has a question for you. She wants to know what would help her talk at school.
Chrissy: (*rather sternly*) Look it.
Tiger: I don't like talking at school but I know I need to. What should I do?
Chrissy: (*to therapist*) I don't know, you tell.
Therapist: I should tell her? O.K., Tiger, will you listen to me real carefully . . . I know it is really, really hard, and you're really kinda scared to do it, but I tell you what, if you really try, and you just say a little bit, and then the next day you say a little bit more, pretty soon you'll be ready to talk all the time, and I think you'll even like it. And I don't think you have to worry about kids teasing you, and I don't think you have to worry about anybody making a big fuss. I just think you'll just really like talking there. . . .
[*Chrissy puts hat on Tiger and is laughing*]
Tiger: Chrissy, I look silly in this hat. Should I wear this hat to school?
Chrissy: Mmmmm.
Tiger: The kids will laugh at me.
Chrissy: No they won't.

Chrissy and the therapist played a card game, and Chrissy quickly learned the rules. At the end of the session, the parents were asked to join Chrissy and the therapist for a game. She was quite involved in the game but would not explain the rules to her parents, and talked only in a whisper to her mother.

Session 16. An excerpt:

Tiger: I talked at school this week.
Chrissy: I don't care. (*looking at therapist*) You talk to her.

In the game at the end of the session with her parents, Chrissy is quiet, again only whispering to her mother.

Session 17. Just prior to this session, Chrissy's mother had telephoned the therapist to inform her that Chrissy had talked "nonstop" to the teacher at school that day.

Chrissy began the session by immediately showing the therapist the two pins she had received at school for talking.

Chrissy: I talked with my teacher this week.
Therapist: About what?
Chrissy: Everything. . . .
Tiger: I heard you talked at school. Tell me how you did it.
Chrissy: I don't know, I just did it!
Tiger: Was it scary?
Chrissy: No.
Tiger: Did it feel good?
Chrissy: Yes. Maybe you can get a sticker if you talk at school.

Chrissy decided to make glasses for Frog; she drew them, cut them out, and placed them on the puppet. The therapist praised Frog for wearing the glasses, stating "I know you can see better with the glasses, and they look very nice on you."

Chrissy became upset when she realized that the therapist was going to talk to her parents at the end of the session. When the therapist acknowledged the anger and tried to label it for her, she at first denied it, but later Chrissy admitted that she was angry with the therapist because she wanted to spend the entire time with her.

In meeting with the therapist, the parents reported that Chrissy continued to talk at school with her teacher individually, in class, and was now also talking to the speech therapist.

Session 18. Excerpts:

Chrissy: (*to Tiger*) Did you talk at school this week?
Tiger: Yes. [*Tiger shows Chrissy a piece of paper with stickers on it for talking*]
Chrissy: Good girl, Tiger. I talked to my teacher and the speech teacher.
Tiger: That's great. . . .

Therapist: I think you were mad at me last week when I had to talk to your mom and dad.
Chrissy: Yes. I don't want you to. I don't like it.
Therapist: Sometimes things like that make you mad. I had to talk to your mom and dad and that made you mad. . . .

Chrissy: Some kid at school called a girl "Four Eyes" because she wears glasses.
Therapist: Do you think she was sad when they called her Four Eyes? Think that made her kind of sad and mad?
Chrissy: NO, she was angry and then that little boy apologized.
Therapist: He apologized? That was a nice thing to do.
Frog: I wouldn't like it if somebody called me Four Eyes, that would make me mad.
Chrissy: You would talk to the teacher, Frog.
Frog: Yeah, but I always talk to the teacher. Remember sometimes I talk too much? The teacher has to say, Frog, you gotta give all the kids a chance, you can't talk all the time, remember?
Chrissy: And then there's Tiger.
Therapist: What happened to Tiger this week? 'Cause once she started talking in school she really likes talking to her teacher—she was so happy. She started talking to everybody.

Chrissy: [*puts on the frog's glasses*] No songs for him until he wears his glasses for awhile.
Therapist: OK. He looks good in his glasses, but it may make him mad if someone teases him because he wears them.

Tiger: I talked to my teacher, and I talked to my speech teacher, and I talked to the kids at school, but can I start talking to other people too?

Chrissy: Yes.

Tiger: Who should I talk to?

Chrissy: Lots and lots of people.

Tiger: Lots of people?

Chrissy: Yeah.

Therapist: (*to Tiger*) I think you should talk to everybody because you have nice things to say.

Chrissy: Yeah, yeah. You talk to somebody, everybody. . . .

Tiger: OK, I tell you what, Chrissy. You ask me next week who I talked to, OK?

Chrissy: OK.

Therapist: (*to Tiger*) Do you want to know who Chrissy's talked to? Well, ask her.

Tiger: Who'd you talk to Chrissy?

Chrissy: Guess.

Therapist: Umm, Mommy and Daddy . . .

Chrissy: And the speech lady.

Therapist: And the speech lady, and Mrs. Smith (teacher), and Bunny . . . and who else. The principal?

Chrissy: How'd you know the principal? I talked to her too. I 'member her name . . .

Tiger: Should I talk to the principal at my school? Is it hard or easy?

Chrissy: It's easy.

Tiger: Oh it's easy. I would like to do it.

Session 20.   Chrissy verbalized that she was still angry but plays positively with the puppets. On the way out of the session she called to the tiger, "Keep talking at school."

Session 21.   Chrissy praised the frog for wearing his glasses, "Very good, Frog."

Session 22.   Chrissy was intently making hearts for the puppets and herself. As the therapist engaged the puppets in conversation about school and speech class, Chrissy appeared to be listening and offered her opinions from across the room. However, she did not want to join the conversation.

Session 23.

Chrissy: Do you have to see my parents today?
Therapist: Yes.
Chrissy: [*makes face*]
Therapist: I know that makes you very mad. Can you tell me that you are mad when I need to talk with your parents?
Chrissy: [*quiet*]
[*Therapist shows how frog makes a face and says he is mad.*]

Parents reported that Chrissy was talking to "everyone," including other patrons at restaurants! She was so talkative at school that at times the teacher needed to encourage her to be quiet.

Session 24.   Chrissy talked with the therapist about the change to every-other-week sessions (therapist and parents have been talking with her about this) and stated that "every other week is a long time."

Session 25.   (Sessions are now scheduled for once every other week.)
Therapist talked with Chrissy about how well she was doing and stressed that she was not coming in as often because of her great progress. A scenario was set up with the lion puppet where he did not want to talk and Tiger showed him how, but Chrissy was uninterested in this.

Session 28.   Therapist had Tiger play out anger at a boy who teased her because she has such long eyelashes. Chrissy had the boy come over to Tiger and apologize.

Session 29.   Chrissy discovered a timer in the room and wanted to time Frog for not talking and then reward him with presents. She then timed Tiger to see how long the puppet could talk. Tiger talked about being sad because she has to leave kindergarten, and how hard it is to say goodbye. Tiger added that first grade would be good. Chrissy listened, but told Tiger that she is sad about leaving kindergarten. She did not seem to be able to focus on the positive side of first grade.

Session 30.   (Sessions are now scheduled for once a month.)
Chrissy again timed Frog for not talking. She worked on a book of

her life, providing current information about herself. When asked about her life before kindergarten she said, "I don't remember."

Parents reported that she continued to do very well. She was talking to most people, and planning when she would talk to others to whom she had not yet spoken (e.g., "I will talk to her for her birthday").

Session 31.   Chrissy talked about missing her kindergarten teacher. The therapist discussed how Chrissy and the therapist would miss each other after therapy ends. Chrissy took a copy of the therapist's business card and promised to call. Chrissy seemed to need reassurance that even though she did not know where the therapist lived, she would still be able to "find" her. Chrissy and the therapist started to make plans for a final "farewell" party to be held at the last session.

Parents report that she had been most responsive to others and they continued to be amazed by the settings in which she talked freely.

Session 32.   Chrissy talks about termination and missing the therapist, requesting reassurance that she can call or visit.

Parents report that Chrissy appears to keep a mental list of those with whom she has yet to speak. Remaining on the list are her first grade teacher (3 more weeks until the beginning of school) and her dentist, whom she has not seen since beginning to talk with adults.

Given her dramatic success in talking and her increasing reluctance to wear diapers at night, the parents were interested in actively treating Chrissy's nocturnal enuresis. They began to use a urine alarm system with Chrissy, with excellent results. They reported that it awakens her immediately, she goes to the bathroom, and thereafter stays dry throughout the night. Chrissy is thrilled about finally being out of diapers at night.

Session 33.   Chrissy, the therapist, and the puppets hold a party. Chrissy repeatedly says, "I will miss you" and writes her last name on a paper so the therapist "will not forget, in case you have another Chris." She draws a picture of the therapist "so I won't forget you," and states she is "happy now. I wasn't before when I wouldn't talk."

Results

Chrissy did not speak with the therapist or in the therapist's presence during the first three assessment sessions. Gradually, she made closer and closer approximations to talking, moving from laughter, noises, whispering, speech sounds, simple utterances, and then at the twelfth session, Chrissy began to talk. Figure 8-1 shows the progression of the child's talking over the course of treatment.

Although Chrissy talked to the therapist regularly after the twelfth session, at first she did not talk to any other new adults in her environment. Between the sixteenth and seventeenth treatment sessions, she began to talk to her teacher, and then gradually to other adults at school and elsewhere.

A Child Behavior Checklist (CBCL), filled out by the parents at the last session, again yielded a nonclinical profile. Compared with the initial CBCL, this profile was also flat, with even fewer items endorsed than had been at the initial assessment CBCL. The items endorsed as "somewhat or sometimes true" were as follows; Can't concentrate, can't pay attention for long; Can't sit still, restless, or hyperactive; Doesn't eat well; Fears certain animals; Problems with eyes (farsighted); Speech problems (dysfluency); and Wets the bed. No items were endorsed as "very true or often true."

Follow-up

Follow-up was obtained via the parents 30 months after the termination of treatment. At that time, Chrissy was talking freely to all individuals with whom she had contact and was doing well with her schoolwork. There had been no relapses in talking, although she was still receiving speech therapy one day a week for her articulation difficulties. The parents had continued to use the urine alarm system for approximately 1 month after termination of treatment with positive outcome. When they discontinued the alarm, Chrissy had remained dry at night for the past 29 months and there had been no relapses of enuresis. No other problems were reported.

Discussion

Chrissy's mutism was treated indirectly through two major avenues. The first was through the creation of a positive therapeutic environment for the child, in which talking was not the major focus. Instead, mastery and accomplishment in other areas were encouraged by the therapist. Although the therapist used positive reinforcement, Chrissy was praised for nonspeech activities (e.g., tying her shoelaces; drawing pictures). Speaking was not assumed to be necessary on Chrissy's part. The therapist's comments were often worded as statements conveying interest, not as questions with the expectation that Chrissy needed to provide an answer. For example, with regard to her statement "Ho Ho," instead of asking "Where are you going?" the therapist would say, "I wonder where you are going. . . . " Also, when Chrissy did speak, the therapist reinforced the *content* of her conversation, not the *fact* that she was talking.

The second therapeutic avenue was via "treating" several puppets for a variety of problems. One puppet, who was shy and nontalkative, was gradually shaped to talk, and as she "learned" to talk, her efforts provided a model for Chrissy. Thus, although many of the behavioral and cognitive interventions reported in the literature were used, they were employed indirectly through modeling, not directly with the child. The decision to treat Chrissy's mutism indirectly was based on the therapist's clinical sense that the child would not respond positively to another adult who tried to "pressure" her to talk. Although this approach might be construed as counter to the behavioral literature, which highlights attempts to initiate and maintain speech in the elective mute individual, it is consistent with the notion that direct attempts to prompt speaking are usually ineffective. Chrissy had not responded in the past to other professional efforts to "convince" her to talk or to shape talking, and she had made clear to her parents that she did not want a big fuss made when she started to talk. It seemed pointless to attempt to coax her into talking.

The therapist tried not to respond to Chrissy's nonverbal behavior by making assumptions about what she was communicating. Even when Chrissy began to make closer and closer approximations to speech, the therapist did not make assumptions about what Chrissy was intending to convey. For example, when she said "Ho Ho," the therapist did not immediately assume that she meant Santa Claus (Session 11). Similarly, when Chrissy made low sounds for a ringing phone (Session 6), the therapist waited until the sounds were more audible before "answering" the phone. This communicated to the child that the therapist was interested but would not try to second-guess the child's intentions or speak for her.

Initially, when Chrissy began talking with the therapist, she continued to refuse to talk with the therapist in front of her parents. Nor was she talking to anyone new outside the therapy sessions. A *stimulus fading* paradigm was used in order to encourage talking in new settings and with new people. The parents were introduced into treatment with Chrissy to play a game at the end of the session with the child and therapist. Although she had been talking with the therapist, when the parents were introduced into the sessions, Chrissy refused to talk. Gradually, she began to whisper to her mother and then eventually to talk with the therapist and both parents in a normal tone of voice. Thus, by the therapist's gradually changing the stimuli controlling speech, Chrissy began to extend her efforts to talk to include speaking with her parents and therapist at the same time. Such a paradigm might have been useful at school had Chrissy not begun to speak there without such an intervention.

The teacher was evidently frustrated by Chrissy's lack of speech, particularly in view of her knowledge that Chrissy was now talking in therapy. Despite an agreement with the therapist not to directly discuss Chrissy's silence with her, one day between the sixteenth and seventeenth treatment sessions the teacher simply told Chrissy that she would need to talk in order to go on to first grade in the coming year; if she did not begin to speak, she might have to remain in kindergarten. Chrissy then spoke to the teacher, apparently in response to the perceived threat.

The puppets modeled various adaptive skills for Chrissy, and she appeared to respond very positively to their behavior. For example, appropriate verbal expression was modeled by the puppets as they labeled feelings in response to certain situations. Thus, the puppets were *shaped in the socially appropriate expression of feelings.* Gradually, Chrissy moved from pointing to pictures of feeling faces, to making faces to match a particular feeling (e.g., mad, sad), and then eventually to verbal labeling of her feelings.

In providing encouragement and *positive reinforcement* for Chrissy and the puppets, the therapist also modeled this behavior for Chrissy. She responded by consistently reinforcing the puppets for their efforts to meet their goals. For example, Chrissy encouraged Tiger with comments such as "Keep talking at school." She offered positive reinforcement in the form of praise to Tiger for talking (e.g., "Good talking, Tiger") and Frog for wearing his glasses (e.g., "Very good, Frog"). This positive reinforcement on her part was unsolicited and seemed to increase as Chrissy continued to feel more positive about her own efforts.

Once Chrissy began to talk, she never specifically dealt with issues related to her previous silence. In fact, she tended to avoid participating in the puppets' conversations related to not talking, except to reinforce Tiger and offer her praise and encouragement. She did deal with the issues of teasing to some extent, although this was largely through comments regarding wearing glasses, something for which she had also apparently been teased. Working with Chrissy on a book of her life was one effort to deal with these earlier issues. Chrissy's response to her life before kindergarten was "I don't remember," another indication that she preferred not to discuss the time before she talked.

There are several limitations of the treatment of this child. First, the three-session assessment could be construed as a type of treatment. During these assessment sessions, the therapist may have conveyed warmth and acceptance of the child. Although the child might interpret this as acceptance of her nonverbal manner, it might also have conveyed the message that therapy was a safe place. Given this, it is probably more accurate to think of the first three sessions as both assessment and treatment, rather than exclusively as assessment. Second, it is possible that factors other than the CBPT contributed to the child's positive gains. By complying with the therapist's request to ignore the mutism, the parents and teacher were in essence extinguishing it. This might be considered a form of treatment. The results could be explained on the basis of either the CBPT or the extinction of her silence. However, given the gradual increase in talking related to what was taking place in the sessions, it seems most likely that the CBPT played an important role in the child's increasing verbalizations.

Finally, maturation cannot be ruled out as an explanation for the child's success in talking. There is no way to determine whether Chrissy would have begun to talk spontaneously without treatment. However, given her dramatic response to specific situations in treatment, and lack of responsiveness to previous interventions, it seems unlikely that maturation alone would explain the positive changes.

CONCLUSIONS

Assessment of elective mute children presents some unique difficulties because of the lack of direct verbal information provided. Such information must be obtained from parent report, school information, and other sources, as well as from the child's nonverbal behavior. Creative use of feeling faces, drawings, and play materials can provide the therapist with a wealth of information. Currently, most behavioral interventions deal directly with the elective mute child's refusal to speak, either by shaping closer approximations to speech or reinforcing talking when it does occur. These interventions can be problematic, in part because they directly address the child's silence. By dealing with the silence directly, the therapist potentially conveys a message that the child is being "coerced" to speak. Such attempts are typically unsuccessful.

Although many behavioral treatments of elective mutism have been successful without cognitive components, the cognitive-behavioral approach expands the treatment to include cognitive interventions that may directly address the child's perceptions about speaking. Elective mute children may have perceptions about their silence that may not be clear to others. In some instances these perceptions may be noted by significant others, such as parents. If the therapist has such information available, the child's perceptions can be understood initially through information conveyed to the therapist.

Chrissy's parents were able to convey information concerning her perceptions about talking to the therapist. The therapist could then use this information in the puppet play. For example, Chrissy's comments to her parents that she did not want a fuss to be made when she talked was used by the therapist with the tiger puppet. The puppet not only modeled the thought but also provided self-statements associated with it (e.g., "I know it will be hard, but it will feel good when I talk").

Through CBPT, children can address feelings associated with their silence, as well as learn more adaptive ways of dealing with their feelings. Initially this may involve nonverbal expression (e.g., facial expressions, drawing feeling faces) and verbal labeling, which is modeled for the child. Later, if the child begins to talk to the therapist, more direct verbal labeling of feelings can be explored.

Several examples of this progression were used in Chrissy's treatment. Before Chrissy was speaking to the therapist, the therapist offered feeling faces (e.g., Session 6). Chrissy was able to point to the face that expressed her feelings. The therapist also modeled self-statements via the puppets, such as "I don't like talking at school, but I know I need to" (Session 15). As the child began to speak, other issues were raised. For example, the therapist knew about the teasing Chrissy had been subjected to because of her speech dysfluency, but did not know about her concerns about wearing glasses. Chrissy brought up the latter issue as it related to one of the puppets wearing glasses, and another child at school being called "Four Eyes" (Session 18). This information could then be used to relate to Chrissy's concerns about her own need to wear glasses.

Elective mutism is clearly a complex disorder. A variety of treatment approaches may be indicated, and the choice of a particular approach may be dictated by many factors. These include the child's age, developmental level, extent of mutism, apparent role of his or her silence, family dynamics, and previous interventions, as well as parental cooperation and motivation. The applicability of CBPT in the treatment of other elective mute children is at present unknown. Further use of this form of treatment would be helpful in determining which variables would be most amenable to a CBPT approach.

9

Cognitive-Behavioral Play Therapy with Children of Divorce

OVERVIEW OF PROBLEM

Almost 40 percent of all children in this country will experience parental marital disruption by their fifteenth birthday (Kurdek, 1986). These children are overrepresented in clinic-referred populations (Felner et al. 1975, Kalter 1977). Further, divorce is considered a severe, acute stressor that often precipitates a range of symptoms in children (*DSM-III-R* 1987). Although children in the first 18 months to 1 year postdivorce are considered most vulnerable, follow-up studies indicate that the negative effects of divorce often diminish over time but do not necessarily disappear. In fact, Wallerstein's (1985) 10-year follow-up study of children of divorce suggests that many children continue to experience negative effects from their parents' divorce well into adulthood.

Although divorce is often thought of as a single category, it is important that divorce be considered within the broader context in which it occurs. For children, parental divorce rarely happens in isolation from other events. Thus, divorce often results in multiple stressors for the child and family. Other life changes concomitant with the divorce may play a role in children's reactions, such as increases in mother–child conflict, changes in the mother's mental status, decrease in financial resources, and new routines, homes, and schools.

173

These stressors can have multiple effects. For example, it is well documented that women usually suffer financially after a divorce. Because approximately 90 percent of children remain with the mother after their parents separate, a vast majority of children experience a loss in family income after a divorce (Soldano 1990). Coupled with the fact that postdivorce income is a powerful predictor of successful adjustment, this suggests that divorce must be considered from a multi-faceted perspective. Another critical factor is parental adjustment after divorce. For example, if the custodial parent did not want the divorce and is experiencing significant depression as a result of it, the child may be adversely affected. Additionally, children who have regular, positive visits with the noncustodial parent appear to have the best adjustment (Felner and Terre 1987).

Preschoolers, especially boys, have a particularly difficult time adjusting after the divorce of their parents (e.g., Wallerstein and Kelly 1980). Wallerstein and her colleagues studied the reactions of children across four age groups, and concluded that preschoolers (ages 2½–5) showed some typical patterns in reaction to divorce. They were noted to regress behaviorally (e.g., toileting accidents), worry about being abandoned by both parents, feel responsible for the divorce, and be upset by even the most routine of separations. Additionally, many of the preschoolers developed sleep disturbances and inhibited play, and became more aggressive and irritable or withdrawn (Wallerstein and Kelly 1975). Preoccupation with the divorce may be noted, as evidenced in increasing aggression as frustration tolerance decreases or in decreasing aggression as the child tries desperately to be "good" so that the parents may reconcile. The likelihood of emotional or behavior problems following divorce appears to be influenced by gender as well as age. In mother–custody homes, girls tend to adjust better than boys. This is true across the age groups studied (preschool through adolescence). Additionally, boys appear to become more aggressive, and girls to be more withdrawn and anxious (Hetherington et al. 1985).

Preschool-age children's cognitive ability to understand factors such as time and causality are hindrances to their ability to truly understand what is happening in their families. At best, children may understand divorce based on the physical separation from and loss of one parent in their lives. The existence of both positive and negative feelings between the parents will be confusing to preschoolers, who have difficulty understanding the coexistence of two apparently contradictory feelings. Because the concept of finality is not well understood by young children, divorce may be seen as temporary. They may be less distressed by any real understanding of what the divorce means, but more affected by specific day-to-day aspects of the divorce (e.g., father not living in the home). The magical thinking of children at this age is particularly problematic. For example, preschoolers often feel that they had some powerful role in the parents' divorce; therefore they have the power to make the parents reconcile.

ASSESSMENT

Assessment information is often gathered from clinical interviews with both parents, if available, and with the child. Although it is frequently the custody-holding parent who initiates contact with a mental health professional, the cooperation of the noncustodial parent is usually crucial. This conveys that the therapist is not partial to either parent. Obtaining information from each parent separately also provides information about the child from two perspectives, which may be quite different. When the parents are both asked to complete a Child Behavior Checklist (CBCL), the therapist not only compares interview information, but CBCL profiles as well. It is also important to gather information about how significant others (i.e., caretakers, teachers) perceive the child's functioning pre- and postdivorce. This is particularly important if the child is seen within the first 2 years following divorce, since children often have the most difficulty during this early stage after a divorce is finalized.

In addition to a more global assessment of the child, the therapist will gather information directly from the child regarding the child's thoughts, feelings, and attitudes about the divorce. With young children this is frequently obtained via play observation and interaction, and rarely in response to specific, directive questions.

Berg (1982, 1989) has addressed the issue of divorce from the perspective of both assessment and treatment. He used individualized assessment of attitudes and situations to develop treatment plans. Berg, whose work is predominantly with school-age children, developed a number of assessment measures for gathering this information. He proposed that assessment take place via a self-report inventory (Children's Beliefs about Parental Divorce scales; Kurdek and Berg 1987); Storytelling task (Family Story Method; Berg 1989); a modification of the Thematic Apperception Test (Berg 1989); and structured interview (Divorce Interview Schedule; Berg 1989).

TREATMENT

Data suggest that children's adjustments are enhanced by a parent's ability to meet the child's daily-living and emotional needs. Therefore part of treatment should be focused on parent and family functioning. This does not negate the need for child treatment but suggests that child-focused intervention should not be done in isolation. Treatment plans need to address both parent and child issues; therapy needs to provide a stable, consistent, supportive relationship that may not otherwise be available to the child. Often the child's needs are not met during the stressful period following a divorce. Ideally, the therapist can help the parents see how they can better help their children.

Cognitive-behavioral therapy for children of divorce is often geared to helping the child gain a realistic view of the situation while dealing with personal thoughts and feelings about the divorce. Older children and adolescents can be helped to see how they react to feelings about the situation and how their behaviors may in fact exacerbate family difficulties. Problem solving around difficult issues (e.g., visitations with the noncustodial parent, stepparents) may be useful for many children.

Berg (1982, 1989) developed an intervention for children of divorce that is an expansion and elaboration of the earlier work of Hambridge (1955). However, Berg's approach has a cognitive-behavioral orientation, with cognitive change as its primary goal. His work relies in large part on structured games and activities designed to assist school-age children in developing problem-solving abilities around divorce issues. Berg contends that the range of appropriate play techniques is unlimited and can be devised by the creative therapist for use with individual children. In his own work, Berg has developed four methods, including (1) The Changing Family Game (Berg 1982); (2) Divorce Stories (Irwin and Berg 1978); (3) Modification of Gardner's (1976) Mutual Storytelling Technique (Berg 1989); and (4) Role-Play (Omizo and Omizo 1987, cited in Berg 1989).

These four methods were created to facilitate divorce-related problem-solving skills. They rely on the techniques of behavioral rehearsal, cognitive restructuring, and reinforcement. Adaptive problem solving is modeled, and children are reinforced for efforts that will be most helpful in their particular situations. Therapy is focused on developing the ability to deal with the six problematic attitudes often found among children of divorce:

1. Peer ridicule and avoidance
2. Paternal blame
3. Maternal blame
4. Self-blame
5. Fear of abandonment
6. Hopes of reconciliation [Berg 1989, pp. 144–145]

In addition to these six areas, Berg contends that the child of divorce encounters difficulties in using good problem-solving skills related to situations surrounding the divorce (e.g., visitation, relations with stepparents). The specific situations to be dealt with—essentially a recapitulation of the divorce process—are presented via cards (Changing Family Game), stories (Divorce Stories; Mutual Storytelling), or role playing (Role-Play).

Cognitive-Behavioral Play Therapy

Studies have suggested that children's reactions to divorce differ from those attributed to them by their parents, and that the parents' views may be influenced by their own level of stress (e.g., Wallerstein and Kelly, 1980). This suggests that relying on parents as sources of information regarding their children's divorce-related cognitions and affect may be fraught with complications (Kurdek and Berg 1987). Further, parental implementation of programming for the young child in a postdivorce situation presents many problems, not the least of which is related to the parent's own mental status and postdivorce thoughts and feelings.

Children in postdivorce situations often have beliefs not only about the divorce but also about their causal role. These beliefs include fear of abandonment by the custodial parent, expectations of peer rejection, a perception that proper behavior will result in parental reconciliation, and unrealistic self-blame for the divorce. If these beliefs are not addressed in treatment, they may continue to interfere with the child's ability to regain some equilibrium following the divorce.

The basic goal of Cognitive-Behavioral Play Therapy (CBPT) with children of divorce is to help them understand their problems, examine their feelings, and modify their beliefs. An additional goal is to learn problem-solving and anger-resolution skills. Bibliotherapy is widely used with children of divorce, and many books not only identify post-divorce feelings but model coping strategies (see Appendix). Such books may be used in a preventive way or as one component of treatment for a child already exhibiting difficulty dealing with the divorce. In addition to books written for children, a range of books also exists for parents, both to help them deal with their own feelings about the divorce and to assist them in facilitating their child's adjustment.

CASE EXAMPLE

Kenny was an almost-6-year-old Caucasian boy referred because of problems at school, subsequent to his parents' divorce. He was an only child. After Kenny's father moved out, his mother noted drastic changes in Kenny, including anger and aggressive behavior at school. The referral was made approximately 4 months after the divorce was finalized; however, the parents had been separated for at least 1 year prior to the divorce. Both parents reported extreme conflict in their relationship. They indicated that they "never could agree on anything," and both acknowledged that the child was frequently caught in the middle. The father once woke Kenny up in the middle of the night and brought him out of his bed to explain to him what was going on between the parents. The father fought for custody of the child, but it was awarded to the mother. Kenny had regular visits with his father, which proved to be a continued source of conflict because of parental disagreement regarding much of what transpired during these visits (e.g., regarding Kenny's bedtime).

Kenny had just started school and was described by his kindergarten teacher as a sweet, sensitive child, who at times could be cooperative and at other times insisted on getting his way and being first. He was noted to grab, kick, and hit to get what he wanted. He frequently cried and was irritable at school. He also seemed preoccupied and at times would blurt out information about his parents (e.g., "I am going to my dad's this weekend"). The teacher reported that Kenny needed consistent, frequent structure and was more like a 3-year-old than like a child who was almost 6. Kenny's thoughts about the divorce were evident in his initial answers to several open-ended questions asked by the therapist. Kenny stated, "Dad divorced my mom. I didn't feel fine"; "Divorced people don't like each other"; and "One time I came into the living room and they told me they were getting divorced." When asked about what made him sad, Kenny said, "When people don't like each other." He appeared sad and withdrawn during the first several sessions. His affect was particularly sad when talking about his parents and the divorce.

Appointments were weekly, with Kenny's parents taking turns bringing him for therapy. Each parent was seen individually during the week he or she provided Kenny's transportation. On the third week, the parents were seen together and Kenny was not seen. Because of the ongoing conflict between the parents over Kenny, much of the work with them focused on the need for a consistent set of rules, smoother transitions between time Kenny spent with his father and mother, the need for a set of his own belongings at each parent's home, and the need for the parents to work out their conflicts.

During Kenny's individual CBPT sessions, the therapist created several role plays of puppets who expressed, rather than acted out, feelings. The situations the puppets dealt with were similar to those described by the parents and teachers as problematic for Kenny. Thus, the puppets were often entangled in school problems, peer difficulties, and situations where they would hit and push, despite being told not to fight. In these scenarios, the puppets gradually learned to verbalize angry feelings rather than hitting and kicking. Although Kenny did not want to participate with the puppets in these role plays, sometimes he would watch as the therapist interacted with the puppets. During the course of treatment, the teacher reported a positive improvement in Kenny's ability to express his feelings. His mother also reported that Kenny was more direct in his verbalizations to her. For example, instead of having a temper tantrum when she needed to go out, he was able to tell her that he was sad because "I am afraid you will leave me." She was able to reassure him and to explain that Kenny would be living with her, despite his visits with his father and his father's expressed wish to have Kenny live with him.

In Kenny's spontaneous play during the therapy sessions, he often played with clay, creating "slime" and "bad" people. He repeatedly built fortresses, with "good" and "bad" guys. At one session, approximately midway through the treatment, the father, who had brought Kenny, was upset because his lawyer had lost some documents. Kenny knew this and spent much of the session mimicking his father's acting upset. He was not able to verbalize anger beyond saying "My dad's mad because the lawyer lost something." He acted it out, however, by banging a hammer on a block. The therapist could verbalize Kenny's anger for him, and model for him, via the puppets, ways that he could better understand his dad's and his own feelings. Although Kenny was able to attend to this, he was less able to tolerate puppet play around specific parental and divorce issues, acknowledging that it is "hard because of the divorce." He would often push away the puppets during attempts to portray these issues through play.

At termination, 8 months after the beginning of treatment, Kenny was reportedly behaving more appropriately at home and school. However, follow-up 18 months after the termination of treatment suggested that although his behavior was somewhat improved, Kenny still had many unresolved issues regarding the divorce. Not surprisingly, there was still much conflict between his parents both in face-to-face interactions and via the court system. Understandably, Kenny's environment was still extremely stressful, as the parents continued their battles over visitation and child-rearing issues. Unfortunately for Kenny, their conflicts were now intensely focused on him.

Discussion

It is interesting to note that the structured therapeutic activities were much more focused on Kenny's anger and acting-out behavior rather than specific feelings about the divorce. At the point at which he was seen, Kenny was not able to deal with puppet play around issues related to his parents' divorce. He could acknowledge that the divorce made him feel "not fine" and that it was "hard." Expressing these feelings was painful but represented a beginning for Kenny. Although therapy seemed to be helpful to him, it was clear that his parents were not able to benefit to any extent from the work they did individually or together with the therapist. Their continued conflict may be the most significant, detrimental, and unfortunate aspect of this case. In spite of positive gains, Kenny's future will be undoubtedly influenced by the fact that he is continually caught in the tug-of-war between his parents.

CONCLUSIONS

The clinician working with children of divorce deals regularly with parental conflict. The literature is replete with examples of the enormous toll these conflicts take on the offspring who become victims of their parents' inability to manage their struggles with an ex-spouse. Additionally, the various stressors that often accompany divorce make children especially vulnerable to its effects. For children, the sequelae of divorce are numerous. It is noteworthy that many adults still experience the effects of their parents' divorce even when it occurred many years earlier.

Cognitive-Behavioral Play Therapy may be useful in allowing the child to learn alternative coping strategies and deal with conflictual situations in a different way. Certainly, this is often the goal even if family change is not possible. Unfortunately, we do not yet know whether learning of such skills will be helpful for the child over the long term. For many years therapists have been aware that treatment of postdivorce sequelae in children will have only temporary effects, if the environment and particularly the parents do not change. Indeed, CBPT may be ineffective as well, although its main advantage is in its efforts to teach the child adaptive coping skills. It is possible that the postdivorce family may not change, but the child may take skills away from treatment that will enhance abilities to deal with stressful family situations.

10

Cognitive–Behavioral Play Therapy with Fearful Children

OVERVIEW OF PROBLEM

Fears are a normal part of childhood. In children, fears are typically mild, age-specific, and transient (King et al. 1988). Particular fears are often seen in children at certain ages, although each child's fears will be determined in part by his or her learning history. Many children are fearful, often presenting with multiple fears. King and associates (1988) estimate that 3–8 percent of the population exhibit excessive fears. As the child gets older, fears change in nature, moving from those that usually occur in reaction to something in the environment to broader, less concrete fears. The infant may exhibit behavior reflective of fear in response to a loud noise or a stranger, whereas the older child may be fearful of imaginary figures ("monsters," "bad people"), events, and objects (Jersild 1968). These age-related fears are often transitory and of short duration. With time, the child's experiences, cognitive development, and expanding resources are helpful in overcoming certain fears.

A distinction is made between fears, which are a normal reaction to real or perceived threat, and phobias, which are fears that are not age related and are irrational because there is no real danger. These terms are often used interchangeably, despite their very different meanings. Additionally, the young child's perception of a fear as "irrational" is questionable given developmental issues that preclude such an under-standing.

Although it has been reported that 43 percent of children aged 6–12 have seven or more fears (Lapouse and Monk 1959), the percentage of children with phobias is reportedly as low as 5 percent in 7–12-year-olds (Miller et al. 1974). The definitions as well as the incidence of fears and phobias in children vary, with much of the research conducted during the 1930s through 1950s (e.g., Jersild and Holmes 1935, Lapouse and Monk 1959). In addition to concerns about the relevance of data collected over 30 years ago, many of the studies are of school-age children. In the most frequently cited studies, only the work of Jersild and Holmes (1935) dealt with children under the age of 6 years. In fact, Jersild and Holmes studied fears in children between the ages of 24–71 months as reported by their mothers. Jersild and Holmes found that some fears (e.g., a dark room) faded as the child got older, whereas others (e.g., snakes) were relatively constant.

In this chapter, childhood fear, a common problem, is addressed. The problem of fears in childhood will be discussed in terms of problem presentation, assessment, and treatment. The indications for Cognitive-Behavioral Play Therapy (CBPT) will be considered and highlighted through case vignettes.

ASSESSMENT

Much literature exists on the assessment of children's fears and phobias (see Morris and Kratochwill 1983). However, a great deal of this literature deals with older children and pays little attention to the preschool-age child. Attention to the young child is warranted given the number of fears reported in this age group. Assessment efforts focused on obtaining information from both the child and parents may provide the background needed for appropriate treatment planning.

Given what appears to be the relatively high incidence of fears in young children, the developmental appropriateness of the child's fears must first be assessed. Fears that are relatively common and age related may decrease as the child gets older (e.g., fear of strangers, fear of the dark); treatment is not necessarily warranted for such fears. On the other hand, a fear may be age appropriate, but if it is excessive, lasts over a long time, and interferes with the child's functioning, it may be clinically significant and worth treating. For example, one would be very concerned about a child who is so afraid of strangers that she is unable to interact with anyone outside the immediate family. If the child's fear interfered with her ability to go to school and interact with teachers and other students, intervention might be indicated.

It is important for the clinician to understand how the child typically deals with the fearful object/event, and what coping strategies the child has developed, if any. The extent and nature of the child's exposure to the feared stimuli will also be critical, and often is a prime determinant in the family seeking treatment for the child's fear. For example, a child who is afraid of dogs but who rarely has the opportunity to interact with a dog is less likely to be referred than a child who is afraid of elevators and lives on the twentieth floor of a high-rise apartment in a large city.

In terms of specific assessment measures, the Child Behavior Checklist (CBCL) (Achenbach and Edelbrock 1983) is used for screening purposes and has several items related to fears and anxiety, and a specific "schizoid/anxious" scale for 4-to-5-year-olds. The CBCL also screens for coexisting behavioral or emotional problems. Clearly it is not sufficient as the sole assessment measure of fears, although it provides a good beginning point. Scales specifically designed to assess fears and phobias in children include a number of self-report behavior checklists and rating scales (see Werry 1986b). Additionally, children can be asked to fill out self-monitoring forms based not on recall but on the documentation of fears as they are occurring. However, none of these specific assessment measures of fear and anxiety for older children is appropriate for use with preschoolers.

Given the developmental level of children at this age, intensive clinical interview and observation are often indicated. For the young child this assessment may come through observation and interaction during play. Play can provide invaluable information about the child's fears. For example, Terry, the encopretic child discussed in Chapter 7, repeatedly had the toy bear fall in the toilet and be "flushed away." Although he could not directly express fear of the toilet, it was evident in his play. This fear had not been obvious to the parents and therefore was not reported to the therapist. As the therapist observed his play, this fear became clearer and could then be dealt with in treatment.

Some fears can be assessed in real life so the therapist can observe the child's actual response to feared stimuli. For example, Richard was a 4½-year-old child who had been sexually abused by his baby-sitter (see Chapters 6 and 11). He expressed fears of using the bathroom and did not like to go into the bathroom without his mother. In one session, Richard went to use the toilet (in a bathroom adjoining the therapist's office). He first went to the waiting room to inform his mother that he needed to use the toilet. Then, when finished, he went back to his mother and stated, "I can't flush. I'm afraid." With reassurance from his mother, he was able to return to the toilet and flush it without assistance. This provided the observing therapist direct knowledge regarding the manifestations of Richard's fear.

TREATMENT

Despite the prevalence of fears in children, these youths are rarely referred to mental health professionals. In a sample of parents, 7 percent indicated concern regarding their child's specific fears, although only 2 percent of service users report such concerns (Schroeder et al. 1983). This may reflect parental lack of knowledge regarding the child's fears, parental awareness of fears as common in this age group, lack of available resources, or a wait-and-see attitude. Unless the child is experiencing serious distress, or the fear is interfering with the child's functioning in some way, psychological intervention may not be warranted. However, when serious interference is noted or the fear is debilitating or generalizing to other areas, referral for psychological treatment is often indicated. A wide range of literature exists on treating children's fears (e.g., Morris and Kratochwill 1983). Much of the recent literature describes behavioral interventions stressing fear reduction. These interventions usually employ one of four approaches: systematic desensitization, contingency management, modeling, and cognitive-behavioral techniques.

Systematic desensitization of fear is based on the assumption that a response can be inhibited by replacing it with an activity that is incompatible with it. Typically, the fear response is anxiety and the incompatible activity is relaxation. Although systematic desensitization is frequently used to treat fears, its use is rarely reported with children below the age of 9 years. Morris and Kratochwill (1991) contend that if systematic desensitization is to be used with younger children, an in vivo exposure should be added so that the child is practicing in a real-life situation. Nonetheless, the literature does not provide many examples of use of systematic desensitization with very young children.

Contingency management for children with fears and phobias most often involves positive reinforcement either alone or in combination with other behavioral approaches. Shaping is often necessary if the child needs assistance in approaching a feared stimulus. This may be the case if the series of behaviors needed to approach is complicated, or if the fear is strong enough to keep the child from approaching at all. In other situations where the child performs certain behaviors in selected settings but not in others, stimulus fading may be used to decrease fear responses. In these cases, the child learns to perform the response in new settings as the characteristics of the successful setting are gradually faded out. When a child has been reinforced for particular fears, the fear behavior may be reduced by ensuring that the child is not reinforced whenever the behavior is performed. Attention, one of the most common forms of reinforcement that the child receives, often helps maintain the behavior. Then, when the attention is removed, the fear may gradually extinguish.

The following case highlights the use of stimulus fading with a fearful child.

Mary was a 4-year-old girl who was fearful when left at her preschool. She would cry and sob when her mother tried to leave in the morning. The mother was asked to stay at the school during session for several days before her presence was faded out. While the mother was there, Mary was reinforced for nonanxious behavior. She was praised for increasing involvement in activities with her peers. Gradually the mother's presence was faded, first to the back of room, later to a room down the hall from the classroom, and eventually out of the building. Previously, Mary had received a great deal of attention from her mother when she was crying. When the attention was removed from the crying and refocused on positive activities, her fear was gradually extinguished.

Similar cases of separation anxiety in young children are often treated with a stimulus-fading paradigm, a procedure that is frequently used by preschool personnel.

Modeling to reduce children's fears has been reported since the late 1960s. Much of the work has been done through symbolic modeling, especially using film, videotape, or imagination (e.g., Bandura and Menlove 1968, Melamed and Siegel 1975). One common use of symbolic modeling is with children facing invasive or painful medical procedures. In Melamed and Siegel's seminal study, children who had been exposed to a 16-minute film called *Ethan Has an Operation* exhibited significant reduction in situational anxiety measures when compared with children in control (no treatment) conditions.

Cognitive-behavioral interventions to treat fears are a more recent addition to the literature and have usually involved approaches based on self-control, self-instruction, and rational-emotive treatments. Self-control focuses on procedures to help individuals learn techniques (e.g., self-statements) that help when they are confronted with feared stimuli, events, or objects. Self-instructional training, originally developed by Meichenbaum and his colleagues (e.g., Meichenbaum and Goodman 1971), was designed to teach children to be reflective in problem solving. Several studies have reported the use of this self-instructional technique in alleviating fears (e.g., Fox and Houston 1981, Genshaft 1982). Finally, rational-emotive therapy has been used with fearful adults (e.g., DiGiuseppe and Miller 1977), but literature regarding its use with children is sparse.

A study of coping skills used by 3-to-11-year-old children to deal with frightening television programs revealed some interesting findings. Wilson, Hoffner, and Cantor (1987) studied the strategies that children used in coping with programs that were frightening to them. They found that cognitive strategies (e.g., "Tell yourself it is not real") increased with age. Noncognitive coping strategies (e.g., "Sit with Mom and Dad") decreased with age. Their findings suggested that 3-to-5-year-olds tended to rely on more noncognitive strategies. The use of self-statements may be more effective with older children. However, coping self-statements relying on social or parental support may be most effective with young children. Wilson and colleagues (1987) were not specifically looking at treatment per se, but their work has important implications for designing treatment strategies.

Indications for Cognitive-Behavioral Play Therapy of Fears

Gaining control over one's fears appears to be a significant component of overcoming these fears. This may involve learning that one can deal with the feared stimuli, as well as learning to manage the associated feelings. Because of the specific skills necessary to overcome fears, much current treatment of childhood fears and phobias is based upon either behavioral or cognitive-behavioral interventions. This literature is largely focused on older children and adolescents and does not include work that integrates cognitive-behavioral and play therapy interventions for younger children.

If specific interventions (e.g., systematic desensitization) are used directly with a young child, these techniques are often not implemented within the context of therapeutic play sessions. In these types of interventions, the child may not have the opportunity to interact directly with the play material and the therapist. One might assume that these directly implemented treatments would provide an opportunity for the child to gain mastery of the feared stimuli. This may in fact be true, although interventions implemented within a more comprehensive play therapy framework may optimize the children's chances of mastering that which they fear. For example, in play therapy the child may master the feared object by taking on the role of one who does not fear it. This is often seen in therapy when children act in ways that suggest they are not afraid. By "pretending" and therefore practicing in this way, the child may in fact begin to learn to overcome the feared stimuli. Loevinger (1976) saw such role play as the origin of self-control. Such "practice" may not be possible when interventions are rigidly structured or when the child does not have the opportunity in therapy for spontaneous play.

CASE EXAMPLES

Both case examples to be considered are children who were discussed briefly in previous chapters. These two children, both of whom were seen in CBPT, were quite different, both in the nature of their fears as well as in the treatment approach utilized.

Billy is a 2-year-5-month-old child (briefly described in Chapter 5). Billy's family had experienced numerous fires near their home. He presented with fears of sirens and fire trucks, as well as sleep difficulties. Besides these difficulties, Billy had begun having soiling and wetting accidents (after having been successfully trained for over 5 months), had become aggressive toward his younger sister, and had started having difficulty separating from his mother. The parents reported that all of these problems had appeared within approximately 10 days after the most recent fire, when Billy had to be awakened and carried from his bed

during the night. Because of his young age and limited language development, his parents were having great difficulty reassuring him. In fact, they
would coddle and hold him when he heard sirens. During the course of
therapy, the therapist had the opportunity to observe Billy's reaction to
sirens when fire trucks went by the office on two separate occasions. Both
times Billy froze, stopped speaking, and had a terrified look on his face.
Each time he repeatedly said "fire truck" and was not able to relax and
resume interaction with the therapist until the sirens passed.

Because of his age, treatment was a combination of CBPT with Billy
and work with his parents. Bibliotherapy was the primary component of
treatment. The choice of stories as the main modality was determined only
after several sessions with Billy, when it became clear that he responded
better to pictures and stories than to other toys and objects in the therapist's office. Because Billy seemed to respond positively to books and
pictures, the therapist wrote a story regarding a child who experienced
similar fires near his home.

The story was read to Billy at each therapy session. The parents also
had a copy of the story and read it to him at home. Additionally, the
parents were assisted in not reinforcing Billy's fear but in attending instead
to his more adaptive, positive behaviors. They were instructed to focus
positive attention on Billy when he was playing nicely and behaving.
Billy's father acknowledged that when he heard a siren he immediately
looked at Billy and expected a reaction from him. Often he anticipated
Billy's screaming before it occurred. The parents were both instructed not
to anticipate Billy's fear but rather to deal with it calmly if Billy became
upset. They would tell Billy in a soothing voice that he would be all right
and the siren would soon be gone. However, they would not pay any more
direct attention to his screaming. As soon as the fire truck passed (usually
within seconds) and Billy calmed down, the parents again attended to him
in a positive way. After they were able to change their reaction to Billy's
response to sirens, the parents began to deal with his wetting and soiling
by creating a star chart with positive attention for appropriate toileting
skills. This positive reinforcement of appropriate toileting quickly proved
to be successful.

The parents terminated treatment after the child was successfully
sleeping through the night, not exhibiting fear at the sound of sirens, and
using the toilet successfully without accidents.

Another case of a fearful child was Jim, the 5-year-old boy who exhibited
a fear of closed spaces. Jim had accidentally been locked in a bathroom by
his younger sister (see Chapters 4 and 5). It was several hours before he
could be removed from the bathroom, and thereafter Jim refused to stay in

any room unless the door remained open. At the time of referral, Jim's fears had escalated, and he would scream intensely and freeze in place when a door was closed behind him or he was about to enter an elevator. Jim was beginning to refuse to ride in the family car.

Jim's treatment was largely based on a simple systematic desensitization paradigm described in Chapter 4 and delineated in Table 4–1. The paradigm was incorporated into play therapy after Jim had developed rapport with the therapist and seemed to enjoy the sessions. The hierarchy consisted of graduated steps from a larger to a smaller room with the therapist in attendance, to a small room without the therapist. Graduated stages of a door being closed were added until the child was comfortable being in the room with the door shut and without the therapist. Because of his age, Jim was not taught relaxation. Instead, play was used, and toys and games were chosen that he seemed to find particularly pleasant and relaxing. Jim was able to tolerate graduated stages in the hierarchy presented, and thus to tolerate the door closer and closer to being shut. Eventually he was able to ride in an elevator with the therapist. (Because he was too young to be in an elevator alone, this was not considered a step the child should learn to master. However, being in a room alone was certainly feasible and therefore was part of the hierarchy.)

Along with the relaxing play activity, Jim learned to make simple, positive self-statements such as "I can stay in this room," "I feel good playing in here," and "I feel good, I am brave" (see Chapter 5). The therapist provided positive feedback (e.g., "That was great," "Good job") after successful completion of increasingly difficult items. When he showed discomfort, there was a return to the previous step, with added intermediate steps to facilitate his progress. Jim seemed to derive satisfaction as he continued to overcome his fear. He was particularly pleased when he could report back to his mother, who waited for him after every session, about his progress. The mother understood the nature of the treatment strategy and had been told to provide specific, positive feedback to Jim as he reported his progress to her. At termination Jim was staying in closed rooms without difficulty, and riding in elevators and cars without complaint.

DISCUSSION

In both Billy's and Jim's cases, specific CBPT approaches were used that directly addressed the fears with which each child presented. In part, the differences in the children's developmental levels and in the nature of the feared situations dictated very different approaches. In Billy's case, the work was extremely straightforward and concrete. In addition to the direct interventions with Billy, parent-implemented work was used to supplement his treatment. Billy is perhaps the youngest documented case of a child treated with CBPT. Jim, on the other hand, was closer to school age, with more sophisticated verbal and cognitive skills. Jim's fears were highly internalized and were generalizing to new situations. In contrast with Billy's situation, Jim's fears did not appear to be based in parental attention or reaction, nor maintained by the parents' behavior. His treatment took place without any work with the parents.

The specific approaches also differed for both of these boys. Through structured play therapy it became clear that Billy responded positively to books and stories, so individually tailored bibliotherapy was adapted. It seemed important to create a story that was as much like Billy's situation as possible. Given his age, the therapist was concerned that published stories, even those specifically regarding fears, written for a general child audience might be too abstract for Billy. In fact, it seemed that to provide Billy the model he might need to overcome his fears, the boy in the story would need to be as much like Billy as possible. Also, the story provided a mastery modeling approach, with the boy in the story able to feel safe, go to bed at night without difficulty, and describe in simple words how he felt about the fires. Other approaches might not have been as understandable for such a young child, and probably would not have been helpful.

For Jim, the treatment relied more on in vivo systematic desensitization (with real-life situations), modeling, and cognitive-behavioral strategies (use of self-statements). Jim was old enough to understand these techniques and seemed to enjoy the approach. For example, as he progressed through the stages of the hierarchy, his sense of accomplishment seemed to increase his confidence and lessen his fear. After each progressive stage, he seemed pleased with the positive feedback from the therapist and his mother. Because actual experiences may be the most helpful for young children, Jim's treatment was kept as closely as possible to the situations in which he was fearful (e.g., closed doors in different-sized rooms, elevators). In order to make the situations as similar to real life as possible for Jim, and to promote generalization, the therapist used various offices in the mental health clinic where the child was seen as well as different elevators in the building. Thus, the combination of play, self-statements, and praise from the therapist and Jim's mother for his accomplishments allowed Jim to overcome his fear of closed doors.

Although the differences in these two treatments may be quite striking, the similarities should not be overlooked. Both interventions were relatively short-term (under 3 months), and both focused specifically on the child's fears. Both relied on creating situations as similar as possible to the child's particular circumstances.

CONCLUSIONS

The overall goal in treating fears is to desensitize the child to the feared stimulus, thereby reducing the fear. Behavioral interventions have been shown to be effective for fearful and anxious children, with systematic desensitization being the most popular. Desensitization is a gradual process, and there are a variety of ways that it can be accomplished. Because muscle relaxation, a main component of systematic desensitization, is not commonly used with children under age 6, other responses incompatible with anxiety may be necessary. Relaxing play is an activity that may be incompatible with anxiety and thus should be explored as an alternative to relaxation in systematic desensitization with very young children. Further, exposure to real-life situations is probably best for the young child, because imagery-based desensitization may be too difficult. Finally, the addition of cognitive approaches in conjunction with behavioral techniques may help the fearful child. The most useful strategies may be those designed to facilitate self-instruction and self-control, and to change (maladaptive) beliefs.

Much of this work is best presented through modeling. It is well documented that modeling is helpful for fearful and anxious children. Although there are a variety of ways to present models, the most accessible and cost-effective is probably through bibliotherapy (see Appendix). In addition to using any of a variety of books specifically written to help children deal with general fears (e.g., nightmares), it is possible to create individualized stories to meet a particular child's needs. The use of videotapes for this purpose is increasing, although at this time commercial videotapes are unlikely to be as accessible as books. Moreover, one can easily write and thereby individualize a simple written story for a child; this is not the case with producing videotape, a far more time-consuming and costly process.

11

Cognitive-Behavioral Play Therapy with Sexually Abused Children

Christine D. Ruma, M.S., M.S.S.A.

OVERVIEW

Recent years have seen a great increase in societal awareness of the problem of child sexual abuse. Although this phenomenon has probably occurred throughout history, only since the late 1970s has it become the focus of public attention. Parallel with the increase in public awareness has been an arousal of interest in the professional community regarding the prevalence, impact, and treatment of child sexual abuse. Thus, a great deal of research is now available regarding the prevalence of child sexual abuse. There is some variance in these data, depending on how abuse was defined, how the data were collected, and how the sample was selected. A review of the literature (Peters et al. 1986) found reporting rates of child sexual abuse for females ranging from 6–62 percent (average 23 percent) and for males from 3–31 percent (average 10 percent). In general, estimates of sexual abuse based on self-report are believed to underestimate the actual prevalence, owing both to the reluctance of individuals to disclose those experiences (even anonymously) and to lapses in memory. Estimates of the prevalence of child sexual abuse range

Note: The author wishes to thank Linda Hartman-Makovec, who worked with many of the children presented in this chapter.

as high as one in four for females and one in six for males. This is based on a broad definition of sexual abuse including contact and noncontact offenses.

Although it is generally believed that boys are abused less frequently than girls, there is reason to believe that the incidence for boys may actually be higher than what is generally reported. This phenomenon is suggested by lower incidences of males in sexual-abuse treatment programs compared with the percentage of males who have reported abuse in surveys of the general population (Finkelhor and Baron 1986). Boys may tend to disclose sexual abuse less often than girls, owing in part to a societal image that dictates that boys are not victims (unlike girls). Because the majority of perpetrators are male, boys are more frequently faced with issues of homosexuality than are girls, since they are more often abused by a same-sex perpetrator. Finally, society still tends to condone sexual contact between older females and younger males. Thus, boys who are sexually abused by a female may be less likely to report it, based on the belief that they should have enjoyed the activity and subsequent confusion regarding whether or not they were actually abused.

While it is well documented that children of all ages, even infants, can be victims of sexual abuse, it appears that school-age children or teenagers are probably at the greatest risk (Finkelhor and Baron 1986, Russell 1983). However, these studies do not take into account the inability of many young children to disclose the abuse or to remember it when asked to recall it later. Thus, the prevalence of sexual abuse for very young children may actually be greater than estimated.

Although preschool children may be at lower risk to be sexually abused than older children, it is still unclear what role their young age plays in determining the impact of the abuse. Some studies suggest that younger children will be less affected by sexual abuse (Adams-Tucker 1982, Gomes-Schwartz et al. 1985). This may be due to their inability to fully understand the impact of what has occurred, owing to their level of cognitive development (Shapiro et al. 1992). Conversely, it has been found that younger children may be more negatively affected by sexual abuse (Friedrich et al. 1986). This may be related to their vulnerability and consequent inability to protect themselves.

One myth that is still present, even amongst professionals, is that sexual abuse is generally perpetrated by strangers. In reality, the majority of reported child sexual abuse cases are perpetrated by an individual who is known and trusted by the child (Sgroi 1982a). This person may be a parent, parental figure, other relative, or any known and trusted person outside the family. Since preschoolers are more closely supervised than older children, they are most likely to be abused by a caretaker (e.g., parent, baby-sitter, or preschool teacher).

IMPACT OF SEXUAL ABUSE

Along with the awareness of the prevalence of sexual abuse has come the recognition of the traumatic impact on the child as well as of the long-term consequences, which may continue into adulthood. Finkelhor and Browne (1986) have identified four traumagenic dynamics (trauma-causing factors) related to sexual abuse, which provide a framework for conceptualizing children's reactions to the abuse. These factors are traumatic sexualization, betrayal, powerlessness, and stigmatization. Using this framework, it is possible to identify the primary ways in which a child has been affected and to direct treatment specifically to these areas.

Porter, Blick, and Sgroi (1982) identified ten impact issues common to victims of child sexual abuse, regardless of their age or sex. These issues are (1) "damaged goods" syndrome, (2) guilt, (3) fear, (4) depression, (5) low self-esteem and poor social skills, (6) repressed anger and hostility, (7) impaired ability to trust, (8) blurred role boundaries and role confusion, (9) pseudomaturity and failure to accomplish developmental tasks, and (10) problems of self-mastery and control. The first five issues are said to be present for all victims, regardless of the relationship of the perpetrator to the child, whereas some aspects of the last five are considered specific to incest.

The traumagenic factors described by Finkelhor and Browne (1986) and the impact issues described by Porter and colleagues (1982) are said to be common to all victims of sexual abuse, but will manifest themselves differently in each child. Frequent symptoms of young children cited in the literature include nightmares and sleep disturbances, regression in toileting and other skills, expressions of anger and fear, and sexualized behaviors (Beitchman et al. 1991, Browne and Finkelhor 1986, Finkelhor 1990, Kendall-Tackett et al. 1993). Recent research has also suggested a close association between childhood sexual abuse and the diagnosis of Post-traumatic Stress Disorder (Eth and Pynoos 1985).

Several factors commonly believed to affect the severity of the child's reaction to sexual abuse have been documented in the literature (Beitchman et al. 1992, Beitchman et al. 1991, Browne and Finkelhor 1986, Kendall-Tackett et al. 1993, Krug 1989). Factors that indicate a more severe reaction include longer duration or more frequent sexual contact; more intrusive sexual acts; the use or threat of force; and the perpetrator being a father or father figure, or mother. As mentioned previously, it is not clear how the child's age affects the impact of abuse on the child. Other factors that must be considered are the child's level of functioning prior to the abuse, and the reaction of the child's family at the time of disclosure. Children whose parents believe them and respond appropriately by protecting them and getting help will clearly have a better adjustment (Everson et al. 1989, Faller 1988, Kendall-Tackett et al. 1993, Wyatt and Mickey 1987). Based on these factors, it is possible for some children to be relatively unaffected by sexual abuse. This is primarily true for children who were abused one or two times, where the abuse was not forceful or intrusive, and where the child was believed and supported upon disclosure with little or no family disruption.

The long-term effects of child sexual abuse have also been documented as emotional disturbances in adults abused as children. Associations have been found between child sexual abuse and adult symptoms of sexual disturbance, confusion regarding sexual identity, anxiety/fear, depression and suicide, eating disorders, dissociations, Post-traumatic Stress Disorder, drug abuse, anger, and impaired ability to trust (Beitchman et al. 1992, Briere and Runtz 1988, Greenwald et al. 1990, Scott 1992).

Clearly, the experience of being sexually abused as a child can have profound and lifelong effects. The remainder of this chapter will discuss the application of Cognitive-Behavioral Play Therapy (CBPT) principles to the assessment and treatment of young children who have been sexually abused. Although most of the work is done with the child, another important aspect is parent education. Parents must learn about child sexual abuse so that they can attempt to protect their child from further abuse and be able to identify the signs and symptoms of abuse if it were to occur in the future. A fuller discussion of parent education is beyond the scope of this chapter.

TREATMENT LITERATURE

The literature regarding treatment for sexually abused children has naturally lagged behind that of the prevalence studies. Most of the available literature does concur that some amount of treatment for this problem is necessary and recommends some combination of individual, group, and/or family treatment. Several comprehensive treatment programs for incest families have been described in the literature (Giaretto 1981, Orenchuk-Tomiuk et al. 1990). Although such frameworks are useful, they also have several limitations. First, these programs are typically for children from incestuous families. Second, although they provide a framework suggesting both order of treatment (e.g., individual, group, and family) and issues to be addressed, they usually do not discuss treatment techniques with which to achieve these goals. Finally, such programs do not allow for the individualized needs of each child and family.

Some of the earliest work regarding the treatment of child sexual abuse can be found in the *Handbook of Clinical Intervention in Child Sexual Abuse* (Sgroi 1982b). This book provides an excellent conceptual framework for the impact issues and treatment goals for the entire family, but it is short on descriptions of treatment techniques for accomplishing these goals. It also applies specifically to victims of incest. More specific treatment activities have been described by James and Nasjleti (1983). However, very little of this work is applicable to young children.

Traditional play therapy has been adapted for use with children who have been sexually abused (Gil 1991, Walker and Bolkovatz 1988). Although both of these sources provide some framework for correcting the child's distorted view of the world, the focus is more on the relationship between the child and the therapist. As expressed by Gil, "there is an attempt to demonstrate to the child through therapeutic intervention the potentially rewarding nature of human interaction. . . . If given a nurturing, safe environment, the child will inevitably gravitate toward the reparative experience" (1991, pp. 51–52).

Finally, cognitive and behavioral theory and treatment approaches have been adapted for use with children who have been sexually abused (Berliner and Wheeler 1987, Deblinger et al. 1990). Berliner and Wheeler use the models of classical conditioning and social learning theory to understand the effects of sexual abuse on children and from this to suggest treatment strategies. Deblinger and associates (1990) reported on the effectiveness of applying cognitive behavioral approaches with nineteen girls with documented histories of sexual abuse, ranging in age from 3 to 16 and with a diagnosis of Post-traumatic Stress Disorder. This study is unique in showing the outcome data, one area where most of the sexual abuse treatment literature falls short. Although both of the above sources suggest that cognitive and behavioral principles can be applied to child sexual abuse, they do not describe how to combine this with play techniques for use with the young child.

IMPLICATIONS FOR COGNITIVE-BEHAVIORAL PLAY THERAPY WITH CHILDREN WHO HAVE BEEN SEXUALLY ABUSED

Cognitive Behavioral Play Therapy principles can be applied to children who have been sexually abused. This approach has several advantages over more traditional play therapy approaches. First, CBPT is directive, while allowing the child control within the structure set by the therapist. The directive aspect of CBPT is beneficial in working with this population, because most children tend to avoid all matters related to the abuse in an effort to avoid anxiety and negative feelings. However, as will be discussed later, control is a central issue in treatment with children who have been sexually abused. The structure provided by CBPT still allows the child to feel in control. Further, children who are part of an incestuous family system typically have not learned to express their feelings, especially negative ones. Cognitive Behavioral Play Therapy provides them with a framework with which to begin to be able to express a full range of emotions. (See Tables 11–1 and 11–2 for cognitive and behavioral interventions, respectively, and examples of their application with children, as described later in this chapter.)

ASSESSMENT

The assessment of children who have been sexually abused is a critical first step in the treatment process. As is true in working with other

TABLE 11-1
Examples of Behavioral Techniques in Cognitive-Behavioral Play Therapy with Sexually Abused Children.

Behavioral Technique	Therapeutic Intervention	Case Example
Systematic desensitization	Child depicts abuse through drawings or play, beginning with least threatening material and gradually dealing with most threatening issues.	(pp. 221–224)
Contingency management	Child earns stars for sleeping in her own bed.	Elaine (pp. 215–216)
Differential reinforcement of other behavior	Child's mother says to child, "I don't like it when you lick me like that, but I like it when you give me a hug."	Elaine (pp. 215–216)
Modeling	Therapist expresses confused feelings about sexual touching through puppet play.	Diane (pp. 226–228)
	Therapist models disclosure of sexual abuse through puppet play.	Richard (pp. 210–212)
Behavioral rehearsal	Therapist coaches child to use abuse prevention skills through puppet play.	Diane (pp. 226–228)

children, the assessment should be an initial phase of therapy as well as an ongoing process throughout treatment. An assessment done for clinical or treatment purposes must be distinguished from one done by child protective workers or police for legal purposes. Both assessments are necessary, but each is unique. Assessments done for legal purposes must focus on the specific details of the abuse and are not typically done by therapists. The following is an overview of information that needs to be gathered in the clinical assessment, and a discussion of approaches to gathering the information. More detailed discussions of clinical assessments with child victims of sexual abuse are available elsewhere in the literature (Friedrich 1990, Schroeder and Gordon 1991, Shapiro 1991).

The clinical assessment should include an understanding of the child's level of functioning prior to the onset and disclosure of the sexual abuse, the child's current level of functioning and presenting symptoms,

TABLE 11-2
**Examples of Cognitive Techniques in Cognitive-Behavioral Play
Therapy with Sexually Abused Children.**

Cognitive Technique	Therapeutic Intervention	Case Example
Identifying and correcting (irrational) beliefs	Child states that doll's private parts were hurt. Therapist responds by stating that although they had been hurt in the past, they are all right now.	Lisa (p. 228)
	Child draws picture of a nightmare in which child was being scared by a man. Therapist draws a similar picture but includes the mother protecting the child.	Carol (pp. 223–224)
Positive self-statements	Child is destroying PLAY-DOH® model of perpetrator and says to therapist, "Don't rip me up." Therapist models positive statement by saying "We won't rip you up. You are a special and good person." Child is encouraged to learn to use positive self-statements.	Lisa (pp. 224–225)
	Child is told that the police would be mad at the perpetrator because he was "bad," but not at child because she had done nothing wrong. Child is taught to make such positive self-statements.	Lisa (pp. 224–225)
Bibliotherapy	Therapist reads stories to child regarding sexual abuse.	(pp. 218–220)
	Therapist helps child complete workbooks regarding sexual abuse experiences.	(pp. 219–220)

the child's beliefs and feelings related to the sexual abuse, and the parent's reactions to the abuse. Although it is helpful to know the details of the sexual acts and coercion methods, this information has usually already been gathered by child protective workers and can be obtained from them rather than requiring the child to disclose this information again. If this information was not provided by the child at the time of the investigation or is not otherwise available, it can be gathered throughout the course of treatment.

Gaining an understanding of the child's previous level of functioning is important in order to set realistic goals for the child. Often it is not known when the abuse actually began, and therefore is difficult to know the child's previous level of functioning. Furthermore, information about the child's previous level of functioning is usually gleaned from parent report, since few of these children were in treatment prior to the abuse. It should also be noted that children may have appeared asymptomatic during the course of the abuse and only began displaying problems upon disclosure. In these cases, the impact of disclosure on the child and the child's understanding of these events must also be assessed. Assessment of the child's previous level of functioning can be gathered through interviews with both the child and parent(s) or through a review of documents such as school or day-care reports.

Assessment of the child's current level of functioning may be done objectively and subjectively through the use of interviews, observations, psychological tests, or structured behavior rating scales such as the Child Behavior Checklist (CBCL) (Achenbach and Eddelbrock 1983). The information gathered in this portion of the assessment will determine what behaviors, if any, need to be addressed in therapy. It will also serve as a baseline from which change can be measured. Some children may appear asymptomatic either outwardly or when questioned in a general way. However, when asked questions specifically related to common symptoms of sexual abuse (e.g., "Do thoughts of what happened to you sometimes pop into your head when you don't want them to?" or "Do you ever find yourself feeling real upset and not know why?") many children will answer affirmatively. Some authors (Shapiro et al. 1990) have suggested that owing to guardedness or defensiveness, children will not report symptoms such as depression on a structured self-report measure, but that this information can be gathered with less structured or projective techniques.

What is more difficult to obtain is information regarding the child's beliefs, thoughts, and feelings about the abuse. However, there are several ways in which this information can be gathered. Shapiro (1991) provides a list of specific questions to ask young children in order to elicit statements expressing their thoughts, feelings, and beliefs related to the sexual abuse. Some information may be gleaned from spontaneous play or statements made by the child. For instance, the child may talk about being bad, or may demonstrate this belief through play situations in which adults tell children that they are bad and then proceed to sexually abuse them. Distortions in children's drawings can be used to understand their perceptions about the abuse. Finally, more projective methods may be used to assess the child's perceptions of the sexual abuse (e.g., Child's Apperception Test, Roberts Apperception Test, Puppet Sentence Completion).

Another method to assess children's distortions related to the sexual abuse is to pose a series of simple multiple-choice questions that can be responded to either verbally or by pointing to specific selections. For example, regarding distortions about blame, the therapist can ask: "If two people were touching each other sexually, whose fault would it be, the big person or little person?" or "If two people were touching each other sexually and the little person got a present for it, whose fault would it be?" The child can respond by pointing to pictures of a big or little person. Other questions used are: "Is sexual abuse a good or bad secret?" or "When you are sexually abused, does that make you a good or bad person?" Children can be asked similar questions about their feelings during the abuse or after disclosure and asked to point to faces that might represent their feelings.

Finally, assessment of the victim cannot be complete without an assessment of parental and family functioning. Important information includes the parents' level of belief that their child was sexually abused and their level of understanding that this is a serious and traumatic event. In gathering this information, it is helpful to inquire whether either or both of the parents have a history of abuse, and if so, how they dealt with it, in order to understand their reaction to their child's sexual abuse. Clinical observations suggest that parents who have not dealt with their own abuse will have a more difficult time supporting their child's recovery. In incestuous families, knowledge regarding the family's level of pathology, their rules regarding boundaries and privacy, and the child's role within the family system are all important pieces of information (Friedrich 1990). An understanding of the changes in the family as a result of disclosure is also important.

Although the initial assessment may take several sessions, it may also be therapeutic in nature and serve to begin the therapeutic process. Frequently, children will disclose more details about the abuse throughout the course of therapy than was originally known. This information needs to be incorporated into the assessment and treatment process. Other significant events may occur during the course of treatment, such as separation of family members or court proceedings. The impact of these events on the child must be assessed and incorporated into the treatment process.

TREATMENT ISSUES

Disclosure

One of the most common difficulties of working with young children who have been sexually abused is their difficulty in disclosing what has happened to them. Some children may give vague disclosures, but the specifics of who, what, and when are not clear. Other children may initially make no disclosure and are brought for treatment because of behavioral or emotional problems. In some cases the therapist may be the first to suspect sexual abuse. Since preschoolers are more likely than other age groups to be abused by a family member or caregiver, it is critical to ascertain the details of the abuse as quickly as possible to prevent further abuse.

The safety of the child and prevention of further abuse must be the first consideration in any treatment with children who have been sexually abused. This may result in a physical separation or ending of contact between the child and perpetrator. In other cases it may be a matter of limiting contact with the perpetrator to supervised visits only. Unfortunately, in cases where the disclosure is unclear or nonexistent, legally the child may have to continue having contact with the person who has abused him or her.

Case Example

Casey, aged 5 years, was brought into therapy owing to the following symptoms: aggressiveness toward and French-kissing her brother, burying a new toy doll in the yard, placing objects in her vagina, and fondling the family pet's genitals. As of her first appointment for therapy, there had been no report to the child protective services nor any spontaneous disclosure on her part. Although a report was immediately made by her therapist to the child protective agency, it was many months before

Casey was able to disclose any information regarding sexual abuse. During the months before Casey disclosed, she continued to have regular visits with her father, whom she later identified as the perpetrator.

Facilitating a Disclosure

Ideally, therapy should begin after completion of the investigation by the child protection workers. However, in cases where the disclosure is unclear or nonexistent, treatment may begin despite the possibility of contamination of the facts for legal evidence. Because this is a very serious and delicate issue, several factors must be taken into consideration. First, the majority of cases involving very young victims are never brought to court owing to the belief that the child will not be a credible witness. Second, if therapy is postponed in the hopes that the child will eventually disclose, the child may suffer even more trauma. Thus, the possible risk to the child's safety must be weighed carefully against the risk of contamination of evidence before the therapist continues.

Despite these difficulties, there may be ways that the therapist can facilitate a disclosure without contaminating evidence. One method is to allow the child more unstructured play in the early stages of assessment. The materials used and the topics introduced could be structured by the therapist. However, the therapist is not attempting to correct or change the child's thoughts or behaviors. Rather, the purpose is to help the child disclose information about what has happened. For instance, the therapist may introduce play with a doll or puppet and the theme such as "this doll is afraid . . . " or "this puppet has a scary secret . . . " or even as leading as "this doll has a problem with touching. . . . " The child can be encouraged to talk about what might be bothering the doll or puppet, and by doing so impose personal experiences on these characters. By introducing through play the themes that are common among sexually abused children, the child may feel more comfortable expressing information without questioning from the therapist regarding personal experiences.

Case Example

Richard (previously described in Chapter 6) is a 4½-year-old boy who had been sexually abused by a baby-sitter while living in New Orleans, but he is unable to disclose the details of the abuse. It is believed that the abuse involved urination and defecation on Richard. Whenever the issue of sexual abuse is brought up directly, Richard regresses and usually begins talking about "poopoo" or "kaakaa." Below are several attempts by his therapist to help him disclose.

Session 3:

Richard: More bad guys in Cleveland.
Therapist: What do they do bad in Cleveland?
Richard: Ah poopoos.
Therapist: Oh, there is poopoo in Cleveland? [*pause*] Do people poopoo in New Orleans?
Richard: Yeah.
Therapist: They do. What do they do with the poopoo?
Richard: Put it, they eat the poopoo . . .
Therapist: They eat the poopoo?
Richard: Yeah.
Therapist: They eat the poopoo in New Orleans. . . . Do they do that in Cleveland?
Richard: Nope.

Session 7:

Bobby: (*therapist using a turtle puppet they call Bobby*) My name is Bobby and I used to live far far away. I knew this lady and she was bad. She used to watch me when my mommy was at work, but she did some very bad things to me.
Richard: (*changing the subject*) Oh, I do three.
Bobby: She did some bad bad things and it made me upset and I want to talk with my mommy about it, but sometimes it's hard to talk about it. And I want to talk to Miss Sally (therapist) about it, but sometimes that's hard too.
Therapist: Bobby, if you talk about it maybe you could tell Richard. Richard would listen.
Richard: [*making noises*]
Bobby: Richard, I want to tell you something.
Richard: What, Kaykay?
Bobby: I used to live far far away, and somebody did something bad to me.

Richard: What did they do?
Bobby: It made me very upset.
Richard: It made you poopoo.
Bobby: She made me poopoo.
Richard: No.
Therapist: What did she do?
Richard: She . . .

Although Richard did not actually disclose in either of these vignettes, he was able to listen to the dialogue by the puppet and therapist. The therapist modeled disclosing and verbalized feelings about how difficult it is to talk about the abuse. In other interchanges in therapy, the therapist verbalized that the child would be believed and supported for disclosing and that he would not be seen as "bad" for what happened (see Table 11–1).

Another approach to facilitate disclosure may be through the use of a parent. Since preschool-age children are less accustomed to talking with adults other than parents or caregivers, they may feel safer talking in the presence of, or directly to, their parents. If the child believes that the sexual abuse should not be discussed (either implicitly or because he or she was told so by the perpetrator), a parent's encouragement may give the child permission to disclose. The therapist may ask the questions and the parent encourage the child to answer, or the therapist may coach the parent on what questions to ask or how to engage the child in the structured play.

The therapist may infer that the abuse has occurred, even when the child has not disclosed despite opportunities to do so. Therapy then can focus on abuse in the third person. For example, this can be done through play, with the therapist describing feelings or distorted cognitions that are common for abused children. Therapy would also include education in abuse prevention skills. This type of intervention may prompt disclosure or at least normalize children's feelings, correct distorted beliefs, and teach them skills to protect themselves or disclose in the future.

Central Issues: Trust and Control

Most sexually abused children struggle with two central issues as a result of their abuse: trust and control. When children are sexually abused by a known and trusted person, the betrayal of their relationship and trust is very great. Also, when a child is sexually abused, all control by the child is taken away for that time. Consequently, the child may struggle to regain control, often in negative ways. Both of these issues permeate all aspects of treatment with these children.

The difficulty with trust is one reason that treatment with sexually abused children may take longer than with children with other problems. The therapist must be aware that trust may be an issue and allow time for the therapist–client relationship to develop. Throughout the course of therapy the child may continue to test the relationship in many ways. For example, children may behave provocatively toward the therapist to see if the therapist is going to harm them.

The issue of trust is also important at the time of termination. Many of these children have been abandoned by one or more caretakers, and if the termination is not handled sensitively, they may experience another abandonment. To avoid this, termination should be discussed well in advance of the last session. It is also helpful to explain to the children that the reasons for termination are not that they were bad in any way, but rather that they have improved significantly enough not to need "extra help." If allowed to plan a special event such as a "party" or "graduation" for the last session, children can anticipate the end of treatment rather than dread it. Such a celebration casts the termination in a positive light for the child.

The issue of control must also be addressed throughout treatment. Children who have been sexually abused have often met with a variety of professionals before beginning therapy (e.g., police, child protective workers, and hospital social workers). Consequently, they may feel as if they are being forced to tell their "story" one more time. Although it is important that the children express information about the abuse and resulting feelings (either through talk or play), it is more important that they are in control of what, how, and when they disclose.

To decrease the child's anxiety in the first session, these trust and control issues must be clarified. Children may come into the first appointment wondering if the therapist knows about the sexual abuse. The anxiety over whether or not the therapist will bring up this issue can be tremendous. For this reason, it is helpful for the therapist to determine the child's understanding regarding entering therapy. Based on the child's response, the therapist should clarify that the child is there because of the sexual abuse (using words that the child can understand) and that the child and therapist will be talking or playing about this during part of their time together. The therapist should also clearly communicate that the child controls the talk and/or play about the abuse. The therapist may then begin to ask the child some questions about the abuse. If the child is clearly uncomfortable, the therapist should help the child verbalize these feelings of discomfort and allow the discussion of the abuse to stop. However, the therapist should let the child know that the topic will be brought up in their next and future meetings, and that the child can again let the therapist know when he or she becomes uncomfortable. If the child expresses that he or she does not want this to happen, the therapist will want to reach some sort of compromise with the child in establishing a time frame or a method so that the child feels comfortable and in control. In any event, the issue should be addressed relatively early in the therapy.

Addressing Sexual Abuse

In the therapy of sexually abused children, it is important that the issue of the abuse be directly addressed. One problem with sexual abuse is the element of secrecy. Open exploration of this issue means that the secret is no longer present. Children must also learn that others will not necessarily reject them when they learn of the abuse. By asking about specific details or feelings, the therapist conveys to the children that they are not alone with their experiences and that it is all right to talk about them. Also, the openness of the therapist in talking about sexual abuse models this behavior for the child. Finally, children can only gain mastery over what has been done to them by expressing the abuse either through words or play.

Addressing Symptomatic Behaviors

Most children who are referred for therapy because of sexual abuse present with a variety of symptomatic behaviors. Common symptoms of young victims include enuresis, encopresis, separation anxiety, nightmares, sexual acting-out, and aggressiveness. Although some of these behaviors may subside as a result of addressing the child's beliefs and feelings regarding the sexual abuse, others may require more direct intervention. Parents can be taught to use simple behavioral interventions with the child. The therapist can also employ these same principles during the therapy sessions. These principles need not relate specifically to the sexual abuse. When children are brought for therapy soon after the abuse has occurred, these symptomatic behaviors are usually relatively short-lived. In some cases, where the risk factors described earlier were low and the child is showing relatively few problems, this sort of behavioral intervention may be sufficient.

Case Example

Elaine, aged 3½, had begun to lick her mother and attempted to French-kiss her. Her mother also observed Elaine doing this to her dolls. When questioned by her mother and the child protection worker, Elaine disclosed that her preschool teacher had done this to her. By the time she began treatment, Elaine was having nightmares, would not sleep in her own bed, and was continuing the sexualized touching of her mother and dolls. (See Figures 11-1 and 11-2 for pretreatment and posttreatment CBCL scores.) Elaine's mother was a single parent who was attentive to her daughter and capable of following through with the recommended behavioral interventions. Elaine was seen with her mother for a total of seven appointments over a 3-month period. Since Elaine was resistant to being alone with the therapist and her verbal skills were not well developed, the majority of the work was done with Elaine's mother. The mother also attended several sessions of a nonoffending parents' support group.

Since the most distressing behavior for Elaine's mother was the sexual touching, that was addressed first. The mother was taught to respond to Elaine's sexual behavior by redirecting Elaine to appropriate kinds of touching. She was also taught to calmly talk to her about this, (e.g., "I don't like it when you lick me like that, but you can give me a hug"). The mother was also taught to reward Elaine with praise when she noticed Elaine playing with her dolls or touching her mother appropriately (see Table 11-1). This behavior subsided quickly once the mother began responding in this manner. Elaine was also able to begin disclosing to her mother about other ways that her teacher had touched her.

To help Elaine sleep in her own room and to decrease the nightmares, the mother instituted a consistent and relaxing bedtime routine, and Elaine earned a star for each night she slept in her own bed. She also designated one evening per week when Elaine could sleep in the mother's bed and

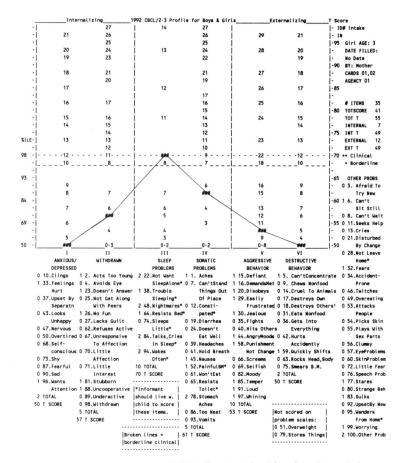

Figure 11-1.   Pre-treatment Child Behavior Checklist for Elaine (3½ years).
Copyright © 1992 T. M. Achenbach. Reprinted by permission.

presented this as a "slumber party." By allowing Elaine in her bed one night per week, the mother was allowing Elaine control over her sleeping situation, without encouraging dependency on sleeping with her mother.

Preparing the Child for Court

One component of therapy with many sexually abused children is preparing them for a court hearing. As mentioned previously, one must be cautious not to influence a child's testimony. However, play therapy

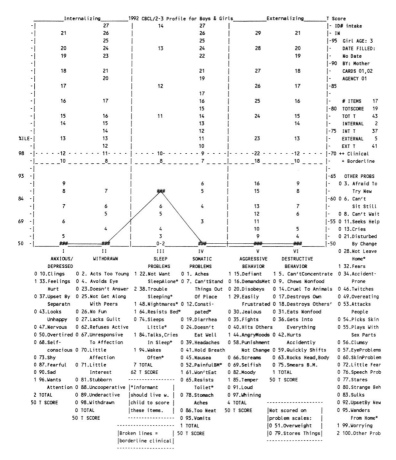

Figure 11–2. Post-treatment Child Behavior Checklist for Elaine (3½ years). Copyright © 1992 T. M. Achenbach. Reprinted by permission.

can be used to help the child understand who will be present in the courtroom, what their respective roles will be, and what the court process entails. This may involve drawing pictures, enacting a skit, or actually visiting the courtroom.

When children are preparing for court, it is important that the therapist help them see that the court process allows them to take control of their lives. It also allows them the opportunity to show the perpetrator how they feel about the abuse, and to let that individual know that he or she can no longer intimidate the child into silence. Because offenders are often not found guilty or are given light sentences, the child should be helped to see that the outcome of a case is less important than the fact that the child has done something very assertive.

TREATMENT TECHNIQUES

Given the limited cognitive abilities of preschool children and the high level of anxiety that sexual abuse arouses, play is an ideal way for them to express their thoughts and feelings. Numerous modalities of play can be used to help the children express what has happened to them. These include: bibliotherapy (books, stories, structured workbooks), drawing, other art media (clay, PLAY-DOH®), and puppets and doll play.

Bibliotherapy

Bibliotherapy is a commonly used method to explore the issues of sexual abuse with young children. Numerous books are available that address this topic. (See Appendix for a list of resources.) The benefits of reading stories to children about sexual abuse are several. First, doing so helps them to see that they are not the only ones that have been sexually abused. It also shows them that they are not alone with their feelings. This is especially true with regard to feelings for the offender (positive, negative, or mixed), feelings of fear, or any positive feelings associated with the abuse (either the sexual acts or the social aspects of the relationship). Often we tell children that this has happened to so many children that they had to write books about it. Most of the stories not only focus on the abuse of the child but also show a positive resolution of the problem (i.e., child telling and getting help). Seeing situations where children were able to end the abuse by talking about it allows the child to see that it is possible to have control over the situation. For children who have not disclosed sexual abuse but where it is suspected, this can be one way to encourage disclosure. The use of bibliotherapy also helps children express their feelings about the abuse through modeling.

Although there are many stories that address the issues of sexual abuse directly, it is not always necessary or desirable to use such stories. An example of an indirect approach is through the book *Therapeutic*

Stories for Children (Davis 1988), a collection of short stories that use metaphors to address the issues of abuse. These stories are especially effective for the highly anxious child who cannot tolerate the reading of a story about abuse. Children may derive the same benefits from these stories as from those that are more direct. One child, aged 3½ years, was able to recall the details of one of these stories when asked about it by her therapist almost 6 weeks after reading it in a therapy session. This same child, although she had not yet given a full disclosure of abuse, requested copies of this story and similar stories to take home and have her parents read to her.

The use of bibliotherapy about sexual abuse will often provide children the courage and permission to talk more openly about their own abuse experiences. The therapist may be able to use the stories to draw parallels with the child's situation and feelings. For children who are unable to tolerate these materials directly but for whom a more direct and less metaphoric approach is indicated, stories may be read in their presence (S. Knell, personal communication, June 1992). This technique was used with Richard (discussed earlier in this chapter). Richard refused to listen when the therapist tried to read a book about different kinds of touch (*Red Flag, Green Flag*, from the Rape and Abuse Crisis Center, 1980) to him. He did, however, sit and listen attentively as the therapist read the book to the puppet (Bobby). In fact, Richard not only listened, but also interacted in "conversation" with Bobby about the material being read. Thus, Richard would not allow the therapist to read the story to him directly but made clear through his interaction with the puppet that he was listening and understanding what was being read. The following vignettes are from this session, which was the fifteenth session.

Therapist: Maybe Bobby (*puppet*) and I will do it.
Richard: (*to Bobby*) OK, you do it all by yourself.
Therapist: OK, Bobby will do it by himself. Hey, Bobby, what's going on?
Bobby: What if I don't want to do it? [*pause*] Well, I don't really want to, but I will do it.

As the therapist began to read the book, Richard continued to play. However, he constantly looked over at the pictures in the book as the pages were turned. As the therapist read, she interjected more personalized information regarding Richard into the conversation with Bobby, the puppet.

> *Therapist*: We are touched by our moms. We are touched by our dads. It's like Richard's daddy came to visit. I bet he gave him a big hug.
> *Richard*: Yes.
> *Therapist*: *Yes, he did?*
> *Richard*: Yeah, and I gave him a hug.
> *Therapist*: (*to Bobby*) Yeah, and Richard gave his dad a hug. . . .
>
> *Therapist*: We are touched by many people.
> *Richard*: At school we aren't allowed to touch. Keep your hands to yourself.
> *Therapist*: You keep your hands to yourself. Did you know that, Bobby? At school you have to keep your hands to yourself. . . .
>
> *Therapist*: Bobby, we did a lot of this book, and Richard was very helpful. Should we keep going or should we stop?
> *Richard*: (*before Bobby has a chance to answer*) Keep going.
> *Therapist*: We should keep going?
> *Richard*: Yeah.

Later, Richard decided that he would "help" Bobby, and he took the crayons and drew "boobies" on a car in the workbook.

Some bibliotherapy, such as the example above, is presented in the form of a workbook or coloring book that can be completed by the child with the therapist's assistance. These can be used after other, more general books in order to further personalize the child's experiences. Examples of workbook tasks might be having children identify people with whom they feel safe or unsafe. Children might also be asked to identify ways or places that they like, or do not like, to be touched. Through the use of these books, children can be encouraged to express how they feel about the times that they have been touched in sexual ways. Again, these tasks are not only therapeutic, but may encourage a child to disclose abusive experiences for the first time. Finally, these workbooks may also increase a child's sense of control by helping them to identify specific ways that they can prevent or stop abuse.

Drawing

Another method of helping children disclose their own personal history of abuse is through the use of self-created picture books (L. Hartman-Makovec, personal communication, March 1990). This task is more often used with children of early school age and older but might be adapted for younger children. Through this task, children are encouraged to tell their story of abuse in small and manageable steps through drawings. They begin with less threatening aspects of the abuse and as anxiety decreases, express more threatening aspects (see Table 11–1). It is also important that children not stop with describing the abuse experience(s), but that they describe the disclosure and the events that followed. This process helps them to look beyond the victim role and to see ways in which they have regained control over their lives.

Through the use of pictures, children may express their cognitive distortions about the abuse in a way they could not do with words. This allows the therapist to identify and correct these distortions. For example, in drawing pictures of the offender and the victim, the child may draw the offender proportionately much larger than he or she truly is. Or children may draw themselves without any arms or hands. This may express the child's feelings of helplessness and vulnerability. The therapist can begin to correct these distortions by having the child "correct" the drawing.

Some beginning nonthreatening pictures that the child can draw in this sequence might be of the child's family or house (if the abuse occurred in the child's home or by a family member). The child should be encouraged to talk about each of the drawings. "Who in your family do you get along with the best/worst and why?" "Which rooms in the house do you like/dislike and why?" Exploration of the picture through this sort of questioning helps the child identify both positive and negative feelings related to the abuse. It also facilitates the child's ability to talk about later pictures.

Continuing along this sequence, the pictures should gradually introduce more threatening material. However, proceeding gradually and allowing the child control, the therapist helps the child to become systematically desensitized to the details of the abuse. The next picture might depict what happened with the perpetrator prior to the abuse starting. This facilitates disclosure of the specific methods of coercion or manipulation used by the perpetrator. The details of this information are useful in correcting the child's distortions regarding self-blame.

Having the child draw pictures about how the abuse started and of the actual abuse will allow for disclosure of the details of the abuse. It is important to encourage the disclosure of as much detail as possible regarding the actual sexual acts. This information is useful therapeutically. If children never disclose the details of the abuse, they may always believe that what happened to them is somehow different from what happened to other children who have been sexually abused. Also, when the therapist knows the details of the abuse, the child's experiences can be normalized. Finally, this information may also be useful in understanding a child's specific symptoms. For instance, one young boy who was wetting his bed disclosed that he had been sexually abused in the bathroom and was afraid to go into that room in the dark for fear that he would again be attacked. The specific details may also be useful for medical and legal purposes.

It is helpful in these pictures to note the child's self-depiction as compared with that of the offender. Having children draw the details of their own and their perpetrator's faces allows for a discussion of their feelings during the abuse and their beliefs about those of their perpetrator. This may also be an opportunity for the therapist to explore and normalize any positive feelings that the child may have had during the abuse.

Having the child depict what happened immediately after the abuse facilitates disclosure of threats and bribes. As mentioned above, this information is important in confronting the child's feelings of self-blame as well as dispelling fears of harm.

In order to help the child see beyond the abuse, it is important not to end the sequence at this point. By having the child tell how the abuse was disclosed or what made it stop, the child may gain a sense of control over the situation. This is especially empowering for children who disclosed directly, or whose behavior helped lead to disclosure. The following example highlights this sense of control. A 7-year-old child who had been anxious to the point of trembling in all previous therapy sessions suddenly stopped trembling after drawing the picture of disclosure and seeing her role in stopping the abuse. She was not observed trembling in future sessions.

It is important to have the child depict any events that may have occurred as a result of the disclosure. This would likely include the investigative process and parents' reactions. Because parental belief and support is prognostically important, this is important therapeutic information. The depiction may also include more disruptive events, such as removal from the home. When removal has occurred, it is important to determine the child's beliefs regarding this removal and to correct whatever distortions may be present. This might also include depicting what happened to the offender and how the child believes that this person feels. Having the child depict therapy may also identify the child's attitudes and beliefs regarding this result of disclosure.

In this sequence the final stage should be to have children draw a picture of something positive in their current life. By focusing on the positive, children are able to see that they can be happy and in control of aspects of their life, despite the trauma of the abuse.

As mentioned previously, this technique may need to be modified for use with the preschool-age child. The therapist may be able to adapt certain aspects of it to the developmental level of the very young child. For instance, children who are unable to draw clear pictures may draw whatever they can and "dictate" to the therapist what is in their picture. The therapist may help the child by drawing the picture or writing the story as described by the child. Discussion of details can be elicited as described above.

Drawing can be used in other ways, as can be seen in the following case examples.

Debbie, aged 7 years, was soon to testify in court against the man who molested her. The therapist helped her draw a picture of the courtroom, with the therapist identifying who would be present and where each person would be seated. The people who were there to help protect her and convict the perpetrator were also identified. Debbie was able to see more realistically what the court would be like, and realize that she was not the person "in trouble."

Carol, aged 6½ years, had been forcibly raped by a man living in her apartment building. She exhibited numerous symptoms including fear, nightmares, and separation anxiety. When drawing pictures of the perpetrator in therapy, the child was encouraged to draw him however she wanted or to do whatever she wanted to the picture. Once she drew him with "an ugly face" and then put staples in his picture. Another time, after drawing his picture she put it on a punching bag and hit it, then stepped on it, ripped it up, and threw water on it, saying "I hate you so much." One other time, after tearing up his picture and throwing it in the garbage can, she asked to dump it in the building's Dumpster. After a week of particularly bad nightmares, the therapist asked Carol to draw a picture of her nightmare. Carol drew a picture of a man scaring a young girl. The therapist then made a similar picture but showed the girl's mother protecting the girl from the man (see Table 11–2). Carol then disclosed being afraid of a man at her church who she knew had been convicted of child sexual abuse. With Carol's permission, the therapist helped her to tell her mother about this fear. Her nightmares decreased after this session.

Other Art Media

Another medium that is useful with young children who have been sexually abused is play with clay or PLAY-DOH®. This activity can be structured so that the child depicts different aspects of the abuse through the clay. Some children feel a sense of control when modeling themselves as bigger than the perpetrator or even destroying the model of the perpetrator. As with drawings, children's feelings and beliefs regarding the sexual abuse can be understood.

Case Example

Lisa, aged 3½ years, had only disclosed that Sam (an adult male at her caretaker's home) had hurt her. The following is a sample of one of several sessions in which Lisa used PLAY-DOH® to play out situations of aggression against Sam:

Therapist: What are we going to make?
Lisa: Sam.
Therapist: Sam?
Lisa: With his clothes off.
Therapist: With his clothes off? What part do you want to make?
Lisa: His wiener, you do the rest.
Therapist: O.K., you make his wiener and I'll make the rest. What kind of a face should he have, happy, mad, or sad?
Lisa: Mad face, then I'll rip him up!

Therapist: Should I make him big or little?

Lisa: Big.

Therapist: What color should his body be?

Lisa: No body!

Therapist: No body? Then how can I make him without his clothes?

Lisa: That one [*pointing to one of the cans of PLAY-DOH®*]

Therapist: [*Therapist completes figure of Sam.*] I'm going to make you. Should you be dressed or undressed?

Lisa: Dressed, with pants and a shirt.

Therapist: This will be like a bad dream that we get rid of. (*Refers to discussion earlier of Lisa's bad dreams*)

Lisa: Don't rip me up!

Therapist: No, we won't rip you up, you're a special and good person. If you are standing next to Sam, what kind of a face are you going to have? (*See Table 11-2.*)

Lisa: Scared!

Lisa: I'm going to get rid of him! [*Grabs clay figure of Sam and begins tearing it up*]

Therapist: When he's all ripped up, how do you feel?

Lisa: Happy!

Therapist: [*Changes face on clay figure of Lisa*] You look like you're mad at Sam. Are you?

Lisa: Yeah! [*to clay figure*] I'm going to throw you in the garbage! [*pounding the clay into its container*] You're going to stay in there! [*yelling*]

Therapist: It seems like you get real mad at him when he has his clothes off.

Lisa: Yeah! [*yelling*] You stay in there, you butthead! (*After completing this, there is a noticeable positive change in her affect.*)

Lisa continued with this play, pretending that the police come and tear Sam up further. The therapist emphasized that the police would be mad at Sam because he was "bad," but that they would not be mad at Lisa because she has done nothing wrong (see Table 11-2).

Puppet and Doll Play

The use of puppets, dolls, or other figures is another medium of structured play that is useful with sexually abused children. These toys can be used in several different ways. The therapist can structure play scenarios around the specific issues with which the child is struggling. For children who are unable to express themselves through drawing, a sequence similar to the drawing technique described above can be used with dolls or puppets. The therapist can correct the child's distortions by modeling corrective thoughts or experiences through play. Children can also practice prevention skills through play. Play scenarios may be structured so that they are clearly about the child; for children who cannot tolerate this level of anxiety, the play may be done in the third person.

Case Example

Diane, aged 6½ years, had been sexually abused repeatedly with another girl by a neighborhood boy who was several years older. The abuse had been going on for quite a while before it came to the attention of Diane's parents. By the time they became aware of it, Diane was engaging in similar sexual acts with numerous other children in the neighborhood who were her age or younger. At the beginning of one of Diane's therapy sessions, her mother reported to the therapist that she had found Diane and several neighbor children engaged in sexual acts the day before. The therapist decided to try to help Diane express her feelings about the abuse through puppet play in order to decrease her sexual acting-out. A puppet skit was done initially with the therapist playing the part of the perpetrator and Diane playing the part of herself. The therapist coached Diane through this puppet skit by telling her to say no and instructing her to use other prevention skills (see Table 11–1). After completing the skit, Diane initiated another one with her being the perpetrator and the therapist playing the part of the victim (Diane changed the puppet's name to Karen). The following is a transcript of this puppet play:

Diane: Hey, Diane, come over here.
Therapist: What do you want, Tommy?
Diane: I'm going to touch you in the wrong places. [*Diane tells therapist to say OK*]
Therapist: OK.
Diane: [*Becomes visibly anxious, shuffles her feet, and looks around*]
Therapist: What are you going to do to me, Tommy?
Diane: You'll see.
Therapist: [*to Diane*] Is Karen scared?
Diane: No.
Therapist: How is she feeling, then?
Diane: H-a-p-p-y [*whispered*]

Therapist: Karen is happy?

Diane: I mean no.

Therapist: But she's going to let him touch her anyway?

Diane: [*nods yes*]

Therapist: Even though she doesn't like it, she's still happy?

Diane: She is happy.

Therapist: Maybe Karen likes the touching?

Diane: [*nods yes*]

Therapist: Go ahead, then, you can touch her. What do you want, Tommy?

Diane: Nothing [*becomes anxious again*].

Therapist: You know, Tommy, sometimes I wonder why you do these things. Does it feel good?

Diane: No.

Therapist: Are you mad at me?

Diane: [*yells*] No!

Therapist: Well, I don't understand why these things happen because we always get in trouble when they do.

Diane: You won't get in trouble.

Therapist: I won't get in trouble?

Diane: No.

Therapist: Well, all the adults get mad. Why do they get mad?

Diane: They aren't going to get mad this time.

Therapist: How do you know? I think you're trying to trick me.

Diane: No.

Therapist: I think you are, because my mom always says not to do these things. Sometimes it does feel kind of good, but I know deep down inside something is wrong, or else everybody wouldn't get mad.

Diane: [*Interrupts*] Well, you better be quiet.

Therapist: I'm not going to be quiet. I think I should tell somebody.

Diane: [*puts hand over mouth of Karen*] She can't talk.

Therapist: Do you think she should talk?

Diane: I don't know. [*Picks up turtle puppets and changes subject*]

Therapist: What's going to happen to Karen, is she going to tell or keep quiet?

Diane: Keep quiet.

Therapist: Do you think that is the best thing to do?

Diane: [*Nods yes*]

Therapist: Do you think that is OK for Tommy to do to Karen?

Diane: No, but she still isn't going to tell.

Therapist: Why won't she tell?

Diane: Because. . . . [*Picks up turtle puppets again and changes subject*]

Therapist: [*With turtle puppet*] Sometimes I want to go in my shell and hide because sometimes I kind of like what Tommy did to me and I kind of feel like doing it to smaller kids. I know that it's wrong, but it feels good. What should I do?

Diane: [*With turtle puppet*] Tell me.

Therapist: Are you going to get mad at me?

Diane: No.

Therapist: Do you understand that sometimes I feel like doing that?

Diane: Yes.

Therapist: I'm glad to have someone like you who understands how I feel. I don't want to do what Tommy did to me because I know when I do that I hurt other people, but sometimes I feel like I can't stop. *(See Table 11-1).*

As they were picking up at the completion of this puppet play, Diane picked up "Tommy" and twisted his head and said she was going to put him in jail.

Through this series of puppet plays, Diane demonstrated her confused feelings about her perpetrator, about enjoying the sexual activity, and about not wanting it to stop. Although Diane clearly needed more work on these issues, the therapist was beginning to help her understand why she was sexually acting out with other children and how this related to her own sexual abuse. Several months later in therapy, Diane requested to view the video of this session. When she watched it, she responded with surprise at how she was unable to demonstrate prevention skills on her own without coaching from the therapist, and at how she had wanted Tommy to touch the girl puppet.

Because many sexually abused children have issues relating to feeling "damaged," it is helpful for the therapist to have access to a play medical kit or something that the child can use to simulate doctor's instruments. For example, while playing with the dolls during one session, Lisa (described previously) used the doctor kit to examine the doll. After doing so, she stated that Sam had hurt the doll in her private parts. Her therapist explained that even though the doll's private parts had been hurt in the past, they were all better now and the therapist and the doll's parents would make sure that Sam did not hurt the doll anymore (see Table 11-2). Another use for doctor kits is to reenact a physical exam. Many of these children will have already experienced, or will soon be experiencing, medical exams, which can be anxiety-provoking. Using dolls, the therapist and child can act out these medical examinations in order to prepare the child or decrease anxiety from an already completed exam.

Because the issues are similar for children who have been sexually abused, it is possible to adapt many of the above treatment techniques to a group setting. Although the majority of groups described in the literature are composed of school-age and adolescent children, some group work has been done with preschool-age victims (Fowler et al. 1983, McFarlane and Waterman 1986). Not only will the children gain the benefits already described, they will also be able to see that they are not the only children who have had these experiences or feelings. Although therapists and other adults frequently tell children these facts, for children of this young age, direct contact with others who have been abused is usually more meaningful.

TERMINATION

As mentioned previously, therapy with sexually abused children may take longer than with children with other presenting problems. Because therapy with children who have been sexually abused usually involves addressing abuse issues as well as more symptomatic behavior, it is important to know when to end treatment. Although parents and children often would like to "forget about" the abuse, this is not a goal of therapy. There are several factors that the therapist should consider in deciding if the child is ready to end treatment.

First, the behavioral symptoms with which the child originally presented should have returned to a normal level. If baseline information was gathered in the initial assessment, it can be tracked periodically throughout treatment. This tracking can be done through the use of a self-report or parent-report measure such as the CBCL. It is likely that symptoms may temporarily resurface during times of stress related to the abuse (e.g., a court hearing or visit with the perpetrator). However, the parent and child should now have the skills to be able to handle these stress-related situations.

The therapist should also assess the child's beliefs regarding the abuse to determine whether distortions are still present. Such an assessment can be similar to that done in the initial assessment phase of therapy. The particular distortions with which the child presented (e.g., self-blame, damaged self) should be corrected.

By the end of treatment, the child should also be able to express personal feelings related to the sexual abuse through either play or talking. Ideally, recall of the events of the abuse should not result in an extreme emotional reaction or denial of feelings. Rather, the child should be able to identify and express a range of emotional reactions related to the abuse.

Even when all of these goals have been achieved, the young child may need to return briefly to therapy at future developmental stages. As children reach new developmental levels, especially in their sexual development, they may need to address again the issues of abuse as they apply to their more advanced cognitive and sexual developmental level. It is common to see a recurrence of problems at the onset of puberty, beginning of menses for girls, and the onset of dating and sexual relationships.

12

Cognitive-Behavioral Play Therapy with Young Children: Theoretical and Practical Issues

THEORETICAL ISSUES

The development of cognitive-behavioral interventions with adults has been a driving force in the field of psychotherapy. The successful use of cognitive therapies, such as those developed by Beck (1963, 1964, 1972, 1976) and Ellis (1958, 1962, 1971), assumes that the individual has the cognitive capacity to distinguish between rational and irrational behavior; logical and illogical thoughts. Whereas it is accepted that adults have the ability to be active participants in the cognitive-behavioral intervention process, it is not safe to assume that children have such capacity. In fact, children might perceive a therapist's discussion of the child's thoughts as punishment or criticism (Braswell and Kendall 1988).

The array of cognitive-behavioral interventions used with adults has expanded to include adolescents and children, and most recently, preschool-age children. Despite some successful new applications with preschoolers, issues have been raised regarding the appropriateness of cognitive-behavioral therapies with young children. The major question is whether or not developmental factors preclude cognitive-behavioral approaches with such young children. Various authors (e.g., Campbell 1990) have argued that cognitive-behavioral interventions are beyond the grasp of most preschoolers. The skepticism regarding cognitive-behavioral interventions with preschoolers is based in large part on the cognitive limitations of children at this age. Children under the age of 6 years are more concrete, egocentric, and less reflective in their thinking. Language-based self-control techniques are often a component of cognitive-behavioral interventions with children. Such language-based interventions may be beyond the abilities of preschoolers, and approaches based on more abstract and sophisticated language and cognitive skills may be doomed to fail (Braswell and Kendall 1988).

Some cognitive-behavioral interventions may be unsuccessful because they ignore important developmental issues. Therapies that rely on abstract thought and complicated language skills do not consider the child's limited cognitive and language abilities. Recently it has been argued that when presented in a developmentally sensitive way, cognitive-behavioral interventions can be used appropriately even with very young children (e.g., Knell and Moore 1990). In the assessment and treatment of preschool-age children, increasing attention is being focused on the importance of maintaining a developmental perspective in child interviewing (e.g., Bierman 1983, Hughes and Baker 1990).

To conduct developmentally sensitive interviews, the interviewer must be able to respond to the limited verbal, organizational, and recall skills of preschoolers. To do so, Bierman (1983) contends, requires specialized interview techniques. Younger children typically require more structured and specific (Copeland 1982), concrete (Pressley 1979, Bierman 1983), and flexible (Hughes and Baker 1990) interventions. These techniques demand an understanding of child development, particularly in regard to cognitive and language functioning.

Understanding receptive and expressive language development is important for conducting developmentally sensitive interviews. Because words may be imbued with a host of meanings for the child, one can never assume that a child understands language in the same way that an adult does. The context within which words are used provides the child with some powerful cues to their understanding. Conversely, familiar words used in novel contexts can be confusing to the child, whose interpretation may be quite different from what the speaker intended. To make language developmentally sensitive, and therefore accessible, children often need concrete referents and more non-verbally oriented materials (e.g., drawings). Interviewing young children demands that the therapist structure questions in a manner that facilitates children's ability to understand. Task complexity must be reduced, concrete referents added, and expectations simplified (Bierman 1983). Tangible stimuli such as dolls and pictures provide children with familiar and concrete examples. Play therapy bridges the gap by providing these examples. The task presented is thus translated for the child into something understandable. Often, nonverbal response options are used; for example, by asking the child to point to one of a number of possible options rather than asking an open-ended question about the same material.

Harter (1977, 1983) has written eloquently about play therapy from a cognitive-developmental perspective. The difficulty young children have in understanding feelings emanates partly from the child's limited capacity to understand that two feelings can occur simultaneously. She proposes a three-stage sequence regarding conflicting feelings. At first, children deny that two feelings can co-occur. Later, they perceive that two feelings can occur sequentially. Finally, children come to understand that two feelings can exist simultaneously. Harter (1977) employs a drawing technique that facilitates children's understanding of seemingly contradictory emotions. She describes this as a "graphic metaphor" that helps the child to visualize and thus understand apparently conflicting feelings such as love/hate, dumb/smart, and sad/happy (Harter 1983). Her work focuses on the transition from play to talk, with interpretations that are initially embedded in play scenarios becoming increasingly more direct.

Thus, the nature of the preschool years creates some interesting issues for those interested in therapy with young children. Play-based treatment approaches are most often used with preschoolers, in large measure because of the developmental level of children at this age. Although play has been used as a treatment modality with children for many years, recent innovations in philosophical and practical issues have reflected a multitude of changes in the field of child psychotherapy. One recent innovation has been the introduction of cognitive-behavioral interventions. The following section will review principles of cognitive-behavioral therapy and consider the implications for its use with preschool-age children.

Principles of Cognitive Therapy

According to Beck and Emery (1985), "Cognitive Therapy is more than a sum of techniques: it is a system of psychotherapy" (p. 167). The strategies and techniques used in cognitive therapy are based on ten principles of psychotherapy, described by Beck and Emery (1985) and discussed below.

The adaptation of cognitive-behavioral therapy for use in play therapy with very young children involves a new look at these principles, which can be divided into those that apply to work with young children, those that apply with modification, and those that do not apply. Each principle retains the original number as set forth by Beck and Emery. Thus, the principles as applied to young children are not presented sequentially so that fidelity to the original numbering is maintained.

Cognitive Therapy Principles that Apply to Young Children

Principle 1. Cognitive Therapy is based on the cognitive model of emotional disorders. This model of emotional disorders is based on the interplay of cognition, emotions, behavior, and physiology. Behavior is mediated through verbal processes, with disturbed behavior considered to be an expression of irrational thinking. Therapy is focused on cognitive change, which is composed in part of altering irrational, maladaptive, or illogical thinking. A wide range of techniques has been developed to modify cognitions.

The cognitive model of emotional disorder is applicable to children. The interplay among cognition, emotions, behavior, and physiology is as important for children and adolescents as it is for adults. However, the role of cognition must be carefully considered for children. The preoperational-stage child's thinking is often illogical or irrational, and verbal mediation of behavior is still quite limited. Because preschoolers can be impulsive, behavior and activity often precede thought and reflection. Even when young children are functioning optimally, their thinking is not like an adult's. Therefore, Cognitive Therapy does not try to make children think like adults. Rather, interventions may focus on helping the child formulate thoughts that would be adaptive to his or her situation. Thus, interventions may need to focus on the absence of adaptive thoughts (cognitive deficits), not just on cognitive errors (distortions).

Principle 2. Cognitive Therapy is brief and time-limited. The course of Cognitive Therapy typically lasts less than 6 months. Brief therapy encourages the individual's self-sufficiency and discourages dependency on the therapist. Because therapy is brief, it is task oriented and focused on problem solving. Beck and Emery (1985) propose several strategies for keeping treatment brief. These include making interventions simple, specific, and concrete; keeping sessions task related; and focusing on manageable problems.

Brief and time-limited treatments for children are also appropriate. In fact, a task-oriented, problem-solving focus is indicated for many of the more common childhood difficulties. Because problems in the preschool years are rarely indicative of serious psychopathology, they can often be dealt with in a brief, time-limited manner.

Principle 3. A sound therapeutic relationship is a necessary condition for effective Cognitive Therapy. Cognitive Therapy relies on the establishment of a warm, therapeutic relationship based on trust and acceptance. As in all forms of psychotherapy, the development of a positive, accepting therapeutic relationship is the best predictor of good treatment outcome (Brady et al. 1980, Rogers et al. 1967). Play therapy is no exception. If a child is to view therapy as a safe, accepting place where communicating about oneself is permissible, the therapist will need to be seen as trustworthy and nonjudgmental.

Principle 6. Cognitive Therapy is structured and directive. It provides a structured, directive format both for individual therapy sessions as well as for therapy as a whole. The degree of structure varies depending on the needs of the individual. For adults, providing structure may involve setting an agenda for each session and focusing on specific targets. For children, there may be specific targets and agendas for each session, although the opportunity for less structured therapy time is also important. During this time, the child may introduce spontaneous material through play that can be incorporated into the more directive, structured interventions.

An example of using structured, directive interventions as well as more open-ended time is highlighted in the treatment of Terry, the encopretic child described previously (Chapter 7). During Terry's therapy, time was used for reviewing star charts (for both Terry and the bear) as well as for introducing specific material by the therapist (e.g., issues related to the bear's feelings about soiled pants). Even with an agenda for sessions, there was ample time for Terry to engage in more spontaneous play, which was used for purposes of both assessment and treatment.

Principle 7. Cognitive Therapy is problem-oriented. Initially, cognitive therapy is focused on resolving current problems. With adults, focusing on current concerns may provide more accurate data and allows the therapist and patient to work together to resolve specific problems. Later, a focus on past and future information may be helpful. The individual and therapist work together to identify and correct maladaptive thoughts and behaviors that may be maintaining a problem or impeding its solution. For adults, Beck and Emery (1985) recommend conceptualizing the problem, choosing a strategy and technique to implement the strategy, and assessing the effectiveness of the technique.

In cognitive-behavioral work with children it is equally important to be problem oriented. When children present with discrete problems (e.g., related to toileting, eating), more global treatment approaches often lose sight of the particular presenting problem. For example, in more traditional play therapies, presenting problems may not be specifically addressed in the treatment. Alternatively, when presenting problems are not discrete, the error that child therapists may make is in being symptom oriented, rather than problem oriented. The presenting problem needs to be understood in the context of the child's life and the circumstances that may be causing or exacerbating the symptoms.

Children may present with a variety of symptoms caused or exacerbated by particular life experiences or stressors (e.g., sexual abuse, parental divorce). In treating the child, one must not lose sight of the stressor or of the context in which it occurred in the child's life. Treatment is unlikely to be effective if it focuses on symptom alleviation alone. For example, in cases of sexually abused children, to provide a comprehensive problem-oriented treatment, the therapist usually needs to focus on issues related to the sexual abuse, such as trust and control, as well as more symptomatic concerns in order to be effective (see Chapter 11).

Principle 8. Cognitive Therapy is based on an educational model. One premise of cognitive therapy is that symptoms develop because the individual has learned inappropriate ways of dealing with life situations. This suggests that one can change coping styles. In this respect, the therapist is a teacher who imparts positive coping skills and alternative behaviors. One aspect of this is teaching the individual to learn from experiences, so that coping skills can be applied on an ongoing basis. Beck and Emery (1985) refer to this as "learning to learn" (p. 186).

The educational model is particularly relevant for children who often need to be taught specific alternative ways of coping. Because the young child cannot generate alternatives and test them out, the therapist will need to provide, often through example, an alternative coping method. Teaching new skills in play therapy is often accomplished via modeling with puppets and other toys. The cases presented throughout this book highlight the role of teaching as one component of Cognitive-Behavioral Play Therapy (CBPT). Thus, for example, the encopretic child (Terry) was taught new toileting skills; the fearful child (Billy) was taught to be calm when fire engines passed, and several of the sexually abused children (e.g., Richard, Diane) were taught skills to help protect them from future maltreatment.

Cognitive Therapy Principles that Apply to Young Children, with Modification

Principle 4. Therapy is a collaborative effort between therapist and patient. Cognitive therapy uses a "team approach" to solve an individual's problems. The patient supplies information; the therapist provides structure and expertise in problem solving. The patient and therapist work together to develop strategies and plans to help the patient deal with difficulties. Collaboration is approached by avoiding hidden agendas, designing treatment plans and homework together, and maintaining a "collaborative environment" (Beck and Emery 1985).

Although collaboration is important with individuals of all ages, with preschoolers the word "collaborative" may be defined quite differently than with older children or adults. The preschooler does not have the cognitive ability to collaborate with the therapist, in the true sense of the word. This may prompt some therapists to be more authoritarian. However, if the therapist ignores the child's wishes or how the child wants to participate, it is unlikely treatment will proceed successfully. The therapist must find a balance between imposing structure on the child and not interfering with the child's spontaneous behavior. With young children this may involve creative efforts to follow the child's lead as well as to convey certain information. This balance helps define how the child and therapist will collaborate.

Cognitive-Behavioral Play Therapy with Richard, the child sexually abused by his baby-sitter, provides an example of collaboration (see

Chapters 6, 10, 11). Richard resisted any attempts by the therapist to introduce information regarding abuse. When material was presented via puppets, books, or conversation, Richard either changed the subject or regressed to speech about "poopoo" or "kaakaa." However, Richard did tolerate the introduction of such materials if he did not need to interact with them directly. The therapist read a book about abuse to a puppet. Richard had indicated that he did not want to have the therapist read the book to him, but he listened and interacted with the puppet about the material in the book. Similarly, Richard listened attentively as the therapist and puppet engaged in conversation about the puppet's past experiences of being mistreated. In this example, the "collaboration" exists in part due to the therapist's flexibility and the child's stated, and implicit, communication about how treatment should proceed.

Some of the collaboration occurs between the parent and therapist, rather than directly between the child and therapist. Because parents and caregivers control the child's environment, their cooperation and collaboration is essential. Collaboration with parents does not replace a collaborative relationship with a child. However, it may supplement the child's treatment. In some situations parents may provide information that is directly used by the therapist in the CBPT sessions with the child. Several examples throughout this book highlight situations where the collaboration of the parents provided invaluable information used by the therapist in CBPT with the child. For example, Chrissy, the elective mute child (Chapter 8), would not speak with the therapist at the initial sessions. However, her parents collaborated with the therapist by providing information, and a treatment plan was developed with the parents. More collaboration between Chrissy and the therapist occurred in later therapy sessions.

Principle 9. The theory and techniques of Cognitive Therapy rely on the inductive method. In Cognitive Therapy, patients are taught a scientific approach to their problems. Beliefs are viewed as hypotheses that can be revised based on new data. "Experiments" are conducted by the patient to test hypotheses. Similarly, the therapist processes information about the patient inductively. Hypotheses are generated by the therapist and tested and revised according to therapy–generated data. The choice of therapeutic techniques is also driven by the inductive method; various techniques are tested until a suitable one is found.

The inductive method is beyond the cognitive capabilities of most young children. Hypothesis testing is considered to be a hallmark of formal operations, a Piagetian stage not evident until early adolescence. So the inductive method cannot be used effectively with the young child in treatment. However, from the therapist's perspective the inductive method is still important. Hypotheses are tested about the child and treatment techniques; case conceptualization and treatment plans are adapted and changed accordingly.

Principle 5. Cognitive Therapy uses primarily the Socratic method. The cognitive therapist uses the question as a lead and avoids direct suggestions and explanations. Questions are often used to help the individual alter maladaptive thinking. For example, the therapist asks, "What is the evidence? What do you have to gain or lose? What can you learn from this?" Such questions eventually become incorporated into the patient's repertoire in order to counter irrational thoughts and develop a more rational, adaptive thinking style.

Direct questions are usually not effective with children, although the use of open-ended questions if phrased in statement format can be helpful for young children. For example, asking the child "What do you think about that?" may not elicit a response, whereas the child is much more likely to respond to "I wonder what you think about that." The latter statement does not necessitate a response in the same way that a question does. Such statements may be considered to be Socratic in nature, albeit quite different from what one traditionally considers to be the Socratic method.

Cognitive Therapy Principles that Do Not Apply

Principle 10. Homework is a central feature of Cognitive Therapy. One important aspect of cognitive therapy is for patients to use new, more adaptive techniques in their everyday functioning outside of therapy. To promote generalization outside of therapy, homework assignments are used. Between-session tasks are geared to reinforce and supplement the work that is taking place in the therapy session. Although homework assignments have been used with children, they are rarely used with preschool-age children. When assignments are given, they are more often completed by the parents, or done by the child with significant contribution from the parent. As a rule, however, they are not an integral aspect of CBPT.

Methods of Cognitive-Behavioral Play Therapy

A wide range of techniques and strategies may be used in CBPT. However, there are several methods through which treatments are usually delivered with children. These include modeling, role-playing, and use of behavioral contingencies (Braswell and Kendall 1988).

Modeling

Most cognitive-behavioral interventions with children include some form of modeling. Although modeling is important in work with children of all ages, it is particularly important for young children with whom verbal therapy cannot be used extensively. In CBPT, modeling is used to demonstrate adaptive coping methods to the child. Although CBPT is not primarily verbal, the model may verbalize problem-solving skills as a particular behavior is demonstrated. Thus, the model demonstrates verbalizations conducive to positive problem solving. Talking out loud in this way provides a number of cues (e.g., auditory, visual), as well as a concrete example of the behavior.

When used in therapy, modeling exposes the child to an individual (often a stuffed animal or other toy) who demonstrates the behavior that the therapist wants the child to learn. It can be particularly useful if the child can relate positively to the model, which is often the case with stuffed animals and toys. Modeling can also be presented in a variety of other forms such as films, books and stories, puppets and dolls.

Role-playing

Through role-playing in therapy sessions, the child practices skills with the therapist and receives ongoing feedback regarding progress. Role-playing between child and therapist is usually more effective with school-age, rather than preschool-age, children. However, role-playing may be delivered through a modeling technique so that the child can observe, and learn from, the models practicing particular skills. For example, the child can observe two puppets practicing a particular skill and receive feedback from the therapist regarding their skills. Chrissy, the elective mute child (Chapter 8), watched as the puppet who did not talk at school "practiced" speaking at school. The puppet role-played speaking, although she admittedly was afraid to do so. In the role-plays, the puppet received feedback and encouragement from the therapist and other puppets. Although Chrissy did not initially engage in this role-play, she observed it.

Behavioral Contingencies

Behavioral contingencies are often a significant component of CBPT. Cognitive-behavioral interventions for children typically contain behavioral contingencies used to reinforce the acquisition of new skills. These may be quite complex or may simply involve the use of social rewards during therapy sessions. Typically, these involve labeling and praise for the child's attempts to develop new skills. Coping self-statements are also positively reinforced. The therapist can use specific behavioral contingencies in the session and also can encourage the parents to set up contingencies in the home and other environments.

PRACTICAL ISSUES

Critical Issues in Effective Cognitive-Behavioral Play Therapy

Case conceptualization is a critical and ongoing process. Treatment plans based on information gathered at initial evaluation usually are modified as case conceptualization is refined with new information. Cognitive-Behavioral Play Therapy is an ongoing process of assessment and treatment, where a given plan should constantly be reevaluated based on updated information from the child, family, and others.

The therapist's agenda should never "override" the child's needs. It is important to see CBPT as more than the implementation of a set of techniques. Cognitive-Behavioral Play Therapy uses a wide array of both behavioral and cognitive interventions. However, a "cookbook" application of these techniques is likely to be ineffective and is *not* in the child's best interest.

Ongoing developmental concerns should be addressed. The child is not a static being, but rather a constantly growing, changing individual. Focusing on the concerns for which the family originally sought treatment is important, but the therapist should not lose sight of the child's ongoing developmental needs.

Different children respond to different treatment modalities, and a good match should be found between child and material. A wide array of materials is available, including toys, pictures, stories, and videotapes. The therapist should not use the same materials because they are accessible or convenient. Rather, materials should be used that meet the needs of the individual child.

Preparation of the Child for Cognitive–Behavioral Play Therapy

What the parent tells the child about treatment is important. Preparation for CBPT is similar to preparation for other types of play therapy. The parents should be encouraged to be straightforward with the child. It is often helpful for parents to explain to the child that they are concerned about his or her problem. The problem should be described to the child in a simple, concrete, nonjudgmental manner. Further, the parents should indicate that they are all going to talk to someone who "helps kids by talking and playing with them." It is important not to lie ("We are going shopping"), threaten ("You need to behave or the doctor won't talk to you"), or bribe ("If you talk to the doctor, I will buy you a treat") the child (Dodds 1985).

Recently, the American Psychological Association published an excellent book entitled *A Child's First Book about Play Therapy* (Nemiroff and Annunziata 1990). The book, written for children aged 4–7, explains the process of play therapy in very simple language. Although it was written by psychodynamically oriented practitioners, its content is applicable to any form of play therapy. Parents might read this book to their child who is about to enter play therapy. The book can be used to introduce play therapy to the child, or as an ongoing support of the child's therapy. It is appropriate for the parent to continue to read it to the child as therapy is underway. Similarly, the book could be read to the child by the therapist within the therapeutic session. A simple, honest approach with concrete referents, such as a book, may help the child understand more about play therapy.

Involving Parents and Other Adults in Treatment

Children are referred to therapy because their behavior is of concern to an adult, often the parent. Therefore, the inclusion of significant adults in the child's treatment is an important consideration. Parents are usually involved from the beginning, when the therapist meets with them to gather assessment data. After the parents are interviewed and the initial evaluation of the child is completed, it is usually best to meet with the parents to present the evaluation findings and agree on a treatment plan. The treatment plan may primarily involve individual CBPT with the child, work with the parent(s), or a combination of CBPT and parent work. Decisions are made based on the therapist's assessment regarding whether or not the parents will need help in modifying their interaction with the child, or whether the child will need assistance in implementing a treatment program outside of therapy.

When the primary work is with the child, it is still important to meet with the parents regularly. During these parent sessions the therapist will obtain information about the child, continue to monitor the parents' interaction with the child, and work on areas of concern. The therapist may also provide support for the parents as well as information on issues related to child development, as needed. Although the nature of the work with parents will vary, parents are usually seen regularly when their child is in CBPT.

Generalization across Settings

One obvious goal of treatment is for the child to maintain the adaptive behaviors learned in therapy in the natural environment after the treatment has terminated. Despite successful outcome in many studies of cognitive-behavioral therapy with children, an overall lack of generalization of treatment effects and a lack of maintenance of gains is often noted (Braswell and Kendall 1988). For children, the maintenance of newly acquired skills may depend in part on the attitudes and behaviors of significant adults in the child's life. Additionally, therapy should be designed to promote and facilitate generalization, rather than the therapist assuming that it will occur naturally.

In order for generalization to occur, specific training may be required. There is no reason to expect that children will generalize from one setting to another, or from reactions from one caregiver to another. The therapist needs to build in mechanisms for this. As noted previously, generalization may be enhanced by interventions that deal with it directly, and that resemble real-life situations as much as possible; significant individuals in the child's natural environment should be involved in treatment and should be a source of reinforcement of the child's adaptive behavior; procedures should be used that promote self-control of behavior; and interventions should continue past the initial acquisition of the skill to ensure that adequate learning has taken place.

Intervention with Chrissy, the elective mute child (Chapter 8), provides a good example. Her initiation of conversation with the therapist did not ensure that she would speak in other situations. The scenarios set up with the puppets were similar to her own situation and included scenes in school in which one of the puppets had difficulty talking. Generalization issues were dealt with directly and in a manner that resembled real life, as the puppet began to talk at school but continued to have concerns about the possible consequences of talking. Significant individuals, including Chrissy's parents and teacher, were included in treatment plans and provided reinforcement for appropriate talking outside of the therapy sessions. The techniques employed promoted self-control by their focus on Chrissy as ultimately controlling her speech and talking "when she was ready." Finally, treatment continued after Chrissy began to talk in therapy, at school, and elsewhere. By not terminating when Chrissy first began to talk, the therapist was able to focus on issues related to the talking and promoted generalization.

Relapse Prevention

Setbacks are part of learning. Both child and parent need to be prepared for setbacks and not be discouraged by them. Part of the original treatment must be geared toward the possibility of such relapses. This may involve preparing the parent and child not only for what to expect, but also for what to do when certain things happen. In so doing, the therapist and family identify high-risk situations that might present a threat to the child's sense of control and ability to manage situations. Marlatt and Gordon (1985) describe "inoculating" individuals against failure, so that when there are roadblocks, the individual does not panic. Although some of this inoculation will occur in CBPT, much of it will probably arise in work with the parents. This would be particularly true for decisions regarding possible resumption of therapy for the child.

Termination

Preparation for termination is usually gradual, with the therapist and child talking about the end of therapy over the course of several sessions. Children and parents (and therapists too) often approach termination with mixed feelings. It is often helpful to remind the child of the number of sessions remaining until the final appointment. With younger children the therapist may need to provide a very concrete reference to the number (e.g., a piece of paper with marks for the number of appointments remaining). Termination may mean intermittent appointments until the therapy is eventually ended. These appointments may be scheduled over a period of time with a particular event in mind (e.g., beginning of school year, remarriage of a parent). Thus, for example, a child who appears to be "ready" to terminate in March, but who has had concerns about each new school year in the past, may be seen sporadically through the spring and summer so that the final appointment can take place *after* the child begins the new school year. By spacing the final appointments several weeks apart, the therapist begins to communicate a message that the child can manage without the therapist. This can also be conveyed by positive reinforcement from the therapist for how well the child has been doing between appointments.

It may be difficult for the young child to think about therapy as finished. Many children are upset by the thought of never seeing the therapist again. For this reason, it is important that children not believe that "bad" behavior will ensure that they will return to the therapist. Some reassurance may be felt by children if they are told that it is all right to send a card to the therapist. Alternatively, they may appreciate knowing that the parent will call periodically to let the therapist know how the child is doing. It is important in CBPT to have an "open door" policy. For children, simply knowing that they can return to treatment can be very reassuring regardless of whether they may ever need to return.

Appendix: Books for Young Children

FEELINGS

Terry Berger, *I Have Feelings* (New York: Human Sciences, 1971).
_____ , *I Have Feelings Too* (New York: Human Sciences, 1979).

These stories cover a range of feelings, both positive and negative, and explain how the children came to feel the way they do in each situation presented. Black and white photographs are used in each book, the first about a boy, the second about a girl. Although geared toward audiences between the ages of 4 and 9, these books seem more suited for the older child, particularly because many of the situations presented would not be understood by very young children (e.g., homework). However, the school-age child will find that these books make connections between events and feelings in a way that will help the child learn from his or her own experiences.

Doris Brett, *Annie's Stories: A Special Kind of Storytelling* (New York: Workman Publishing, 1988).
_____ , *More Annie Stories: Therapeutic Storytelling Techniques* (New York: Magination, 1992).

Annie's stories developed out of the author's efforts to calm the fears of her own daughter. What emerged was a set of stories (expanded in *More Annie Stories*) covering a range of situations such as nightmares, fears, divorce, hospitalization, and birth of a sibling. The author includes recommendations for the parent in handling the situation, as well as a story in which a child models positive coping skills. Also included are suggestions for personalizing the stories to meet the needs of individual children. Although a bit long for very young children, these stories can easily be adapted to suit the needs of any child. They may be used successfully in therapy with the child drawing pictures to illustrate the text.

Barbara Cain, *Double-dip Feelings: A Book to Help Children Understand Emotions* (New York: Magination, 1990).

Children are often confused by the existence of what seem to be mutually exclusive feelings. *Double-dip Feelings* presents a series of experiences (e.g., birth of sibling, first day of school, move to a new home) and the different feelings that may arise in reaction to the event. The stories and pictures may capture children's uncertainty about such confusing feelings, and help them learn to be more comfortable when such emotions arise. The book includes simple as well as more sophisticated feelings (such as pride and embarrassment) and is written in an interesting and nonthreatening way.

Nancy Carlson, *I Like Me!* (New York: Penguin, 1988).

The character in this very simple picture book is a pig who knows how to have fun and take care of herself. When she makes mistakes, she bounces back with confidence. Through her adventures, she teaches children that they too can feel good about themselves.

Joan Fassler, *The Boy with a Problem* (New York: Human Sciences, 1971).

Johnny is a boy with a problem. He seeks advice from many, but he does not feel better and his problem does not go away. Finally, Johnny finds someone who will really listen to him, "all the way up to the top of the hill . . . and all the way down to the bottom of the hill." This is a charming story, highlighting the importance of listening to children before quickly dispensing advice. We are never told what Johnny's problem is. This ambiguity helps children to connect their own problems to the text.

Barbara Shook Hazen, *Happy, Sad, Silly, Mad: A Beginning Book about Emotions* (New York: Wonder Books, 1971).

This book provides a range of emotions and gives examples of what might make a child feel them. It invites the child to explore a host of feelings and helps explain the connection between events and emotions. It is a helpful beginning explanation of feelings for young children.

Ann McGovern, *Feeling Mad, Feeling Sad, Feeling Bad, Feeling Glad* (New York: Walker & Co., 1977).

Divided into four sections (mad, sad, bad, glad), this book portrays a variety of situations, with photographs that depict these feelings. Each section contains poems that capture common situations and help children associate events and feelings. It is similar to *Happy, Sad, Silly, Mad* in that it is a good introduction to feelings for young children.

PLAY THERAPY

Matthew Galvin, *Ignatius Finds Help: A Story about Psychotherapy for Children* (New York: Magination, 1988).

One of the first books written about seeing a psychotherapist, *Ignatius Finds Help* is aimed, in part, at helping the child understand what therapy will be like. The story is somewhat lengthy, but it will hold the interest of a young child. Ignatius is a little bear with behavioral and family problems. When his family is referred to Dr. Pelican, a therapist in the forest where Ignatius lives, Ignatius learns a great deal about managing his behavior and dealing with his feelings. Some helpful problem-solving skills are interwoven into the therapy, which clearly give the message that therapy is more than just playing. This story is a useful adjunct to therapy, particularly if read by a parent to prepare the child for play therapy.

M. A. Nemiroff and J. Annunziata, *A Child's First Book about Play Therapy* (Washington, DC: APA, 1990).

The American Psychological Association has published this excellent book that explains play therapy to young children. It is simple and well illustrated, portraying a range of families and therapists. Written for 4–7-year-olds, it explains the therapy process from a child's perspective and includes information about why children see therapists, what happens in therapy, and confidentiality. It can be used by therapists to help explain play therapy to a child, or by parents to prepare a child for treatment or encourage a child's involvement in treatment.

SEPARATION ANXIETY

Ellen Kandoian, *Maybe She Forgot* (New York: Cobblehill/Dutton, 1990).

With simple text and beautiful color illustrations, this is a story of a young girl waiting for her mother after her first dance class. We see through the illustrations that Jessie's mother's car has a flat tire as she tries but fails to pick up Jessie on time. As Jessie expresses the common fear of the young child ("I'm afraid maybe she forgot") her mother appears, proclaiming that she could never forget about Jessie. The message is clear, simply stated, and reassuring to the child fearful of separation.

Irene Wineman Marcus and Paul Marcus, *Into the Great Forest: A Story for Children Away from Parents for the First Time* (New York: Magination, 1992).

This book is a symbolic fairy tale about the feelings that children may experience when going to school for the first time. Possible solutions are suggested. Other separation experiences can be substituted for school entrance. Reassurances about the child's fear and angry and confusing feelings are offered.

SHYNESS

Phyllis Krasilovsky, *The Shy Little Girl* (Boston: Houghton Mifflin, 1970).

This charming story is about a little girl who is too shy to interact with other children. When she meets another girl who also does not have friends, she befriends her and discovers that she enjoys her company. This sensitive story captures the feelings of the young girl's gradual evolution.

Charlotte Zolotow, *A Tiger Called Thomas* (New York: Lothrup, Lee & Shepard, 1963).

After moving to a new home, Thomas is shy and worried that no one will like him. He refuses to leave his house and sits on the porch, watching the neighborhood children enjoying themselves. In this delightful Halloween story, Thomas bravely ventures out into the neighborhood and learns that under the disguise of his costume, people still recognize and like him. This story provides young children with the useful message that they can be liked for themselves and need not "hide" from others.

FEARS

Lawrence Balter, *Linda Saves the Day* (New York: Barron's 1989).

Linda's fear of dogs is the basis of this story that takes an interesting turn when Linda is forced to choose between saving a dog or confronting her own fear. Her mother helps her through her fears by allowing her to confront her feelings and to systematically reduce the fear through active coping skills, including creative imagination.

Crosby Bonsall, *Who's Afraid of the Dark?* (New York: Harper & Row, 1980).

This delightful book, in the "I Can Read" series, is about Stella who is afraid of the dark. Stella "hears little, scary sounds and sees big, scary shapes." The fact that Stella is a dog does not stop her owner from seeking advice from a little girl who helps teach Stella how not to be afraid. The book is written in clear, simple language, with the message that anyone, even a dog, can overcome fears.

Alison Coles, *Michael in the Dark* (Tulsa, OK: EDC, 1984).

Michael is afraid of the dark, and he is particularly troubled by his fear one night when he is left with a new baby-sitter. When his parents return, they help him see that the witches are only the wind blowing through the trees, the burglars are the creaking stairs, and the monster is his own stuffed animal. Through this understanding, Michael learns to relax and not be afraid of the dark. The approach is to demystify the fears and help the child learn what the noises and sights really are.

Jacl Dutro, *Night Light: A Story for Children Afraid of the Dark* (New York: Magination, 1991).

Based on the principles of Dr. Milton Erickson, this book taps the inner resources of the child to change images of fear to ones of interest, fun, and comfort. In an interesting twist, Kalispel, a child of the underground, is afraid of the light. He imagines dangerous and monstrous things that happen in the light of day, but an adventure teaches him about the beauty of light. Paradoxically, another child, afraid of the night, finds that the source of his fear can become transformed into pleasure.

Joan Fassler, *Don't Worry, Dear* (New York: Human Sciences, 1971).

This book is about a little girl who sucks her thumb, wets her bed, and stutters. Rather than following the advice offered by some, Jenny's mother uses her own brand of intervention. She is warm and accepting of her daughter's problems and assumes that eventually she will outgrow them. The message is clearly focused on the child's need to make changes at her own pace. This book is particularly reassuring for the child experiencing some minor adjustment difficulties, but may not be as useful for the child in need of more active intervention.

Stephen R. Lankton, *The Blammo-surprise! Book: A Story to Help Children Overcome Fears* (New York: Magination, 1988).

This delightful book is about a young girl, Terry, who is afraid of the circus, although it could be about any of a number of children's fears. Through Terry's conversation with her friend Knowsis, her feelings are aroused and subsequently eliminated. Knowsis creates a wonderful book, the Blammo-surprise! Book, which he offers to Terry to help her deal with her fears. The book builds creatively on principles of systematic desensitization to eliminate fears. A surprise ending helps incorporate what is learned into building on the child's self-concept. In addition to being fun, this book has a powerful message for children with any fears, large or small.

Ted Lobby, *Jessica and the Wolf: A Story for Children Who Have Bad Dreams* (New York: Magination, 1990).

Jessica has nightmares that persist, and she and her parents devise a plan that includes her faithful teddy bear, her parents' support, confidence, and some "personal magic." The attraction of this simple story is in its message that active problem solving can pay off, and that children carry within themselves the tools to overcome their fears and problems.

Irene Wineman Marcus and Paul Marcus, *Scary Night Visitors: A Story for Children with Bedtime Fears* (New York: Magination, 1990).

In this story, Davey tries to rid himself of scary night visitors—monsters and fierce animals—by visualizing their creation, such as the configuration of clothes on the chair. Nothing works for him until he learns that it is safe to have thoughts and wishes, even if they are frightening ones. He learns that he can experience frightening feelings directly, without relying on his scary night visitors.

Jane Werner Watson, Robert E. Switzer, and J. Cotter Hirschberg, *Sometimes I'm Afraid* (New York: Golden Press, 1971).

The premise of this book is that fears grow when they are locked away and shrink when discussed in a quiet, calm manner. The book covers a wide range of children's fears and stresses the idea that communication, understanding, and support are crucial. It is a useful starting point for discussing children's fears with them.

TOILETING

Alida Allison, *The Toddler's Potty Book* (Los Angeles: Price Stern Sloan, 1984).

This large-size book is one of the simplest yet most straightforward of the toileting books. Its message is clear (dry pants are good, using the toilet is positive) and the language is exceptionally direct. Even the very young child (18–24 months) will be able to follow this story. A brief list of books related to toileting is included for parents.

Joae Graham Brooks, *No More Diapers* (New York: Delacorte Press/Seymour Lawrence, 1971).

Two simple stories designed for 1½–2½-year-old children are included in this book. So that any child can identify with the main character, one story is for boys and the other is for girls. The author indicates that this is done so that "the child's attention remains focused on the theme of bowel and bladder control without being diverted by the introduction of sexual differences." The book contains useful information for parents. The stories are clear and simple, with straightforward illustrations.

Judith Caseley, *Annie's Potty* (New York: Greenwillow Books, 1990).

This book has a helpful twist: a focus on a child who is not interested in the potty, real underwear, or being a "big girl." Annie is more interested in diapers. But when she does change her mind, she faces a mishap in which she learns that one can have an accident and still be a big girl. The book is both realistic and reassuring.

Joanna Cole, *Your New Potty* (New York: Mulberry Books, 1989).

The photographs in this book are excellent, capturing both the expressions and behavior of children and parents. Furthermore, the pictures present families of a range of racial and ethnic backgrounds. The main story concerns two children, a boy and a girl, learning to use the toilet. A brief note to parents highlights the major points of toilet training.

Matthew Galvin, *Clouds and Clocks: A Story for Children Who Soil* (New York: Magination, 1989).

Although there is a wide array of books for very young children related to toilet training, little has been written for encopretic children. *Clouds and Clocks* was written to provide children who soil with a sense that others have this problem. The story describes one child who solves his encopresis through the help of a physician, a therapist, and his family.

Vicki Lansky, *Koko Bear's New Potty* (New York: Bantam Books, 1986).

This book approaches toilet training as an urge toward independence and self-reliance that is inherent in each child. The author believes that helping the child understand what is expected will encourage the child's wish to be trained. The book has tips for parents on each page, with the suggestion that these be skimmed quietly while reading aloud to the child. This story is simple and clear and delightfully illustrated, as Koko learns the benefits of using a toilet. This book has a very positive approach. Koko even learns that everyone has accidents and that one does not need to feel sad about them.

Virginia Miller, *On Your Potty!* (New York: Greenwillow Books, 1991).

Bartholomew is a bear whose favorite word is "Nah" when asked if he needs to use the potty. When George, his big bear friend, says "ON YOUR POTTY," Bartholomew finds that he cannot go. However, he learns that when *he* needs to go, he can make it to the potty on time, a lesson in the child's sense of readiness modeled through an animal. When he realizes that he needs to go to the bathroom, Bartholomew says to himself, "On your potty," a message that models a form of self-talk for the child acquiring mastery of toileting.

Fred Rogers, *Going to the Potty* (New York: G. P. Putnam's Sons, 1986).

Illustrated with photographs of children and parents of various racial and ethnic backgrounds, this book is one in a series of Mister Rogers's first experiences for children. The photographs accompany a text that is straightforward, encompassing a range of experiences (e.g., cloth vs. paper diapers, potty-chair vs. chair that fits on the toilet).

Anna Ross, *I Have to Go* (New York: Random House/Children's Television Workshop, 1990).

This book features Little Grover and his Sesame Street Muppet friends, who are cleverly used as Little Grover passes up many an interesting adventure because he "has to go." The focus of the story is that Little Grover makes his final destination and uses the toilet "all by himself." This story might be most effective for children who have mastered some of the basics of toileting, rather than those who are just beginning.

DIVORCE

Laurene Krasny Brown and Marc Brown, *Dinosaurs Divorce: A Guide for Changing Families* (Boston: Little Brown and Company, 1986).

This picture book deals with the confusion, misconceptions, and fears that may accompany divorce. It is cleverly illustrated from the perspective of dinosaur families, and deals with many aspects of divorce.

Linda Walvoord Girard, *At Daddy's on Saturdays* (Niles, IL: Albert Whitman & Company, 1991).

A beautifully illustrated story that follows a young girl as she deals with her parents' divorce. The story is simple, and includes typical thoughts and feelings of both the parents and the children in divorce situations.

Beth Goff, *Where Is Daddy? The Story of a Divorce* (Boston: Beacon, 1969).

This story captures some of the most difficult aspects of divorce for the very young child, such as the sudden loss of one parent and fears of being abandoned. It offers no solutions, but shows how children may behave in inappropriate ways because of confusion about their parents' divorce. For example, the main character, Jane, turns her anger on her beloved dog by hitting him when he does not obey her. Although set in a traditional family setting, this story offers much for children to identify with, even if their family structure differs from Jane's.

Barbara Shook Hazen, *Two Homes to Live In: A Child's Eye View of Divorce* (New York: Human Sciences, 1978).

This story focuses on the feelings of the child experiencing her parents' divorce, as well as the sense of being torn between her mother and father. As she grows accustomed to the separation and the fact that both parents have different homes, she learns how to be with each parent, and learns to accept a situation that she does not like.

June Nobel, *Two Homes for Lynn* (New York: Holt, Rinehart, & Winston, 1979).

With the help of an imaginary friend, Lynn learns to divide her time between her divorced parents. This story, written for older preschool and young school-age children, does not pretend that Lynn likes this situation, for of course, she wants her parents to be back together. However, it shows how Lynn learns to cope with the family splitting in two.

Trudy Osman, *Where Has Daddy Gone?* (Nashville, TN: Ideals Children's Books, 1989).

This book is another child's eye view of divorce, and acknowledges parental as well as the child's feelings. It also highlights the ways that communication is vitally important for the child experiencing the confusion that often accompanies a divorce.

Janet Sinberg, *Divorce Is a Grown Up Problem* (New York: Avon Books, 1978).

This story contains helpful information (e.g., the divorce was not my fault) and deals sensitively with feelings. Although there is no age range provided by the author, it is probably more useful for older preschoolers (4–5-year-olds). Useful information for parents is offered in the preface.

Jane Werner Watson, Robert E. Switzer, and J. Cotter Hirschberg, *Sometimes a Family Has to Split Up* (New York: Crown Publishers, 1988).

This story focuses on the fact that not all families are composed of a mother and father. The child feels that his parents do not love him anymore because they are always quarreling. He learns that their subsequent divorce is not his fault.

ELECTIVE MUTISM

Steve Barry, *The Boy Who Wouldn't Speak* (Toronto, Ontario: Annick, 1992).

Owen is a boy who never speaks, and despite his father's concern, his mother and others are confident that he will talk when he is ready. In this wonderfully illustrated story, Owen meets and befriends a couple of giants who move onto his street. This story weaves in a lesson about stereotypes ("they're just like everyone else, but bigger") as Owen finally has something important to say. This book, written more as a fantasy than to focus on a psychologically relevant issue, might be construed as minimizing the problems of the elective mute child. It should be used cautiously, perhaps as more appropriate with the child who has reluctant speech, rather than one who is truly an elective mute.

Charles E. Schaefer, *Cat's Got Your Tongue? A Story for Children Afraid to Speak* (New York: Magination, 1992).

This story is written by a psychologist to address specifically the issues of the elective mute child. In the book, Anna is afraid to go to school for the first time and does not talk to anyone there. She is helped by a therapist who uses puppets and pictures with her until she eventually speaks with him and later to her classmates and teacher. The story is sensitively written and illustrated attending to the difficulties Anna faces as well as the help she receives from a gentle, reassuring therapist.

SEXUAL ABUSE

Jeanette Caines, *Chilly Stomach* (New York: Harper & Row, 1986).

This is an excellent story that encourages children to share their secret feelings with those they trust. Colorful illustrations and simple content make it useful for very young as well as school-age children.

Frances S. Dayes, *Private Zones* (New York: Warner Books, 1982).

This book addresses the concept of private zones as those parts of the body we cover by bathing suits. Although it attempts to explain the concept of private in terms that very young children can understand, this book may actually be used better with school-age children.

Nancy Davis, *Once Upon a Time: Therapeutic Stories* (Oxon Hill, MD, 1988).

This is a compilation of numerous short stories dealing with various aspects of physical, sexual, and emotional abuse. None of the stories speaks directly about abuse. Each one uses symbolism and has an explanation of the various symbols as a guide for the therapist. Most stories are one to two pages long and are about animals, making them very easy for even the youngest children to enjoy. These stories provide a nonthreatening means of addressing issues of abuse with children of all ages. Since the stories do not have illustrations, children can be encouraged to draw their own pictures, which can be used as a diagnostic tool in therapy.

Jan Hindman, *A Very Touching Book . . . for Little People and for Big People* (Durkes, OR: McClure-Hindman Associates, 1985).

This very informative book describes three kinds of touching: good, bad, and secret. The concept of private parts is also explained, giving the correct anatomical names for male and female genitalia. It also focuses on the importance of disclosing secret touching. Although this book is fairly lengthy, making it difficult to read to a child in its entirety, it can be read in sections. It has wonderful illustrations, which will help keep a child's interest.

Patricia Kehoe, *Something Happened and I'm Scared to Tell* (Seattle, WA: Parenting Press, Inc., 1987).

This book is written for the 3–7-year-old child who is a suspected victim of sexual or physical abuse. It is designed to encourage disclosure, and not to prevent abuse. It also gives concepts that will help the child with emotional recovery from abuse.

Diana L. McCoy, *The Secret: A Child's Story of Sex Abuse for Children Ages 7 through 10* (Knoxville, TN: Magic Lantern, 1986).

This story of father–daughter incest is unique in that it addresses most of the major issues faced by victims of sexual abuse, including mixed feelings about the abuse and disclosure, behavioral and emotional symptoms, and the process that occurs following disclosure, including changes within the family and treatment. This book is excellent for the older school-age child.

Rape Crisis Center, *Red Flag, Green Flag People* (Fargo, ND: Rape and Abuse Crisis Center, 1980).

This coloring book uses the concept of red and green flags to explain different kinds of touches and people. It allows preschool children to personalize types of touch that they like and do not like and people they do and do not like to have touch them.

Pamela Russell and Beth Stone, *Do You Have a Secret? How to Get Help for Scary Secrets* (Minneapolis, MN: CompCare, 1986).

This book focuses almost exclusively on the concept of secrets and the importance of telling adults about those secrets that make the child feel uncomfortable. It emphasizes that although children may have been threatened about telling, they still should not keep certain secrets. The book identifies various adults in most children's lives whom they can safely tell and the importance of telling more than one person if the first person does not help them. The illustrations are in black and white and the text is simple enough that it can easily be used with young as well as school-age children.

Jane Satullo, Russell Roberts, and Pat A. Bradway, *It Happens to Boys Too* (Pittsfield, MA: Rape Crisis Center of the Berkshires Press, 1987).

This unique book addresses those issues of sexual abuse that are common to male victims. It may be reassuring to boys in its message that other males have been sexually abused. Although too advanced for the preschooler, it can be beneficial to school-age and older boys. There is also a section for parents of male victims.

Jo Stowell and Mary Dietzel, *My Very Own Book about Me* (Spokane, WA: Lutheran Social Services, 1987).

This is one of several available workbooks for children who have been sexually abused. It covers the topics of children's rights, private parts, and telling about sexual abuse. Children are given the opportunity to write responses, color and draw pictures, and read short scenarios about sexual abuse. An excellent tool for therapists, this book also has a page by page guide for parents so that they can use it with their own children. Geared more toward school-age children, parts of this book can be used with younger children.

Phyllis E. Sweet, *Something Happened to Me* (Racine, WI: Mother Courage Press, 1981).

The purpose of this book is to help reduce the fear, shame, and confusion of children who have been sexually abused and restore their feelings of dignity and self-worth. This is a well-written book, using simple and short sentences so that even very young children can understand it. It touches on the emotional aspects of abuse and is very nonthreatening in its approach.

Oralee Watcher, *No More Secrets for Me* (Boston: Little Brown and Company, 1982).

This is an ideal book in that it is a compilation of four short stories, each about sexual abuse. The stories depict both male and female victims. The perpetrators are also male and female and include known and trusted individuals as well as family members. In each story, the child expresses a range of feelings felt by most victims and portrays the telling to a responsible adult who is able to help. The stories are relatively short so that they will hold the attention of most children.

References

Achenbach, T. M. and Edelbrock, C. (1983). *Manual for the Child Behavior Checklist and Revised Child Behavior Profile.* Burlington, VT: University Associates in Psychiatry.

Achenbach, T. M., and Lewis, M. (1971). A proposed model for clinical research and its application for encopresis and enuresis. *Journal of the American Academy of Child Psychiatry* 10:535–554.

Achenbach, T. M., McConaughy, S. H., and Howell, C. T. (1987). Child/adolescent behavioral and emotional problems: Implications of cross-informant correlations for situational specificity. *Psychological Bulletin* 101:213–232.

Adams-Tucker, C. (1982). Proximate effects of sexual abuse in childhood: a report on 28 children. *American Journal of Psychiatry* 193:1252–1256.

Alexander, F., and French, T. M. (1946). *Psychoanalytic Therapy: Principles and Applications.* New York: Ronald.

Allen, F. (1942). *Psychotherapy with Children.* New York: Norton.

American Psychiatric Association (1987). *Diagnostic and Statistical Manual of Mental Disorders.* 3rd ed.–rev. Washington, DC: American Psychiatric Association.

Anastasi, A. (1982). *Psychological Testing.* 5th ed. New York: Macmillan.

Axline, V. (1947). *Play Therapy.* Boston: Houghton-Mifflin.

———— (1964). *Dibs in Search of Self.* New York: Ballantine.

Ayllon, T. A., Simon, S. J., and Wildman, R. A. (1975). Instructions and reinforcement in the elimination of encopresis: a case study. *Journal of Behavior Therapy and Experimental Psychiatry* 6:235–238.

Azrin, N. H., and Foxx, R. M. (1974). *Toilet Training in Less than a Day.* New York: Simon and Schuster.

Azrin, N. H., Sneed, T. J., and Foxx, R. M. (1974). Dry-bed training: rapid elimination of childhood enuresis. *Behaviour Research and Therapy* 12:147–156.

Baer, D. M., Wolf, M. M., and Risley, T. R. (1968). Some current dimensions of applied behavior analysis. *Journal of Applied Behavior Analysis* 1:91–97.

Bandura, A. (1969). *Principles of Behavior Modification.* New York: Holt, Rinehart, and Winston.

——— (1977). *Social Learning Theory.* Englewood Cliffs, NJ: Prentice Hall.

Bandura, A., and Menlove, F. (1968). Factors determining vicarious extinction of avoidance behavior through symbolic modeling. *Journal of Personality and Social Psychology* 8:99–108.

Barden, R. C., Zelko, F. A., Duncan, S. W., and Masters, J. C. (1980). Children's consensual knowledge about the experiential determinants of emotion. *Journal of Personality and Social Psychology* 39:968–976.

Baumeister, J., and Jamail, J. (1975). Modification of "elective mutism" in the classroom setting: a case study. *Behavior Therapy* 6:246–250.

Beck, A. T. (1963). Thinking and depression. *Archives of General Psychiatry* 9:324–333.

——— (1964). Thinking and depression. Part 2: theory and therapy. *Archives of General Psychiatry* 10:561–571.

——— (1972). *Depression: Causes and Treatment.* Philadelphia: University of Pennsylvania Press.

——— (1976). *Cognitive Therapy and the Emotional Disorders.* New York: International Universities Press.

——— (1978). *Depression Inventory.* Philadelphia: Center for Cognitive Therapy.

——— (1988). *Love Is Never Enough.* New York: Harper & Row.

Beck, A. T., and Emery, G. (1985). *Anxiety Disorders and Phobias: A Cognitive Perspective.* New York: Basic Books.

Beck, A. T., Rush, A. J., Shaw, B. F., and Emery, G. (1979). *Cognitive Therapy of Depression.* New York: Guilford.

Bedrosian, R. (1981). The application of cognitive therapy techniques with adolescents. In *New Directions in Cognitive Therapy,* ed. G. Emery, S. D. Hollon, and R. C. Bedrosian, pp. 68–83. New York: Guilford.

Beitchman, J. H., Zucker, K. J., DaCosta, G. A., et al. (1992). A review of the long-term effects of child sexual abuse. *Child Abuse and Neglect* 16:101–118.

Beitchman, J. H., Zucker, K. J., Hood, J. E., et al. (1991). A review of the short-term effects of child sexual abuse. *Child Abuse and Neglect* 15:537–556.

Bellak, L., and Bellak, S. S. (1949). *Children's Apperception Test (CAT).* New York: CPS.

Berg, B. (1982). *The Changing Family Game: A Problem-Solving Program for Children of Divorce.* Dayton, OH: Cognitive-Behavioral Resources.

_____ (1989). Cognitive play therapy for children of divorce. In *Innovations in Clinical Practice*, vol. 8, ed. P. A. Keller and S. R. Heyman, pp. 143–173. Sarasota, FL: Professional Resource Exchange.

Berliner, L., and Wheeler, J. R. (1987). Treating the effects of sexual abuse on children. *Journal of Interpersonal Violence* 2:415–434.

Bernal, M. E., Klinnert, M. D., and Schultz, L. A. (1980). Outcome evaluation of behavioral parent training and client-centered parent counseling for children with conduct problems. *Journal of Applied Behavior Analysis* 13:677–691.

Bierman, K. L. (1983). Cognitive development and clinical interviews with children. In *Advances in Clinical Child Psychology*, vol. 6, ed. B. B. Lahey and A. Kazdin, pp. 217–250. New York: Plenum.

Bierman, K. L., and Furman, W. (1984). The effects of social skills training and peer involvement on the social adjustment of preadolescents. *Child Development* 55:151–162.

Bixler, R. (1949). Limits are therapy. *Journal of Consulting Psychology* 13:1–11.

Botvin, G. J., and Tortu, S. T. (1988). Preventing adolescent substance abuse through life skills training. In *Fourteen Ounces of Prevention: A Casebook for Practitioners*, ed. R. H. Price, E. L. Cowen, R. P. Lorion, and J. Ramos-McKay, pp. 98–110. Washington, DC: American Psychological Association.

Brady, J. P., Davison, G. C., Dewald, P. A., et al. (1980). Some views on effective principles of psychotherapy. *Cognitive Therapy and Research* 4:269–306.

Braswell, L., and Kendall, P. C. (1988). Cognitive-behavioral methods with children. In *Handbook of Cognitive Behavior Therapy*, ed. K. S. Dobson, pp. 167–213. New York: Guilford.

Briere, J., and Runtz, M. (1988). Symptomatology associated with childhood sexual victimization in a nonclinical adult sample. *Child Abuse and Neglect* 12:51–59.

Browne, A., and Finkelhor, D. (1986). Initial and long-term effects: a review of the research. In *A Sourcebook on Child Sexual Abuse*, ed. D. Finkelhor et al., pp. 143–179. Beverly Hills: SAGE.

Brunskill, S. D. (1984). Play therapy for the hospitalized child. *American Urological Association Allied Journal* 5:17–18.

Buhler, C. (1951a). Manual for World Test. *Journal of Child Psychiatry*, 2:69–81.

_____ (1951b). A comparison of the World Test with the teacher's judgment concerning children's adjustment. *Journal of Child Psychiatry* 2:36–65.

Burns, D. (1980). *Feeling Good*. New York: New American Library.

Campbell, S. (1990). *Behavior Problems in Preschool Children*. New York: Guilford.

Cantwell, D., Baker, L., and Mattison, R. (1979). The prevalence of psychiatric disorder in children with speech and language disorders: an epidemiological study. *Journal of the American Academy of Child Psychiatry* 18:450–461.

Chethik, M. (1973). Amy: The intensive treatment of an elective mute. *Journal of the American Academy of Child Psychiatry* 12:482–498.

Cohen, N. J., Davine, M., and Meloche-Kelly, M. (1989). The prevalence of unsuspected language disorders in a child psychiatric population. *Journal of the American Academy of Child and Adolescent Psychiatry* 28:107–111.

Cohen, N. J., Sullivan, J., Minde, K., et al. (1981). The relative effectiveness of methylphenidate and cognitive behavior modification in the treatment of kindergarten-aged hyperactive children. *Journal of Abnormal Child Psychology* 9:43–54.

Conger, J. C. (1970). The treatment of encopresis by the management of social consequences. *Behavior Therapy* 1:386–390.

Copeland, A. P. (1982). Individual differences factors in children's self-management: toward individualized treatments. In *Self-Management and Behavior Change; From Theory to Practice*, ed. P. Karoly and F. H. Kanfer, pp. 207–239. New York: Pergamon.

Cox, F. N. (1953). Sociometric status and individual adjustment before and after play therapy. *Journal of Abnormal and Social Psychology* 48:354–356.

Craighead, W. E., Kimball, W. H., and Rehak, P. J. (1979) Mood changes, physiological responses, and self-statements during social rejection imagery. *Journal of Consulting and Clinical Psychology* 47:385–396.

D'Antonio, I. J. (1984). Therapeutic use of play in hospitals. *Nursing Clinics of North America* 19:351–359.

Davis, N. (1988). *Once Upon a Time: Therapeutic Stories*. Oxon Hill, MD: Nancy Davis.

Deblinger, E., McCleer, S. V., and Henry, D. (1990). Cognitive behavioral treatment for sexually abused children suffering post-traumatic stress: preliminary findings. *The American Academy of Child and Adolescent Psychiatry* 29:747–752.

deJonge, G. A. (1973). Epidemiology of enuresis: a survey of the literature. In *Bladder Control and Enuresis*, ed. I. Kolvin, R. C. MacKeith, and S. R. Meadow, pp. 39–46. Philadelphia, PA: Lippincott.

DiGiuseppe, R. A. (1981). Cognitive therapy with children. In *New Directions in Cognitive Therapy*, ed. G. Emery, S. D. Hollon, and R. C. Bedrosian, pp. 50–67. New York: Guilford.

DiGiuseppe, R. A., and Miller, N. J. (1977). A review of outcome studies on rational-emotive therapy. In *Handbook of Rational-Emotive Therapy*, ed. A. Ellis and R. Greiger, pp. 72–95. New York: Springer.

DeRubeis, R. J., and Beck, A. T. (1988). Cognitive Therapy. In *Handbook of Cognitive Behavior Therapy*, ed. K. S. Dobson, pp. 273–306. New York: Guilford.

Dodds, J. B. (1985). *A Child Psychotherapy Primer*. New York: Human Sciences Press.

Doleys, D. M. (1983). Enuresis and encopresis. In *Handbook of Child Psychopathology*, ed. T. Ollendick and M. Hersen, pp. 201–226. New York: Plenum.

Doleys, D. M., and Arnold, S. (1975). Treatment of childhood encopresis: full cleanliness training. *Mental Retardation* 13:14–16.

Dorfman, E. (1958). Personality outcomes of client-centered child therapy. *Psychological Monographs* 72, No. 458.

Douglas, J. W. B. (1973). Early disturbing events and later enuresis. In *Bladder Control and Enuresis*, ed. I. Kolvin, R. C. MacKeith, and S. R. Meadow, pp. 109–117. Philadelphia, PA: Lippincott.

Drabman, R., Spitalnik, R., and O'Leary, K. D. (1973). Teaching self-control to disruptive children. *Journal of Abnormal Psychology* 82:110–116.

Edelman, R. F. (1971). Operant conditioning treatment of encopresis. *Journal of Behavior Therapy and Experimental Psychiatry* 2:71–73.

Elkind, D. (1981). Egocentrism in children and adolescents. In *Children and Adolescents: Interpretive Essays on Jean Piaget*, 3rd ed., ed. D. Elkind, pp. 74–95. New York: Oxford University Press.

Ellis, A. (1958). Rational psychotherapy. *Journal of General Psychology* 59:35–49.

———— (1962). *Reason and Emotion in Psychotherapy*. New York: Lyle Stuart.

————(1971). *Growth through Reason: Verbatim Cases in Rational-Emotive Therapy and Cognitive-Behavior Therapy*. New York: Lyle Stuart.

Emery, G., Bedrosian, R., and Garber, J. (1983). Cognitive therapy with depressed children and adolescents. In *Affective Disorders in Childhood and Adolescence—An Update*, ed. D. P. Cantwell and G. A. Carlson, pp. 445–471. New York: Spectrum.

Erikson, E. (1950). *Childhood and Society*. New York: Norton.

———— (1964). The meaning of play. In *Child Psychotherapy*, ed. M. Haworth, pp. 3–11. New York: Basic Books.

Esman, A. H. (1983). Psychoanalytic play therapy. In *Handbook of Play Therapy,* ed. C. E. Schaefer and K. J. O'Connor, pp. 11–20. New York: Wiley.

Eth, S., and Pynoos, R. S. (1985). *Post Traumatic Stress Disorder in Children*. Washington, DC: American Psychiatric Press.

Evers, W. L., and Schwarz, J. C. (1973). Modifying social withdrawal in preschoolers: the effects of filmed modeling and teacher praise. *Journal of Abnormal Child Psychology* 1:248–256.

Everson, M. D., Hunter, W. M., Runyon, D. K., et al. (1989). Maternal support following disclosure. *American Journal of Orthopsychiatry* 59:197–207.

Faller, K. C. (1988). Decision-making in cases of intrafamilial child sexual abuse. *American Journal of Orthopsychiatry* 58:121–128.

Felner, R. D., Stolberg, A., and Cowen, E. L. (1975). Crisis events and school mental health patterns of young children. *Journal of Consulting and Clinical Psychology* 43:305–310.

Felner, R. D., and Terre, L. (1987). Child custody dispositions and children's adaptation following divorce. In *Psychology and Child Custody Determinations: Knowledge, Roles and Expertise*, ed. L. A. Weithorn, pp. 106–153. Lincoln, NE: University of Nebraska Press.

Fielding, D. M., and Doleys, D. M. (1988). Elimination problems: enuresis and encopresis. In *Behavioral Assessment of Childhood Disorders*, 2nd ed., ed. E. J. Mash and L. G. Terdal, pp. 586–623. New York: Guilford.

Finkelhor, D. (1990). Early and long-term effects of child sexual abuse: an update. *Professional Psychology: Research and Practice* 21:325–330.

Finkelhor, D., and Baron, L. (1986). High risk children. In *A Sourcebook on Child Sexual Abuse*, ed. D. Finkelhor et al., pp. 60–88. Beverly Hills, CA: SAGE.

Finkelhor, D., and Browne, A. (1986). Initial and long-term effects: a conceptual framework. In *A Sourcebook on Child Sexual Abuse*, ed. D. Finkelhor et al., pp. 180–198. Beverly Hills, CA: SAGE.

Fixsen, D. L., Phillips, E. L., and Wolf, M. M. (1972). Achievement place: the reliability of self-reporting and peer-reporting and their effects on behavior. *Journal of Applied Behavior Analysis* 5:19–30.

Flavell, J. (1963). *The Developmental Psychology of Jean Piaget*. Princeton, NJ: Van Nostrand.

Forehand, R., and McMahon, R. J. (1981). *Helping the Noncompliant Child: A Clinician's Guide to Parent Training*. New York: Guilford.

Forsythe, W. I., and Redmond, A. (1974). Enuresis and spontaneous cure rate: study of 1129 enuretics. *Archives of Disease in Childhood* 49:259–263.

Fowler, C., Burns, S. R., and Roehl, J. E. (1983). The role of group therapy in incest counseling. *International Journal of Family Therapy* 5:127–135.

Fox, J., and Houston, B. (1981). Efficacy of self instructional training for reducing children's anxiety in an evaluative situation. *Behaviour Research and Therapy* 19:509–515.

Foxman, B., Valdez, R. B., and Brock, R. H. (1986). Childhood enuresis: prevalence, perceived impact and prescribed treatments. *Pediatrics* 77:482–487.

Fraiburg, S. (1959). *The Magic Years*. New York: Charles Scribner's Sons.

Frank, L. K. (1939). Projective methods for the study of personality. *Journal of Consulting Psychology* 8:389–413.

Freeman, A., Pretzer, J., Fleming, B., and Simon, K. M. (1990). *Clinical Applications of Cognitive Therapy*. New York: Plenum.

Freud, A. (1928). *Introduction to the Technique of Child Analysis*. New York: Nervous and Mental Disease Publishing Co.

––––––– (1946). *The Psychoanalytic Treatment of Children*. London: Imago.

Freud, S. (1909). Analysis of a phobia in a 5-year-old boy. *Standard Edition 10*. London: Hogarth, 1955.

––––––– (1922). *Beyond the Pleasure Principle*. London: Hogarth, 1948.

Friedrich, W. N. (1990). *Psychotherapy of Sexually Abused Children and Their Families*. New York: W. W. Norton.

Friedrich, W. N., Berliner, L., Urquiza, A. J., and Beilke, R. L. (1988). Brief diagnostic group treatment of sexually abused boys. *Journal of Interpersonal Violence* 3:331–343.

Friedrich, W. N., Urquiza, A. J., and Beilke, R. L. (1986). Behavior problems in sexually abused young children. *Journal of Pediatric Psychology* 11:47–57.

Gardner, R. (1971). *Therapeutic Communication with Children: The Mutual Storytelling Technique*. New York: Science House.

_____ (1972). The mutual storytelling technique in the treatment of anger inhibition problems. *International Journal of Child Psychotherapy* 1:34–64.

_____ (1976). *Psychotherapy for Children of Divorce*. New York: Jason Aronson.

Gelman, R., and Baillargeon, R. (1983). A review of some Piagetian concepts. In *Handbook of Child Psychology. Vol. 3: Cognitive Development*, ed. J. H. Flavell and E. M. Markman, pp. 167–230. New York: Wiley.

Genshaft, J. L. (1982). The use of cognitive behavior therapy for reducing math anxiety. *School Psychology Review* 11:32–34.

Giaretto, G. (1981). A comprehensive child sexual abuse program. In *Sexually Abused Children and Their Families*, ed. P. B. Mrazek and C. H. Kempe, pp. 179–198. Oxford: Pergamon.

Gil, E. (1991). *The Healing Power of Play*. New York: Guilford.

Ginott, H. (1959). The theory and practice of therapeutic intervention in child treatment. *Journal of Consulting Psychology* 23:160–166.

_____ (1961). *Group Psychotherapy with Children*. New York: McGraw-Hill.

Gomes-Schwartz, B., Horowitz, J. M., and Sauzier, M. (1985). Severity of emotional distress among sexually abused preschool, school-age, and adolescent children. *Hospital and Community Psychiatry* 36:503–508.

Greenwald, E., Leitenberg, H., Cado, S., and Tarran, M. J. (1990). Childhood sexual abuse: long-term effects on psychological and sexual functioning in a nonclinical and nonstudent sample of adult women. *Child Abuse and Neglect* 14:503–513.

Hambridge, G. (1955). Structured play therapy. *American Journal of Orthopsychiatry* 25:601–617.

Harris, S. L., and Ferrari, M. (1983). Developmental factors in child behavior therapy. *Behavior Therapy* 14:54–72.

Harter, S. (1977). A cognitive-developmental approach to children's expression of conflicting feelings and a technique to facilitate such expression in play therapy. *Journal of Consulting and Clinical Psychology* 45:417–432.

_____ (1983). Cognitive-developmental considerations in the conduct of play therapy. In *Handbook of Play Therapy*, ed. C. Schaefer and K. J. O'Connor, pp. 95–127. New York: Wiley.

Hayden, T. L. (1980). Classification of elective mutism. *Journal of the American Academy of Child Psychiatry* 19:118–133.

Hetherington, E. M., Cox, M., and Cox, R. (1985). Long-term effects of divorce and remarriage on the adjustment of children. *Journal of the American Academy of Child Psychiatry* 24:518-530.

Hug-Hellmuth, H. (1921). On the technique of child analysis. *International Journal of Psycho-Analysis* 2:287-305.

Hughes, J. N., and Baker, D. B. (1990). *The Clinical Child Interview*. New York: Guilford.

Ireton, H., and Thwing, E. (1972). *Minnesota Child Development Inventory*. Minneapolis: H. Ireton and E. Thwing.

Irwin, E., and Berg, B. (1978). *Children's Divorce Stories*. Unpublished audiotapes.

Jacobson, E. (1938). *Progressive Relaxation*. Chicago: University of Chicago Press.

James, B., and Nasjleti, M. (1983). *Treating Sexually Abused Children and Their Families*. Palo Alto, CA: Consulting Psychologists Press.

Jenkins, S., Bax, M., and Hart, H. (1980). Behaviour problems in preschool children. *Journal of Child Psychology and Psychiatry* 21:5-18.

Jersild, A. T. (1968). *Child Psychology*. 6th ed. Englewood Cliffs, NJ: Prentice-Hall.

Jersild, A. T., and Holmes, F. B. (1935). Children's fears. *Child Development Monograph* No. 20.

Johanek, M. F. (1988). Treatment of male victims of child sexual abuse in military service. In *Vulnerable Populations*, vol. 1, ed. S. M. Sgroi, pp. 103-114. Lexington, KY: Lexington Books.

Jones, M.C. (1924). The elimination of children's fears. *Journal of Experimental Psychology* 7:382-390.

Kalter, N. (1977). Children of divorce in an outpatient psychiatric population. *American Journal of Orthopsychiatry* 47:40-51.

Karoly, P., and Harris, A. (1986). Operant methods. In *Helping People Change*, 3rd ed., ed. F. Kanfer and A. Goldstein, pp 210-247. New York: Pergamon.

Kazdin, A. E. (1975). *Behavior Modification in Applied Settings*. Homewood, IL: The Dorsey Press.

Kendall, P. C. (1981). Assessment and cognitive-behavioral interventions: purposes, proposals and problems. In *Assessment Strategies for Cognitive-Behavioral Interventions*, ed. P. C. Kendall and S. D. Hollin, pp. 1-12. New York: Academic.

———— (1991). *Child and Adolescent Therapy*. New York: Guilford.

Kendall, P. C., and Braswell, L. (1985). *Cognitive-Behavioral Therapy for Impulsive Children*. New York: Guilford.

Kendall-Tackett, K. A., Williams, L. M., and Finkelhor, D. (1993). Impact of sexual abuse on children: a review and synthesis of recent empirical studies. *Psychological Bulletin* 113:164-180.

King, N. J., Hamilton, D. H., and Ollendick, T. H. (1988). *Children's Phobias: A Behavioral Perspective*. New York: Wiley.

Klein, M. (1932). *The Psycho-Analysis of Children*. London: Hogarth.

Klonoff, E. A., Knell, S. M., and Janata, J. W. (1984). Fear of nausea and vomiting: the interaction among psychosocial stressors, developmental transitions, and adventitious reinforcement. *Journal of Clinical Child Psychology* 13:263-267.

Klonoff, E. A., and Moore, D. J. (1986). "Conversion reactions" in adolescents: a biofeedback-based operant approach. *Journal of Behavior Therapy and Experimental Psychiatry* 17:179-184.

Knell, S. M. (1992). Puppet sentence completion task. Unpublished manuscript.

Knell, S. M., and Moore, D. J. (1988). Childhood trichotillomania treated indirectly by punishing thumb sucking. *Journal of Behavior Therapy and Experimental Psychiatry* 19:305-310.

_____ (1989). *Cognitive-behavioral play therapy*. Paper presented at the Annual Conference of the American Association of Psychiatric Services for Children, Durham, NC, March.

_____ (1990). Cognitive-behavioral play therapy in the treatment of encopresis. *Journal of Clinical Child Psychology* 19:55-60.

Kohlenberg, R. (1973). Operant conditioning in human anal sphincter pressure. *Journal of Applied Behavior Analysis* 6:201-208.

Kolvin, I., and Fundudis, T. (1981). Elective mute children: psychological development and background factors. *Journal of Child Psychiatry* 22:219-232.

Koss, M. P., and Butcher, J. N. (1986). Research on brief psychotherapy. In *Handbook of Psychotherapy and Behavior Change*, ed. S. L. Garfield and A. E. Bergin, pp. 627-670. NY: Wiley.

Kovacs, M. (1985). The children's depression inventory. *Psychopharmacology Bulletin* 21:995-998.

Krug, R. S. (1989). Adult male report of child sexual abuse by mothers: case descriptions, motivations and long-term consequences. *Child Abuse and Neglect* 13:127-135.

Kurdek, L. A. (1986). Custodial mothers' perceptions of visitations and payment of child support by noncustodial fathers in families with low and high levels of preseparation interparent conflict. *Journal of Applied Developmental Psychology* 9:315-328.

Kurdek, L. A., and Berg, B. (1987). Children's beliefs about parental divorce scale: Psychometric characteristics and concurrent validity. *Journal of Consulting and Clinical Psychology* 55:712-718.

Labbe, E. E., and Williamson, D. A. (1984). Behavioral treatment of elective mutism: a review of the literature. *Clinical Psychology Review* 4:273-292.

Lapouse, R., and Monk, M. A. (1958). An epidemiologic study of behavior characteristics in children. *American Journal of Public Health* 48:1134-1144.

_____ (1959). Fears and worries in a representative sample of children. *American Journal of Orthopsychiatry* 29:803-818.

_____ (1964). Behavior deviations in a representative sample of children: variations by sex, age, race, social class, and family size. *American Journal of Orthopsychiatry* 34:436–446.

Lehman, E. (1944). Psychogenic incontinence of feces (encopresis) in children. *American Journal of Diseases of Childhood* 68:190–198.

Lesser-Katz, M. (1986). Stranger Reaction and elective mutism in young children. *American Journal of Orthopsychiatry* 56:458–469.

Levitt, E., Beiser, H., and Robertson, R. (1959). A follow-up of cases treated at a community guidance clinic. *American Journal of Psychiatry* 29:337–347.

Levy, D. (1938). Release therapy in young children. *Psychiatry* 1:387–389.

———— (1939). Release therapy. *American Journal of Orthopsychiatry* 9:713–736.

Lewinsohn, P. M. (1974). A behavioral approach to depression. In *The Psychology of Depression: Contemporary Theory and Research*, ed. R. J. Friedman and M. M. Katz, pp. 157–185. New York: Wiley.

———— (1975). Engagement in pleasant activities and depression level. *Journal of Abnormal Psychology* 84:718–721.

Lillywhite, H. S., Young, N. B., and Olmsted, R. W. (1970). *Pediatrician's Handbook of Communication Disorders*. Philadelphia: Lea & Febiger.

Loevinger, J. (1976). *Ego Development: Conceptions and Theories*. Washington, DC: Jossey-Bass.

Lovitt, T. C., and Curtis, K. A. (1969). Academic response rate as a function of teacher- and self-imposed contingencies. *Journal of Applied Behavior Analysis* 2:49–53.

Lowenfeld, M. (1939). The world pictures of children. *British Journal of Medical Psychology* 18:65–101.

———— (1950). The nature and the use of the Lowenfeld World Technique in work with children and adults. *Journal of Psychology* 30:325–331.

McArthur, D. S. (1976). A comparison of the stimulus influence of three thematic projective techniques with children. Ph.D. dissertation. California School of Professional Psychology.

McArthur, D. S., and Roberts, G. E. (1982). *Roberts Apperception Test for Children Manual*. Los Angeles: Western Psychological Services.

MacFarlane, J. W., Allen, L., and Honzik, M. P. (1954). *A Developmental Study of the Behavior Problems of Normal Children between Twenty Months and Fourteen Years*. Berkeley, CA: University of California Press.

MacFarlane, K., and Waterman, J. (1986). *Sexual Abuse of Young Children: Evaluation and Treatment*. New York: Guilford.

Marlatt, G. A., and Gordon, J. R. (1985). *Relapse Prevention: Maintenance Strategies in the Treatment of Addictive Behaviors*. New York: Guilford.

Matson, J. L. (1982). Independence training vs. modeling procedures for teaching phone conversation skills to the mentally retarded. *Behavior Research and Therapy* 20:505–511.

Meichenbaum, D. (1971). Examination of model characteristics in reducing avoidance behavior. *Journal of Personality and Social Psychology* 17:298–307.

_____ (1985). *Stress Inoculation Training*. New York: Pergamon.

Meichenbaum, D., and Goodman, J. (1971). Training impulsive children to talk to themselves: a means of developing self-control. *Journal of Abnormal Psychology* 77:115–126.

Melamed, B. G., and Siegel, L. J. (1975). Reduction of anxiety in children facing hospitalization and surgery by use of filmed modeling. *Journal of Consulting and Clinical Psychology* 43:511–521.

Miller, L. C., Barrett, C. L., and Hampe, E. (1974). Phobias of childhood in a prescientific era. In *Child Personality and Psychopathology: Current Topics*, ed. A. Davids, pp. 72–95. New York: Wiley.

Morris, R. J., and Kratochwill, T. R. (1983). *Treating Children's Fears and Phobias*. New York: Pergamon.

_____ (1991). Childhood fears and phobias. In *The Practice of Child Therapy*, ed. T. R. Kratochwill and R. J. Morris, pp. 76–114. New York: Pergamon.

Moustakas, C. (1959). *Psychotherapy with Children*. New York: Harper & Row.

Mowrer, O. H., and Mowrer, W. M. (1938). Enuresis: a method for its study and treatment. *American Journal of Orthopsychiatry* 8:436–459.

Murray, H. A. (1943). *Thematic Apperception Test Manual*. Cambridge, MA: Harvard University Press.

Nelson, R. O. (1977). Methodological issues in assessment via self-monitoring. In *Behavioral Assessment: New Directions in Clinical Psychology*, ed. J. D. Cone and R. P. Hawkins, pp. 217–240. New York: Brunner/Mazel.

Nemiroff, M. A., and Annunziata, J. (1990). *A Child's First Book about Play Therapy*. Washington, DC: American Psychological Association.

Neubauer, P. (1979). The role of insight in psychoanalysis. *Journal of the American Psychoanalytic Society* 27:29–41.

Nickerson, E. T. (1973). Recent trends and innovations in play therapy. *International Journal of Child Psychotherapy* 2:53–70.

O'Connor, D. J. (1991) *The Play Therapy Primer*. New York: Wiley.

O'Connor, R. D. (1969). Modification of social withdrawal through symbolic modeling. *Journal of Applied Behavior Analysis* 2:15–22.

O'Leary, S. G., and Dubey, D. R. (1979). Applications of self-control procedures by children: a review. *Journal of Applied Behavior Analysis* 12:449–465.

Ollendick, T. H., and Cerney, J. A. (1981). *Clinical Behavior Therapy with Children*. New York: Plenum.

Orenchuk-Tomiuk, N., Matthey, G., and Christensen, C. P. (1990). The resolution model: a comprehensive treatment framework in sexual abuse. *Child Welfare* 69:417–431.

Parton, M. (1932). Social participation among preschool children. *Journal of Abnormal and Social Psychology* 27:243–269.

Paul, G. L. (1967). Outcome research in psychotherapy. *Journal of Consulting Psychology* 31:109–118.

Perlmutter, D. (1985). Enuresis. *Clinical Pediatric Urology*, 2nd ed., ed. P. D. Kelalis, L. R. King, and A. B. Belman, pp. 311–325. Philadelphia: W. B. Saunders.

Peters, S. D., Wyatt, G. E., and Finkelhor, D. (1986). Prevalence. In *A Sourcebook on Child Sexual Abuse*, ed. D. Finkelhor et al., pp. 15–59. Beverly Hills, CA: SAGE.

Phillips, R. D. (1985). Whistling in the dark? A review of play therapy research. *Psychotherapy*, 22:752–760.

Piaget, J. (1926). *The Language and Thought of the Child*. London: Routledge and Kegan Paul.

———— (1928). *Judgment and Reasoning in the Child*. London: Routledge and Kegan Paul.

———— (1930). *The Child's Conception of Physical Causality*. New York: Harcourt, Brace, & World.

Piersel, W. C., and Kratochwill, T. R. (1981). A teacher-implemented contingency management package to assess and treat selective mutism. *Behavioral Assessment* 3:371–382.

Piper, W. (1950). *The Little Engine that Could*. New York: The Platt and Munk Co.

Plank, E. M. (1971). *Working with Children in Hospitals*. 2nd ed. Cleveland, OH: The Press of Case Western Reserve University.

Porter, E. (1986). *Treating the Young Male Victim of Sexual Assault: Issues and Intervention Strategies*. Orwell, VT: Safer Society.

Porter, F. S., Blick, L. C., and Sgroi, S. M. (1982). Treatment of the sexually abused child. In *Handbook of Clinical Intervention in Child Sexual Abuse*, ed. S. M. Sgroi, pp. 109–146. Lexington, KY: Lexington Books.

Pressley, M. (1979). Increasing children's self-control through cognitive interventions. *Review of Educational Research* 49:319–370.

Rank, O. (1936). *Will Therapy*. New York: Knopf.

Rape and Abuse Crisis Center. (1980). *Red Flag Green Flag People: A Personal Safety Program for Children*. Fargo, ND: Rape and Abuse Crisis Center.

Rehm, L. P. (1982). Self-management in depression. In *Self-Management and Behavior Change: From Theory to Practice*. ed. P. Karoly and F. H. Kanfer, pp. 522–567. New York: Pergamon.

Richards, C. S. & Hansen, M. K. (1978). A further demonstration of the efficacy of stimulus fading treatment of elective mutism. *Journal of Behavior Therapy and Experimental Psychiatry* 9:57–60.

Risley, T. R., and Hart, B. (1968). Developing correspondence between the non-verbal and verbal behavior of school children. *Journal of Applied Behavior Analysis* 1:267–281.

Rogers, C. (1951). *Client-Centered Therapy.* Boston: Houghton-Mifflin.

Rogers, C. R., Gendlin, G. T., Kiesler, D. V., and Truax, C. B. (1967). *The Therapeutic Relationship and Its Impact: A Study of Psychotherapy with Schizophrenics.* Madison, WI: University of Wisconsin Press.

Rosenberg, J. B., and Lindblad, M. B. (1978). Behavior therapy in a family context: treating elective mutism. *Family Process* 17:77–82.

Roth, D., and Rehm, L. P. (1980). Relationships among self-monitoring processes, memory, and depression. *Cognitive Therapy and Research* 4:149–157.

Rubin, K. H., Fein, G. G., and Vandenberg, B. (1983). Play. In *Handbook of Child Psychology.* Vol 4. *Socialization, Personality, and Social Development,* ed. E. M. Hetherington, series ed. P. Mussen, pp. 693–774. New York: Wiley.

Russell, D. E. H. (1983). The incidence and prevalence of intrafamilial and extrafamilial sexual abuse of female children. *Child Abuse and Neglect* 7:133–146.

_____ (1984). *Sexual Exploitation: Rape, Child Sexual Abuse, and Workplace Harassment.* Beverly Hills, CA: SAGE.

Russo, S. (1964). Adaptations in behavioral therapy with children. *Behavior Research and Therapy* 2:43–47.

Rutter, M. (1977). Delayed speech. In *Child Psychiatry: Modern Approaches,* ed. M. Rutter and L. Hersov, pp. 698–716. Oxford, England: Blackwell Scientific Publications.

Sanok, R., and Striefel, S. (1979). Elective mutism: generalization of verbal responding across people and settings. *Behavior Therapy* 10:356–371.

Sarason, I. G., and Ganzer, V. J. (1973). Modeling and group discussion in the rehabilitation of juvenile delinquents. *Journal of Counseling Psychology* 20:442–449.

Sattler, J. M. (1988). *Assessment of Children,* 3rd ed. San Diego, CA: J. M. Sattler.

Schaefer, C. E. (1979). *Childhood Enuresis and Encopresis: Causes and Therapy.* New York: Van Nostrand.

Schaefer, C. E., Gitlin, K., and Sandgrund, A., eds. (1991). *Play Diagnosis and Assessment.* New York: Wiley.

Schaefer, C. E., and Millman, H. (1977). *Therapies for Children.* San Francisco: Jossey-Bass.

Schaefer, C. E., and O'Connor, K. J. (1983). *Handbook of Play Therapy.* New York: Wiley.

Schroeder, C. S., and Gordon, B. N. (1991). *Assessment and Treatment of Childhood Problems.* New York: Guilford.

Schroeder, C. S., Gordon, B. N., Kanoy, K., and Routh, D. K. (1983). Managing children's behavior problems in pediatric practice. In *Advances in Developmental and Behavioral Pediatrics,* vol. 4, ed. M. Wolraich and D. K. Routh, pp. 25–86. Greenwich, CT: JAI.

Schwartz, S., and Johnson, J. H. (1985). Common developmental problems. In *Psychopathology of Childhood,* ed. S. Schwartz and J. H. Johnson, pp. 89–112. New York: Pergamon.

Scott, K. D. (1992). Childhood sexual abuse: impact on a community's mental health status. *Child Abuse and Neglect* 16:285–295.

Selman, R. (1980). *The Growth of Interpersonal Understanding.* New York: Academic.

_____ (1981). The child as friendship philosopher. In *The Development of Children's Friendships*, ed. J. Gottman and S. Asher, pp. 242–272. New York: Cambridge University Press.

Sgroi, S. M. (1982a). Family treatment of child sexual abuse. In *Social Work and Child Sexual Abuse*, ed. J. R. Conte and D. A. Shore, pp. 109–128. New York: Haworth.

_____ , ed. (1982b). *Handbook of Clinical Intervention in Child Sexual Abuse.* Lexington, KY: Lexington Books.

Shapiro, J. P. (1991). Interviewing children about psychological issues associated with sexual abuse. *Psychotherapy* 28:55–66.

Shapiro, J. P., Leifer, M., Martone, M. W., and Kassem, L. (1990). Multimethod assessment of depression in sexually abused girls. *Journal of Personality Assessment* 55:234–248.

_____ (1992). Cognitive functioning and social competence as predictors of maladjustment in sexually abused girls. *Journal of Interpersonal Violence* 7:156–164.

Shirk, S. R. (1988). Introduction: a cognitive-developmental perspective on child psychotherapy. In *Cognitive Development and Child Psychotherapy*, ed. S. R. Shirk, pp. 1–16. New York: Plenum.

Siegel, L. J. (1976). Preparation of children for hospitalization: a selected review of the research literature. *Journal of Pediatric Psychology* 1:26–30.

_____ (1983). Psychosomatic and psychophysiological disorders. In *The Practice of Child Therapy*, ed. R. J. Morris and T. J. Kratochwill, pp. 253–286. New York: Pergamon.

Skinner, B. F. (1938). *The Behavior of Organisms.* New York: D. Appleton Century.

Slavson, S. R., (1948). Play group therapy for young children. *Nervous Child* 7:318–327.

Soldano, K. W. (1990). Divorce: Clinical implications for treatment of children. In *Psychiatric Disorders in Children and Adolescents,* ed. B. D. Garfinkel, G. C. Carlson, and E. B. Weller, pp. 392–409. Philadelphia, PA: W. B. Saunders.

Spielberger, C. D. (1973). *STAIC Preliminary Manual.* Palo Alto, CA: Consulting Psychologists Press.

Spielberger, C. D., Gorsuch, R. R., and Lushene, R. E. (1970). *Manual for the State-Trait Anxiety Inventory (Self-evaluation Questionnaire).* Palo Alto, CA: Consulting Psychologists Press.

Stewart, M. A. (1975). Treatment of bedwetting. *Journal of the American Medical Association* 232:281–283.

Straughan, J. H., Potter, W. K., and Hamilton, S. H. (1965). The behavioral treatment of an elective mute. *Journal of Child Psychology and Psychiatry* 6:125–130.

Taft, J. (1933). *The Dynamics of Therapy in a Controlled Relationship*. New York: Macmillan.

Wadsworth, B. J. (1989). *Piaget's Theory of Cognitive and Affective Development*. New York: David McKay.

Walker, C. E., Milling, L. S., and Bonner, B. L. (1988). Incontinence disorders: enuresis and encopresis. In *Handbook of Pediatric Psychology*, ed. D. K. Routh, pp. 363–397. New York: Guilford.

Walker L. E., and Bolkovatz, M. S. (1988). Play therapy with children who have experienced sexual assault. In *Handbook of Sexual Abuse of Children*, ed. L. Walker, pp. 249–269. New York: Springer.

Wallerstein, J. S. (1985). Children of divorce: preliminary report of a ten-year follow-up of older children and adolescents. *Journal of the American Academy of Child Psychiatry* 24:545–553.

Wallerstein, J. S., and Kelly, J. B. (1975). The effects of parental divorce: experiences of the preschool child. *Journal of the American Academy of Child Psychiatry* 14:600–616.

_____ (1980). *Surviving the Breakup*. New York: Basic Books.

Weisberger, E. (1987). *When Your Child Needs You*. Bethesda, MD: Adler & Adler.

Wenar, C. (1982). Developmental psychopathology: its nature and models. *Journal of Clinical Child Psychology* 11:192–201.

Werry, J. S. (1986a). Physical illness, symptoms and allied disorders. In *Psychopathological Disorders of Childhood*, ed. H. C. Quay and J. S. Werry, pp. 232–293. New York: Wiley.

_____ (1986b). Diagnosis and assessment. In *Anxiety Disorders of Childhood*, ed. R. Gittelman, pp. 73–100. New York: Guilford.

Williamson, D. A., Sanders, S. H., Sewell, W. R., et al. (1977a). The behavioral treatment of elective mutism: two case studies. *Journal of Behavior Therapy and Experimental Psychiatry* 8:143–149.

Williamson, D. A., Sewell, W. R., Sanders, S. H., et al. (1977b). The treatment of reluctant speech using contingency management procedures. *Journal of Behavior Therapy and Experimental Psychiatry* 8:151–156.

Wilson, B. J., Hoffner, C., and Cantor, J. (1987). Children's perceptions of the effectiveness of techniques to reduce fear from mass media. *Journal of Applied Developmental Psychology* 8:39–52.

Wolpe, J. (1958). *Psychotherapy by Reciprocal Inhibition*. Stanford, CA: Stanford University Press.

_____ (1982). *The Practice of Behavior Therapy*, 3rd ed. Oxford, England: Pergamon.

Woltman, A. G. (1969). The use of puppetry in therapy. In *Conflict in the Classroom*, ed. N. J. Lond, W. C. Morse, and R. G. Newman, pp. 202–208. Belmont, CA: Wadsworth.

_____ (1972). Puppetry as a tool in child psychotherapy. *International Journal of Child Psychiatry* 1:84–96.

Wright, H. L. (1968). A clinical study of children who refuse to talk. *Journal of the American Academy of Child Psychiatry* 7:603–617.

Wright, L., and Walker, C. E. (1976). Behavioral treatment of encopresis. *Journal of Pediatric Psychology* 4:35–37.

Wulbert, M., Nyman, B. A., Snow, D., and Owen, Y. (1977). The efficacy of stimulus fading and contingency management in the treatment of elective mutism: a case study. *Journal of Applied Behavior Analysis* 6:435–441.

Wyatt, G. E., and Mickey, M. R. (1988). Ameliorating the effects of child sexual abuse: an exploratory study of support by parents and others. *Journal of Interpersonal Violence* 2:403–418.

Index

Achenbach, T. M., and Lewis, M., 130
Achenbach, T. M., McConaughy, S. H., and Howell, C. T., 30
Activity scheduling, cognitive therapy, 77–78
Adams-Tucker, C., 200
Affective Domain, the, 26–27
Alexander, F., and French, T. M., 40
Allen, F., 12, 14
Anastasi, A., 93
Anxiety
  disorders, 72, 235–239
  muscle relaxation and, 56
Assessment, 103–105, 117
Assessment of young children for therapy
  apperception tests for, 94–95
  case example of, 106–114
  Child Behavior Checklist and, 91–92, 105–106
  for divorce-related problems, 175–176
  for elective mutism, 148
  for elimination problems, 126–127, 130–132
  for fear, 186–188

feeling scales/drawing and, 99–100
individually administered measures and, 92–93
interview for, 102–103
Minnesota Child Development Inventory and, 92
parent-report measures and, 91–92
play assessment and, 100–102
principles of, 90–91
projective measures in, 93–94
Puppet Sentence Completion Test and, 95–99
Roberts Apperception Test for Children, and, 95
Sentence Completion Test and, 95
for sexual abuse problems, 205, 208
Axline, V.
  on direct therapy, 40
  on group therapy, 15
  on limit-setting therapy, 14
  on nondirected therapy, 13–14
  on praise in play therapy, 50
  on the therapeutic relationship, 46
Ayllon, T. A., Simon, S. J., and Wildman, R. A., 130

281

About the Author

Susan M. Knell is a clinical psychologist and current Director of the Diagnostic Assessment Center of the Child Guidance Center of Greater Cleveland. Previously, she was Director of Training at the Center. Dr. Knell teaches and supervises graduate students at Case Western Reserve and Cleveland State Universities, where she holds appointments in psychology. She is the author of professional publications, including a number of chapters and articles describing the cognitive-behavioral approach to play therapy, which she developed. Dr. Knell received her A.B. from Mount Holyoke College and her Ph.D. from Case Western Reserve University. She completed predoctoral training at The Neuropsychiatric Institute, University of California at Los Angeles, where she was also an NIMH postdoctoral fellow. She lives in University Heights, Ohio with her husband and daughter.